LADY KIMBERLY MOTES DOTY, AURORA BRAND & CONOR FINNEGAN

A Children's Guide To

A Godly Way of Life

What Jesus Taught Children About Living A Godly Life

A CHILDREN'S GUIDE TO A GODLY WAY OF LIFE

Lady Kimberly Motes Doty
Aurora Brand &
Conor Finnegan

LADY KIMBERLY MOTES DOTY, AURORA BRAND & CONOR FINNEGAN

ISBN   paperback
ISBN 979-8390506844   paperback
ISBN 979-8853828452   hardcover
ASIN B0C3SFNGXY   digital

Copyright © 2023 by Lady Kimberly Motes Doty and Lady Kimberly Industries, LLC
All rights reserved. No part of this publication may be reproduced, distributed, or transmitted in any form or by any means, including photocopying, recording, or other electronic or mechanical methods without the prior written permission of the publisher and authors.

Prologue

Embark on an exhilarating journey that will ignite the flames of curiosity in the hearts of children everywhere! Dive into the spiritual realms of God, Jesus, and the Holy Spirit, where secrets are unveiled and fascinating tales come to life. But that's not all - prepare to be enchanted by the captivating world of angels and discover the profound wisdom Jesus shared about the incredible creatures that roam our planet.

"A Children's Guide to a Godly Way of Life" is not just another ordinary book. It is a treasure trove of knowledge and wonder, carefully crafted to quench the thirst for understanding that resides within every child's soul. With each turn of the page, their imagination will ignite, propelling them on a lifelong voyage of love and devotion to God, and an insatiable hunger for unraveling the mysteries of the divine.

Join us on this unforgettable expedition, where the extraordinary meets the ordinary and awe-inspiring revelations await. Brace yourself for a delightful adventure that will leave children yearning to explore the depths of their faith, as they uncover the awe-inspiring truths about God, Jesus, and the captivating teachings that hold the key to a truly godly way of life.

Introducing children to the wonders of God and the teachings of the Bible is a vital aspect of their spiritual development. That's why *"A Children's Guide to A Godly Way of Life"* is the ideal resource to nurture their curiosity and guide them towards a deeper understanding of faith.

In today's world, children are increasingly inquisitive about God and the meaning behind creation. They long to comprehend the principles outlined in the Bible and strive to make righteous choices. By introducing them to the commandments and the valuable lessons Jesus taught us about living a godly life, we can provide them with a solid foundation in their spiritual journey.

"A Children's Guide to A Godly Way of Life" effortlessly intertwines the commandments and the teachings of Jesus, making it an engaging and natural way to introduce children to the core principles of Christianity. It ignites a love for the scriptures and instills within them a deep appreciation for God, Jesus, and the Holy Spirit.

You are not only equipping your children with the knowledge and understanding of God's teachings, but also fostering a genuine love for the Bible. *"A Children's Guide to A Godly Way of Life"* lays the groundwork for a lifelong relationship with faith and ensures children have a strong moral compass to navigate the challenges of life.

Don't miss this opportunity to provide your children with a comprehensive guide to living a godly way of life. Read "A Children's Guide to A Godly Way of Life" with your children and watch as they grow in their love for God and their commitment to following His commandments.

Page Intentionally Left Blank

Table of Contents

Prologue	iv
Table of Contents	vii
Dedication	xxxiii
Acknowledgement	xxxiv
To My Beloved Grandchildren	xxxiv
To My Husband	xxxv
God	**1**
Who is God?	1
God Isn't Human Like Us	1
No One Has Ever Seen God	1
God is Spirit	2
What is a Spirit?	2
God Exists Outside of Time	3
God is the One & Only God	4
God Will Never Lie or Break His Promises	5
Everything Created By God Is Good	7
Angels	**9**
Teach us How to Behave	9
Guard & Protect Us	10
Anger	**13**
Anger Is Just Another Emotion	13
Jesus Taught Us How to Control Anger	14
Managing Anger	15
Jesus Clears the Temple Courts	15
Jesus' Lesson on Dealing with Anger	15
Step 1: Recognizing Anger:	15
Step 2: Controlling Anger:	16
Step 3: Expressing Disapproval:	16
Step 4: Teaching and Guiding:	16

Step 5: Showing Compassion:	16
Conclusion:	17
Managing Anger	17
Jesus Heals on the Sabbath	17
Anger Without A Good Reason	20
Controlling Our Anger	22
Knowing All The Facts	22
Animals	24
God's Love and Care For All Animals	24
Compassion Towards Animals	25
Responsibility As Caretakers	26
Appreciating The Beauty Of Creation	27
Asking	28
God's Rules For Asking	28
Ask In Jesus Name	30
Ask in Faith & Without Doubting	30
Ask in Faith	30
Ask with How Much Faith?	31
Ask having No Doubt	32
Ask in Faith & Without Doubt	33
Ask For The Right Things	35
Ask According to God's Will	36
Ask Keeping God's Commandments	38
Attitude	39
Baptism	41
Blasphemy	42
What Is Blasphemy	42
Blasphemy Against The Holy Spirit	44
Born Again	45
Children	47
Be Humble, Loving, Trusting	48
Don't Harm Children	49

A CHILDREN'S GUIDE TO A GODLY WAY OF LIFE

- Be Kind To Children ... 50
- Help Children ... 50
- Protect Children ... 51
- Childlike Faith, Love & Trust ... 51
- Commandments ... 54
  - Love God With All Your Heart, Soul, Mind ... 54
  - Honor Dad & Mom ... 55
  - Rule Over Everything on Earth ... 56
    - Take Care Of The Earth ... 56
    - Fill The Earth ... 56
    - Take Care of All The Animals ... 57
  - The Ten Commandments ... 57
    - You shall have no other gods before me ... 57
    - Thou shalt not make yourself an idol ... 58
    - Thou shalt not take the name of the Lord thy God in vain ... 59
    - Remember the Sabbath day and keep it Holy ... 60
    - Honor your father and mother ... 61
    - Thou shalt not kill ... 62
    - Thou shallot not commit adultery ... 63
    - Thou Shalt Not Steal ... 64
    - Thou shalt not bear false witness against thy neighbor ... 64
    - Thou shall not covet ... 65
  - Repair or Replace Damaged Borrowed Items ... 66
  - Right to Defend Yourself & Property ... 67
  - Breach of Trust ... 68
  - Widows & Orphans ... 69
    - Don't Harm Widows or Orphans ... 69
    - Don't Oppress Widows, Fatherless, Foreigner Or Poor ... 69
  - Don't Charge Interest To The Poor ... 71
  - Don't Curse gods or Ruler of Your People ... 72
  - Be Honest & Don't Spread Rumors ... 73

Don't Follow The Crowd	74
Show Kindness Even To Enemies	75
Treat Everyone With Fairness and Kindness	76
Let Your Land Rest In The 7th Year	77
Rest on the 7th Day	78
Do Not Invoke The Name Of Other gods	79
Worship & Love God & He Will Keep You Healthy	80
Stay True to God & Don't Let Anything Lead You Away	81
If You Accidentally Take Something, Return it + Extra	82
Be Honest and Responsible For Your Actions	83
Be Pure, Good, & Righteous Like God Is	84
Respect & Honor Your Parents	85
Don't Worship Idols or Make Statues of Them	86
Leave the Corners of Your Fields & Vineyards for the Poor	87
Wait 3 Years to Harvest or Eat Fruit When You Plant New Trees	88
Don't Make Cuts Or Tattoos On Your Body For The Dead	89
Respect & Honor Places of Worship	90
Avoid People Who Pretend To Have Powers	91
Be Kind & Considerate To Older Generations	92
Be Fair & Honest	93
Don't Do Wrong Things Because It's Customary	94
The Lord Bless & Keep You	95
The Lord Bless You With Good Things	95
The Lord Keep You Safe	95
Keep Your Promises	96
Keep Your Promises To God	96
Keep Your Promises to Everyone	96
Everything You Say Is A Promise	96
Create Cities of Refuge	97

A CHILDREN'S GUIDE TO A GODLY WAY OF LIFE

Have Proof Before You Blame Someone	98
Do Not Accept Ransom for the Life of a Murderer	99
Listen Carefully to Live In Harmony	100
Be Kind and Caring Towards Animals	101
The Lord our God is THE One Lord	102
The Greatest Commandment	103
Love God With All Your Heart, Soul & Strength	103
Love Your Neighbor As Yourself	103
Teach Important Things to Your Family	105
Do Good & Wise Things In Your Daily Lives	106
Write Commandments Everywhere	107
Do Not Test God	108
Do Not Desire / Keep False Gods or Idol Items	109
Do Not Bring Anything Bad Into Your Homes	110
Remember to Say Thank You to God	111
Be Kind and Loving to New People	112
Fear, Serve & Cleave To God	113
Love & Obey God	113
Serve God With All Your Heart	113
Keep God's Commandments	113
Share Your Blessings & Help Others In Need	114
Always Do What Is Right & Good	115
Do Not Alter God's Commandments	116
Do Not Add To God's Commandments	116
Do Not Subtract From God's Commandments	116
Walk After The Lord Your God	117
Only Worship God	117
Only Listen to God	117
Don't Allow Anything To Lead You Away From God	118
Stay Faithful To God	119

Don't Do Things For The Dead	120
Respect & Honor God	120
Do Not Cut Or Hurt Yourself For The Dead	120
Take Care Of Yourself	121
Do Not Eat Unhealthy Things	121
Eat Healthy Food	121
How To Know If Something Comes From God	122
Prophets Can Only Say Things That Come From God	122
Prophets Can Only Speak In God's Name	122
Avoid Occult Practices	124
Stay Away From Charmers	124
Stay Away From Mediums	125
Stay Away From People Who Talk To The Dead	125
Stay Away From People Who Inquire of The Dead	125
Have Clean & Pure Hearts	126
Keep Your Promises	127
Do What We Say We Will Do	128
Always Keep Your Promises	128
What We Say We Will Do Is A Promise To God	128
When Borrowing, Don't Take Necessities	129
Be Kind, Loyal & Loving To Others	129
Always Be Loving & Loyal	129
Always Be Loving & Faithful	130
Will Win Favor & Good Name With God & Man	130
Obey your parents & pay attention to their teachings	131
Remember God's Commandments	132
Keep God's Words In Our Hearts	132
Follow God's Commandments	132
Treasure God's Wisdom	132
Obey God's Commandments	132
Obey God's Words, Do His Words & Live Accordingly	133

Obey God's Words & Teachings	133
Put God's Teachings Into Action	133
Live Our Lives According To His Teachings	133
Speak truth, Don't Plot Evil & Don't Swear False Judgements	134
Tell The Truth	134
Do Not Plan or Do Evil Against Each Other	134
Do Not Swear Falsely	134
Let Your Light Shine Before Others	136
Show Others The Good Things You Do	136
Commandments About Being Angry	137
Don't get angry with someone or say mean things	137
Make peace w/ others before doing something special for God	137
Be kind, forgive, and show love to everyone	137
Treating People With Respect & Kindness	138
Treat Everyone With Respect and Kindness	138
Solve Problems In A Peaceful And Calm Way	138
Keep Your Word	139
Don't Take Revenge	139
Treat Everyone The Way You Want To Be Treated	139
Be Generous & Help Those In Need	139
Love Your Enemies & Pray For Them	139
Do Not Judge Or Criticize Others	142
Be Loving & Forgiving To Everyone	143
Love Your Enemies	143
Do Good To Those Who Hate You	143
Bless Those Who Curse You	143
Pray For Those Who Mistreat You	143
Turn The Other Cheek	144
Give To Everyone Who Asks	144
Treat Others As You Want To Be Treated	144
Love Your Enemies	144
Love Your Enemies	146
Treat Others The Way You Want To Be Treated	146

Love Your Enemies and Pray For Them	146
Don't Judge or Criticize Others	146
Give To Everyone Who Asks	146
The Golden Rule	148
Choose Path That Leads To Happiness & Eternal Life	148
Be Careful Who We Trust	148
Look For People Who Do Good Things	148
Build A Solid Foundation	150
False Prophets	150
Obey & Do What Jesus Teaches	150
Listen To Jesus' Words & Put Them Into Practice	150
Following Jesus	152
Be Willing To Face Any Challenge	152
Live our lives in a way that Jesus taught us	153
Don't Do Wrong Or Hurtful Things	154
Focus On Good and Positive Things	154
Children Are Very Special To God	154
God's Angels Are Always Watching & Taking Care of Children	154
How To Solve Problems With Others	156
Solve Problems Peacefully with Love	156
Forgive Each Other	156
Forgive Someone Endlessly	158
Love of Money	159
Love & Care For Others More Than You Love Money	159
Be Kind & Help Those In Need	159
Wise & Faithful Servant	163
Be A Good Servant & Be Ready For His Return	163
Be Kind & Loving Towards Others	163
To Be In Charge, Serve With a Loving Heart	165
Helping People In Need Is Helping Jesus	167
Having A Good Heart	169
God 1st & He Will Always Take Care Of You	171

Judging Others	173
Do Not Judge & You Will Not Be Judged	173
Don't Condemn & You Won't Be Condemned	174
Forgive & You Will Be Forgiven	174
Give & It Will Be Given To You	174
Give Love & Kindness & Get Back Even More	174
The Parable of the Good Samaritan	176
Love God With All Your Heart	177
Love Our Neighbors As Ourselves	177
Married People Stay Together	178
Don't Judge By What You See	179
Love Others The Way Jesus Loves Us	179
Keep God's Commandments If We Love Jesus	180
Remain Close To Jesus He Will Help Us Grow	181
Stay Close To Jesus & He Will Give You Your Needs	182
Do What Jesus Tells Us To Do To Be Close Him	183
Be Kind & Caring Towards Everyone	184
Following Jesus Might Not Be Easy	184
Love Jesus	185
Listen To Jesus	185
Be Kind To Others	185
Don't Be Afraid	185
Don't Do Bad Things	186
Taking Care Of Ourselves	186
Take Care Of Your Body	186
Make Good Choices	187
Keep Learning & Growing To Become Better	187
Love In Action	188
Love & Be Kind To Everyone	188
Use Your Talents	188
Be Happy and Hopeful	188

Pray & Talk To God	188
Help & Share	189
Be Nice To Those Who Are Mean	189
Don't Try To Get Even	189
Live In Peace	189
Don't Seek Revenge	189
Overcome Evil With Good	189
Love Fulfills The Law	191
Love Others	191
Be Honest	191
Do Not Steal	191
Respect Your Parents	191
Be Good To Everyone	192
Do Not Be Jealous	192
Stay Away From Bad Things	192
Those Stronger In Faith	194
Strong In Faith Help Those With Weaker Faith	194
Strong in Faith Help Others Grow Stronger In Their Faith	194
Do Not Indulge In Revelry	195
Do Not Worship Idols	195
Do Not Do Bad Things	195
Do Not Complain	195
Remember Stories & Teachings From Bible	195
The Good Of Others	196
Love Others	196
Look Out For Others	196
Do Good Things	197
Think Of Others First	197
Eat or Drink - Do All For Glory Of God	197
Love & Thank God For The Food and Drink	197
Don't Hurt Others' Feelings Regarding Food	198
Be A Good Example	198
Don't Do Things That Go Against Your Beliefs	198

Don't Think Like Children	200
Make The Best Decision Based Upon Our Maturity	200
Avoid From Evil	200
Make Smart Choices	200
Love Is The Most Important	202
Be Strong and Brave	202
Stay Firm In Your Faith	202
Be Loving And Kind	202
Do Everything In Love	202
Jesus Has Set Us Free	203
Love God	203
Be Kind	203
Share	203
Be Honest	203
Be Patient	204
Be Gentle	204
Have Self Control	204
Do What Is Right & Make Good Choices	205
If Someone Is Caught Up In Sin	206
Be Kind and Help Others	206
Share Each Other's Burdens	206
Live a Life Worthy of the Calling	207
Be A Good Friend	207
Be Patient and Peaceful	207
Stick Together	207
Do Not Sin In YOur Anger	208
Don't Get Mad Easily & Be Kind To Others	208
When In Disagreement, Solve It Peacefully	208
Don't Steal	208
Say Nice Things & Encourage Others	208
Be Forgiving & Understanding	209
Always Be Kind & Caring Towards Others	209
Follow God's Example	210

Be Kind & Loving to Everyone	210
Don't Say Or Do Mean or Hurtful Things To Others	210
Don't Use Bad Or Rude Language	210
Don't Listen To Or Be Influenced By Bad Things	210
Always Show Gratitude To God	211
God Dislikes People Who Do Bad Things & Disobey Him	211
Stay Away From Doing Bad Things	**212**
Avoid Doing Bad Things	212
Try To Show Others What Is Right And Good	212
Be Careful How You Live	**213**
Be Careful How You Act	213
Use Your Time Wisely	213
Understand What God Wants	213
Don't Be Silly Or Rude	214
Be Thankful	214
Sing & Praise God	214
Be Kind To Each Other	214
Be Strong In The Lord & In His Mighty Power	**216**
Be Strong	216
Put On God's Armor	216
Superhero Armor	**217**
The Armor Of Truth, Righteousness, & Peace	217
The Armor of Faith	218
Helmet Protects Our Minds	218
Sword Fights Against Evil	218
Prayer to Talk to God & Give Thanks	219
Conduct Yourselves Worthy Of Christ	**220**
Love Jesus	220
Be United	220
Be Brave	221
Don't Be Worried	221
Continue To Work Out Your Salvation	**222**
Work Hard & Be Good	222

Be Happy & Don't Complain	222
Shine Like A Star	222
Rejoice In The Lord Always	224
Always Be Happy And Joyful	224
Be Kind And Gentle To Everyone	224
Don't Worry About Anything	224
Instead Of Worrying, Pray To God	224
Say Thank You To God	225
The God Of Peace Will Be With You	226
Think About Good Things	226
Be Kind To Others	226
Don't Worry, Pray Instead	226
Thank God For Everything	226
Practice What Is Right	227
God's Peace Is With You	227
Live Your Lives In Christ Jesus	228
Love & Follow Jesus	228
Trust & Believe In Jesus	228
Take Off Your Old Self	229
No More Lying	229
No More Anger	229
No More Mean Words	229
No More Gossiping	229
No More Bad Attitude	230
Bear With Each Other & Forgive One Another	231
Be Kind & Gentle To Others	231
Be Patient & Wait Calmly	231
Forgive Others For Their Mistakes	232
Love Others With All Your Heart	232
Let Peace Be In Charge Of Your Heart & Mind	232
Be Thankful For All The Good In Your Life	232
Teach Others About God's Love & Be Happy To Share Jesus	232
Do Everything With All Your Heart To Please God	233

Always Do Your Best	234
Be Kind & Love One Another Just As Jesus Loves Us	234
Please God	235
Live In Order To Please God	235
Be Kind, Helpful & Good	235
Be Pure & Good Hearted	235
Don't Give In To Bad Desires	235
Control Your Body In A Holy & Honorable Way	237
Treat Our Bodies With Respect To Please God	237
Don't Hurt Or Take Advantage Of Others	237
Lead A Quiet Life	239
Love One Another	239
Work Hard & Mind Your Own Business	239
Live A Peaceful Life	239
Mind Your Manners	240
Depend On God	240
Do The Right Things	241
Hold In The Highest Regard Those Who Work Hard	242
Listen & Respect Your Leaders	242
Be Peaceful & Kind To Everyone	242
Encourage & Help Others	243
Respect & Appreciate God's Message	243
Always Be Joyful & Happy	243
Pray To God & Talk To Hm	243
Give Thank To God For Everything	243
Don't Ignore God's Teachings	244
Test & Hold On To What Is Good	244
Stay Away From Evil & Bad Things	244
A Warning Against Idleness & Laziness	245
Always Listen & Follow Jesus Teachings	245
Stay Away From People Who Don't Work or Aren't Helpful	245
Be Responsible & Help Your Family & Community	245

Be Patient & Kind	245
Do The Right Things & Make Good Choices	246
Keep Busy With Helpful Activities	246
Share With Those In Need	246
Treat Everyone With Respect & Fairness	246
Be Kind, Loving & Helpful To Everyone	246
Oppose False Teachers	248
Love & Be Kind	248
Be Honest	248
Be Thankful	248
Listen To Your Parents & Teachers	248
Share & Be Generous	249
Forgive Others	249
Be Patient	249
Be Brave & Stand Up For What Is Right	249
Instructions For Prayer	250
Pray For Everyone	250
Be Thankful	250
Train Yourself To Be Godly	251
Don't Believe Everything	251
Stay Away From Wrong Or Harmful Things	251
Spend Time With God & Pray	251
Treat Everyone With Kindness & Love	251
Learn about God and the Teachings of Jesus	252
User Your Gifts To Help	252
Take Care of Yourself	252
Be A Good Example	252
Be Kind & Respectful To Those Who Support You	254
Be Kind & Respectful To Older People	254
Show Love & Support Of Your Parents & Grandparents	254
Treat Others The Way You Want To Be Treated	254
Listen & Obey To Wise Adults	254
Be Grateful & Thankful For What You Have	254

Respect & Honor Spiritual Leaders	255
Be Honest & Truthful	255
Stay Away From Harmful & Hurtful Things	255
The Lord Knows Who Are His	256
Keep God's Commandments	256
Confess The Name Of The Lord	256
Turn Away From Wickedness	257
Flee Bad Things & Pursue Godly Things	259
Run Away From Bad Things	259
Do What Is Right	259
Love & Trust God With All Your Heart	259
Be Patient & Gentle	259
Don't Argue or Fight	260
Teach Others About God's Love	260
Have Nothing To Do With Ungodly People	261
Be Kind	261
Respect Your Parents	261
Be Thankful	261
Don't Brag or Boast	261
Be Honest	262
Don't Be Mean Or Hurtful	262
Demonstrate With Faith & Patience	263
Always Do Your Best	263
Have Hope	263
Be Patient & Wait Calmly	264
Never Give Up	264
Trust In God	264
Draw Closer To God	266
Be Close To God	266
Believe &Trust In Our Hopes and Dreams	266
Encourage & Help Other Be Kind and Do Good Things	266
Spend Time With Others Who Believe In God	267
Live In Peace With Everyone	268

When You Feel Sad or Weak	268
Stay On The Right Path	268
Try To Get Along With Everyone	268
Help Others Know About God's Love	269
Make Sure No One Is Immoral	269
Keep Loving One Another As Brothers & Sisters	271
Love One Another	271
Be Kind To Strangers	271
Remember Those Having A Tough Time	271
Don't Be Jealous or Envious Of What Others Have	273
Keep Yourself Free Of Love Of Money	273
Be Satisfied With What You Have	273
God Will Never Leave You	273
Respect The People Who Teach Us About God	274
Respect Our Leaders	274
Appreciate Our Teachers	274
Be Strong In Our Choices	275
Show Love & Kindness To Others	275
Be Faithful In Our Relationships	275
Do Not Be Jealous	275
Be Content With What We Have	276
Don't Be Carried Away By Strange Teachings	277
Be Careful What We Believe	277
Have Kind & Loving Hearts	277
Not By Eating Ceremonial Foods	277
Always Follow The Teachings of Jesus	278
Do Good & Share With Others	279
Always Remember To Thank God	279
Remember To Be Kind To Others	279
Obey Teachers	279
Everything Good & Perfect Is From Above	281
Do Not Be Deceived	281
Every Good & Perfect Gift Is From Above	281

God Created Everything	281
God Is Always The Same	282
God Gave Us LIfe	282
Quick To Listen, Slow To Speak & Anger	283
Be Quick To Listen	283
Be Good & Follow God's Teachings	284
Get Rid Of All Moral Filth & Evil	284
Humbly Accept The Word Planted In You	284
Do Not Merely Listen To The Word	284
Do What It Says	285
Treat Everyone Fairly	286
Don't Show Favoritism	286
Don't Judge By How People Look Or What They Have	286
Don't Judge People By Their Appearance	287
Don't Discriminate	288
Love Your Neighbors As Yourself	289
Treat Others The Way You Want To Be Treated	289
Don't Show Favoritism	289
Obey The Rules and Laws	289
Don't Judge Others	290
Speak With Kindness & Encouragement	290
Submit Yourself To God	291
Obey God	291
Resist The Devil	291
Draw Near To God	291
Cleanse Your Hands	292
Purify Your Hearts	292
Be Humble	292
Don't Speak Evil Against One Another	292
Be Humble And Respectful Towards God	294
Do Not Boast About Your Future Plans	294
We Can't Predict What Will Happen In The Future	294
Always Acknowledge God Is In Control Of Everything	295

Be Patient Until The Lord's Coming	296
Be Patient	296
Don't Complain	296
Listen To The Teachings of The Prophets	296
Be Strong & Patient	297
When You Say You Will Do Something, Do It	297
Do Not Swear	297
Prayer Of A Righteous Person	299
Be Honest	299
Be Kind	299
Forgive Others	299
Pray for Each Other	300
Be Holy	301
Think Before We Act	301
Be In Control Of Ourselves	301
Trust In Jesus	301
Be Good and Kind	302
Don't Let Bad Habit Control Us	302
Living In Harmony With One Another	303
Be Like Minded	303
Be Sympathetic	303
Love One Another	304
Be Compassionate	304
Be Humble	304
Do Not Repay Evil With Evil Or Insult With Insult	304
Repay Evil With Blessing	305
Don't Say Mean Or Hurtful Things	305
Turn From Evil & Do Good	305
Seek Peace & Pursue It	305
God Is Always Watching Us	305
Explain Why You Believe In God	307
Love God	307

Be Ready To Explain Why You Believe In God	307
Be Kind & Respectful	307
Do Good & Avoid Evil	307
Trust In God	308
Always Show Others How Good We Are	308
Living For The Will Of God	309
Be Ready To Suffer	309
Don't Give In To Sin	309
Love & Serve Others	309
Use Your Gifts To Help	310
Be Hospitable	310
Speak Good Words	310
Use Everything For God's Glory	310
Grown-Ups Have Wisdom To Share	313
Be Humble	313
Be Careful & Don't Worry	313
Be Alert & Watch For Bad Things	314
You Are Not Alone, God Is Always With You	314
Be Spotless, Blameless & At Peace With God	316
Spotless	316
Blameless	316
At Peace With Him	317
Grow in Grace & Knowledge	318
Grow In God's Grace	318
Grow In Knowledge of Jesus	318
Don't Love Anything More Than You Love God	319
Reminder To Keep Following Jesus	320
Stay Close To Jesus	320
Keep Believing In Jesus	320
Be Proud Of Yourself For Believing In Jesus	320
How To Know Who Are God's Children	322
Love Each Other	322
Don't Be Like Bad People	322

Help Those In Need	322
Believe In Jesus	323
Obey God's Commandments	323
Show Love For Others With Our Actions	323
Trust in Jesus	323
Love One Another The Way God Loves Us	324
Test What You Hear To Know It's From God	326
How We Should Love Others	327
Love Comes From God	327
Spread Love Everywhere To Everyone	327
Knowing God Is Knowing Love	327
If You Don't Love, You Don't Know God	328
Loving Others & Loving God	329
Love One Another As God Loves Us	329
Love Comes From God	329
No One Has Seen God	329
Love One Another	330
God Lives In Our Heart	330
Believe & Say Jesus Is God's Son	332
Love God	332
Believe Jesus Is God's Son	332
Love Others As God Loves Us	333
God Lives In Your Heart	333
Love Everyone As Much As We Love Our Family	335
Nothing Has Importance Over God	336
Doing What Is Good	337
Do Not Copy Bad Things	337
Copy Good Things	337
Building You Faith	338
Keep Building Your Faith	338
Pray In The Holy Spirit	338
Keep Yourselves In God's Love	339

Show Mercy To Others	339
Help Others In Need	340
Be Ready For Jesus To Come Back To Earth	341
Jesus Is Coming Soon	341
Hold On To Your Beliefs	341
Stay Faithful to God	341
Be Eager To Do Right	343
Value Things That Are Important To Jesus	343
Buy White Clothes From God & Wear Them	343
Ask God For Wisdom & Understanding	344
God Corrects & Punishes Us Because He Loves Us	344
Thirsty for God's Love	345
Go To God When We Need His Love & Forgiveness	345
Share God's Love & Forgiveness	345
Come Receive God's Love & Forgiveness	345
Death	347
Death Isn't The End, But A New Beginning	347
Our Souls Live forever In Heaven If We Believe In Jesus	348
Jesus Comforts Us When We Are Sad	348
How Jesus Dealt With Death	349
Eating & Drinking	354
Our Words & Actions Can Make Us Unclean	354
Be Thankful For Our Food & Share With Others	354
Love and Care For Our Bodies	355
Physical Food vs Spiritual Sustenance	356
Enemies	359
Love Your Enemies & Pray For Them	359
Love Your Enemies & Do Good To Them	360
Feed & Give Your Enemies Drink	360
Faith / Believe	361
Faith Is Trusting Without Needing Proof	361
Faith Is Believing Even If We Can't See It	361
Blessed Are Those Who Haven't Seen Yet Believed	362

Everything Is Possible When You Believe	363
Family	364
Family Extends Beyond Our Biological Relatives	364
Fear	367
God Will Strengthen You & Help You	367
Put Your Trust In God	368
God Gave You A Spirit Of Power, Love & Self Control	368
You Are Very Special & Important To God	369
Be Strong & Courageous, God Is With You	369
Put Your Trust In God	370
Pray To God About Everything	370
Fear Is The Opposite Of Faith	371
Forgiveness	374
If You Want God's Forgiveness, You Must Forgive	374
Don't Judge	375
God Loves Us So Much, He Forgives Us	375
Choosing Not To Hold On To The Hurt & Anger	376
To Bring Healing & Peace To Our Hearts	376
Grace	379
Healing	383
Blind Bartimaeus Receives His Sight	383
Jesus Heals A Sick Woman	384
Heaven	386
No More Sadness or Pain	386
Heaven Has Room For Many	386
Heaven Is Beyond Our Imagination	387
Heaven Brings Us Complete Joy & Eternal Pleasures	387
The Kingdom of God is Heaven	389
If We Put God's Kingdom First, He Will Take Care Of Us	389
Have Childlike Faith To Enter God's Kingdom	389

The Kingdom Of God Can Be In Our Hearts	390
Holy Spirit	392
What is the Holy Spirit?	392
Judging	394
Don't Judge By What You See	394
Don't Judge Others	394
Judging Others	395
Do Not Judge & You Will Not Be Judged	395
Do Not Judge Or Criticize Others	396
Love Peace & Truth	397
Speak the truth to each other	397
Render true and sound judgment in your courts	397
Do not plot evil against each other	398
Do not love to swear falsely	398
Miracles	399
Jesus Turning Water Into Wine	399
Jesus Feeding Thousand With A Few Loaves & Fish	400
Jesus Healing The Sick & Raising The Dead	401
Outcast	403
Jesus Talks With a Samaritan Woman	403
The Parable of the Lost Son	403
The Lord Is Near The Brokenhearted	405
An Outcast - Whom No One Cares	406
Jesus Forgives and Heals a Paralyzed Man	406
Give Yourself The Gift Of Self Love	407
Pray	409
Where To Pray	409
Have Faith & Believe That God Answers Our Prayers	409
The Parable of the Persistent Widow	410
How To Pray To God	411

Salvation	413
What Is Salvation?	413
Everyone Has Sinned	413
To Accept The Gift Of Salvation	413
Self Love	415
What Is Self Love	415
How Do We Know God Wants Us to Have Self Love?	416
Taking Care Of Ourselves	416
Take Care Of Your Body	416
Make Good Choices	416
Keep Learning & Growing To Become Better	417
Walk As Children Of Light	418
Sins	419
Breaking God's Laws	419
No One Is Perfect	419
7 Things God Hates	420
Haughty Eyes	420
Liars	420
Murderers	420
Hearts That Devise Wicked Plans	421
Rushing To Do Something Bad	421
False Witness	421
Those Who Cause Fights Or Arguments	421
Things God Wants Us To Do	422
Confess Our Sins	422
God Is Fair & True To His Word	423
God Will Forgive Us Our Sins	423
Help Us Become Better People	423
Everyone Has Made Mistakes	424
About the Authors	425
Lady Kimberly Motes Doty	426

Aurora Brand   427

Conor Finnegan   430

Dedication

To the Almighty God,

With utmost gratitude and reverence, I humbly dedicate this book, *"A Children's Guide To A Godly Way of Life"*, and every facet of my existence, to You.

Your boundless love and unfathomable grace have rescued me time and time again, weaving a tapestry of salvation throughout my journey.

In every stroke of my pen, whether crafting these pages or any other piece inspired by Your divine touch, Your presence is my guiding light. The Holy Spirit whispers wisdom into my being, illuminating the path to truth and understanding.

I am in awe, dear God, of the purpose behind Your salvation and the calling You have placed upon my life. By Your sheer mercy, I remain alive and well, blessed with the ability to write and fortunate enough to stroll upon sandy shores, where Your profound inspiration graces my soul.

May this dedication be a testament to my profound gratitude and unwavering faith in You, the source of all inspiration and the anchor of my very existence.

Yours faithfully,
Lady Kimberly

Acknowledgement
To My Beloved Grandchildren

I would like to express my heartfelt gratitude to my beloved grandchildren, Braden, Aurora, Conor, and Cade, who have been the driving force behind the creation of *"A Children's Guide To A Godly Way Of Life."*

It is truly remarkable to witness the innate curiosity and genuine interest that children possess when it comes to understanding God, Jesus, and the Holy Spirit. Their thirst for knowledge extends even further to encompass the angels, the significance of animals in Jesus' teachings, and the profound wisdom imparted by Him.

With utmost dedication, this book endeavors to satisfy their inquisitive minds, igniting their imagination and nurturing their curiosity to delve deeper into the realms of God, Jesus, and the Bible. My hope is that this journey will plant the seeds for a lifelong devotion to God and an insatiable thirst for knowledge about Him.

To my cherished grandchildren, thank you for inspiring me to embark on this endeavor. May this book serve as a stepping stone towards a meaningful and everlasting relationship with God, as well as an unwavering passion for unraveling the mysteries of His teachings.

To My Husband

I am forever indebted to my incredible husband, whose unwavering support has made this book a reality. Thank you for standing by my side, not only as my sounding board and editor, but also as the provider of endless glasses of tea. Your patience knows no bounds, as you graciously tolerate my wild and crazy ideas for new books and all the quirky Southern habits that surely drive a New Yorker like you up the wall! Despite the challenges we face, including my health issues and my persistent urge to accomplish everything before "I go", you continue to be my rock. From the deepest depths of my heart, I sincerely appreciate you.

God

Who is God?

"God is spirit, and those who worship him must worship in spirit and truth." John 4:24 ESV

God Isn't Human Like Us

One of the first questions everyone has is: Who is God? This is also one of the most difficult questions to answer because the answer is in terms that isn't easy to understand.

It isn't easy to understand because of the way we think about how we exist today.

God isn't human like us, He exists differently than we do.

No One Has Ever Seen God

No one has ever seen God except for Jesus. The Bible tells us this in John 1:18 where it says "No one has ever seen God. God's only Son, the one who is closest to the Father's heart, has made him known."

John 1:18 — GW "No one has ever seen God. God's only Son, the one who is closest to the Father's heart, has made him known."

As humans, we like to think about things in a certain way. We think that everything in this world exists just like we do, with a beginning and an end. We measure things with time - there's a time when we're alive, a time when we're not, and a time when we exist in a certain form. But you know what? God is different. God doesn't exist in a way that we can measure. It's like God is beyond time, beyond our understanding. Isn't that amazing?

It shows us that there's something so special and incredible about God that we can't even fully grasp. It's like a beautiful mystery that inspires us to keep wondering and exploring. So let's embrace this idea and remember that there's something truly magical about God's existence that goes beyond our imagination.

God is Spirit

God is spirit. As spirit, He is not tied to time and space the way we are. The Bible tells us this in John 4:24 where it says "God is spirit".

John 4:24 ESV "God is spirit, and those who worship him must worship in spirit and truth."

What is a Spirit?

What is a spirit? Where the Bible tells us that "God is spirit" is means he does not have a physical body, he is without flesh and bones. He is invisible. He is present everywhere.

To help understand how God is a Spirit, imagine that you have a friend who is really, really special. You can't see your friend, but you can feel their presence and love all around you. That's kind of like God!

According to the Bible, God is described as a spirit. A spirit is something that doesn't have a body like we do. It's like a special energy that is everywhere, even though we can't see it. Just like the wind, we can't see the wind, but we can feel it and see the effects it has, like when it blows the leaves on the trees or makes our hair move.

God is like that too. Even though we can't see God, we can feel Him and see the things He does. We can feel His love in our hearts and see the beauty of nature that He created. We can also talk to God through prayer and listen to His guidance in our lives.

So, just like you can't see the wind but you know it's there, you can't see God but you can feel His love and presence all around you. He's always with you, watching over you and caring for you, even when you can't see Him.

So these two things tell us that God doesn't have a body like we do, He is invisible because He is a spirit. Also, He can be in every space and all spaces at the same time. God doesn't have to be in one space at a time like we have do. Pretty cool, right!

God Exists Outside of Time

Imagine you have a favorite book, and it has a really exciting story. Now, when you read the story, you start from the beginning and go through each page, right? But guess what? God is not like a storybook with a beginning and an end. He is way more amazing than that!

In the Bible, the very first verse is Genesis 1:1, it says, "In the beginning, God created the heavens and the earth." This verse tells us that God made everything we see around us: the sky, the land, the trees, the animals, and even you and me! But here's the interesting part - God Himself doesn't have a beginning like we do.

You see, time is something that we use to measure moments and events. We have a past, present, and future, right? But God is so big and powerful that He exists outside of time. It's like He created time itself when He made everything else. It's a little hard to imagine, I know!

Just like we can see the characters in a book, but they can't see us, God can see everything that has happened, is happening now, and will happen in the future. He knows every single moment of our lives, even before they happen, because He is outside of time. Isn't that amazing?

So, when it says "In the beginning, God created the heavens and the earth," it means that God has always been there, even before the very first moment in time. He's like the author of the book, who knows the whole story from beginning to end.

Remember, even though it might be a little tricky to understand, just like how we can't see the wind but we know it's there, we can have faith that God exists outside of time. And that's what makes Him so special and powerful!

I hope that helps you understand a little bit about how God is different from us and how He created everything.

Genesis 1:1 ESV, "In the beginning, God created the heavens and the earth".

God is the One & Only God

Have you ever wondered about God and why we believe He is the one and only God? Let me explain it to you using Revelation 22:13 from the Bible.

In the last book of the Bible called Revelation, there is a special verse that helps us understand this. Revelation 22:13 says, "I am the Alpha and the Omega, the first and the last, the beginning and the end." Now, that might sound a little confusing, but let's break it down.

Imagine you are playing a game, and you are the very first person to start playing. You are also the very last person to finish playing. That means you are the original, the one who started it all, and you are also the one who will finish it all. You are the only one who can do that, right?

Well, in this verse, God is saying that He is the Alpha and the Omega, the first and the last, the beginning and the end. This means that He is the original, the one who created everything and started everything. And He is also the one who will be there at the very end, when everything comes to an end.

So, just like when you are the first and the last in a game, you are the only one who can be in that position, God is telling us that He is the one and only God. That's pretty amazing, right?

This verse from Revelation helps us understand that God is special because He is the beginning and the end of everything. He is the one who created the world and all the amazing things we see around us. And He will always be there for us, no matter what.

So, whenever you have any questions about God being the one and only, you can look at this verse and remember that He is the Alpha and the Omega, the first and the last, the beginning and the end.

Revelation 22:13 ESV "I am the Alpha and the Omega, the first and the last, the beginning and the end."

God Will Never Lie or Break His Promises

Imagine you have a really trustworthy friend who always keeps their promises. You know that when this friend says they will do something, they will always do it. They never change their mind or lie to you. That's how God is too!

In Numbers 23:19, it says that God is not like us humans. He's not someone who lies or changes his mind like we do. When God says something, he means it, and he will always do what he says. Just like our trustworthy friend, God will never lie to us.

When God promises us something or says he will do something, we can trust him completely because he will never let us down. He will always fulfill his promises and keep his word. We can have faith in God and know that he is always honest and true to his word.

Numbers 23:19 ESV God is not man, that he should lie, or a son of man, that he should change his mind. Has he said, and will he not do it? Or has he spoken, and will he not fulfill it?

Everything Created By God Is Good

Everything, no matter what, is good if it is created by God. Respect what God gives you and be thankful. 1 Timothy 23:19 tells us everything created by God is Good and nothing is to be rejected if it is received with thanksgiving. Learning to receive it with thanksgiving is the key. We don't always understand all the inner workings of why and how God created everything, do we?

In this little short story, we can begin to understand how everything created by God is Good.

Once upon a time, there was a little girl named Aurora who loved exploring nature. She would often go on adventures in the backyard, searching for bugs, picking flowers, and admiring the beauty all around her. One sunny day, Aurora sat down with her mom and asked, "Mom, why did God create so many different things?"

Her mom smiled and replied, "Aurora, God created everything in this world, and do you know what? Everything He made is good!"

Aurora's curious eyes widened. "Everything? Even bugs and spiders?"

"Yes, even bugs and spiders," her mom confirmed. "You see, Aurora, God designed every creature with a specific purpose. Bugs help pollinate flowers, spiders catch pesky mosquitoes, and each animal plays a role in maintaining the balance of nature."

Aurora pondered for a moment, then asked, "What about vegetables? Sometimes I don't like eating them."

Her mom chuckled and said, "Well, Aurora, even vegetables are part of God's creation. They provide us with essential nutrients and help us grow strong and healthy. That's why we should always be thankful when we eat them."

Aurora nodded, understanding that everything God created has a purpose and is meant to be appreciated. She realized that sometimes things might seem strange or scary, but they all have a role to play in this beautiful world.

From that day forward, whenever Aurora encountered something she didn't understand or felt unsure about, she remembered what her mom taught her: "For everything created by God is good, and nothing is to be rejected if it is received with thanksgiving."

Aurora's adventures in nature became even more exciting as she began appreciating every tiny creature, every colorful flower, and every delicious vegetable. She felt grateful for the incredible variety that God had placed in the world, knowing that it all had a special place and purpose.

And so, Aurora continued to explore, with a heart full of gratitude for the goodness of God's creation.

This little short story shows us what 1 Timothy tells us about that everything created by God is good. It also shows us why we need to respect and be thankful for everything God gives to us. God only creates good things and He expects us to accept and be thankful for the things he gives us and provides for us, even if we don't fully understand why these things are good for us.

1 Timothy 4:4 ESV For everything created by God is good, and nothing is to be rejected if it is received with thanksgiving,

Angels

Angels are spiritual beings created to serve God especially as a messenger and as a guardian to humans.

Teach us How to Behave

An angel is a spiritual being serving God especially as a messenger and as a guardian of humans.

Imagine you are playing a game with your friends, and you want everyone to play fair and follow the rules. Just like this, God wants us to live on earth in the same way that things are done in heaven. He wants us to be kind, loving, and obedient just like the angels.

You know, angels are special beings that God created to serve Him in heaven. They always listen to God's commands and do everything He asks of them. They never argue or complain, but they do everything with joy and willingness. They are always ready to help others and show God's love to everyone around them.

In the same way, God wants us to behave like angels here on earth. He wants us to be obedient to His commands and do things His way. When we pray the verse "Thy will be done in earth, as it is in heaven," we are asking God to help us live according to His will, just like the angels do in heaven.

When we act like angels, we become a reflection of God's love and goodness to others. We become kind, patient, and helpful, just like the angels. We treat others with respect and show them God's love through our actions.

So, remember, when you pray this verse, you are asking God to guide you in living like an angel here on earth. You are asking Him to help you follow His commands, be obedient, and spread His love to others. And just like the angels, you will bring joy and goodness to the world around you.

Matthew 6:10 KJV, Thy will be done in earth, as it is in heaven.

In heaven, God's will is done by angels, isn't it? The angels never talk back or question God, do they? Angels perform their tasks right away, with joy, with thanks and without question. As children, we are to do the things our Mom and Dad ask us to do the same way angels do for God.

Guard & Protect Us

The Bible also says God will send His angels to guard us and protect us. In Psalms and in Luke the Bible tells us "God will command his angels to guard you".

Whenever you are scared or needing some extra confidence, God sends His angels to help you. Isn't it comforting to know God always has His angels there guarding you, protecting you and just being there when you need them?

This little short story will help you understand how God uses his angels to help guard and protect us.

Once upon a time, there was a little boy named Cade who loved to hear stories about angels. He would often ask his mommy how God uses angels to keep us safe. One day, his mother sat him down and shared a beautiful story that explained it all.

"Listen carefully, Cade," his mother began. "In the Bible, the verse Psalms 91:11 says, 'For God will give command his angels concerning you to guard you in all your ways.' This means that God loves us so much that He sends angels to watch over us and protect us in everything we do."

Cade's eyes widened with curiosity as he asked, "Mommy, how do these angels protect us? Can we see them?"

His mother smiled and replied, "Well, Cade, angels are special beings that we cannot see with our eyes, but we can feel their love and protection. They are like invisible superheroes sent by God. When we are in danger or need help, God commands his angels to watch over us and keep us safe."

Cade looked amazed and asked, "But how do they know when to protect us, Mommy?"

His mother continued, "In another verse from the Bible, Luke 4:10, it says, 'For it is written, "He will command his angels concerning you to guard you carefully."' This means that when we trust in God and have faith in Him, He guides the angels to be with us at all times. They know when we are scared, feeling lonely, or going through tough times, and they come to our aid."

Cade's eyes sparkled with excitement as he imagined angels surrounding him. "Can I talk to them, Mommy? Can I ask them for help?"

His mommy nodded and said, "Absolutely, Cade! God loves when we talk to Him and His angels. You can pray to God and ask Him for protection and help. Sometimes, you might even feel a warm presence or a sense of peace, and that is the angels letting you know that they are there with you."

Cade hugged his mommy tightly and said, "I'm happy to know that God's angels are always watching over us. It makes me feel safe and loved."

His mommy smiled and said, "That's the beautiful thing, Cade. God's love is so vast and amazing that He sends His angels to guard and protect us. Remember, whenever you feel scared or need help, just close your eyes and ask God to send His Angels to come and protect you and they will be right there with you protecting you and keeping you safe."

Psalms 91:11, For God will give command his angels concerning you to guard you in all your ways.

Luke 4:10, For it is written, "He will command his angels concerning you to guard you carefully:

Anger

Anger is a God given emotion that gives us energy to protect ourselves, someone else, or to take action against something that is happening that is wrong.

Anger Is Just Another Emotion

Anger is just another emotion we have just like being happy or sad. It is not a bad emotion. It can often protect us or the people we love. Jesus even taught us anger is not a bad emotion. Anger is what happens to us when we are threatened, offended, wronged, or denied something we really want or need. What we do with our anger can sometimes be bad though.

Jesus taught us how to control our anger and tells us to deal with it the right way. When we are angry we can often feel like we are out of control and have no power to control what is happening to us. Jesus taught us how to deal with our anger so we take back control over what is happening to us.

Anger is a God given emotion that gives us energy to protect ourselves, someone else, or to take action against an injustice. An injustice is something that is happening that is wrong. Anger is an important emotion because it tells us when something is wrong.

When we are hurt physically, we feel pain. Like the pain alerts us we are physically hurt, anger alerts us that something outside of ourselves is wrong and we need to do something to make it right.

When we think of Anger as being a gift from God instead of being a bad emotion, we deal with it differently.

Jesus Taught Us How to Control Anger

When we look in the Bible, we see Jesus taught us anger is not a bad emotion. Anger is just another human emotion that we needed to learn how to control and deal with appropriately.

In the Bible, Jesus teaches us about anger. One day, Jesus went to a special place called the temple. When he arrived, he saw something that made him really angry. There were people selling things and exchanging money inside the temple, which was supposed to be a place for prayer and worship.

Jesus was upset because these people were not showing respect for God's house. So, he did something really interesting. He didn't start yelling or throwing things around. Instead, he used his anger to teach others an important lesson.

Jesus went up to the people who were selling and trading and he overturned their tables and scattered their money. He told them, "My house should be a house of prayer for all nations, but you have turned it into a den of robbers."

By doing this, Jesus showed everyone that he was passionate about God's house and how it should be treated. He used his anger to make a point and teach others about what was right.

You see, anger is not always a bad thing. Sometimes, it can help us stand up for what is right, just like Jesus did. But the important thing is that we need to use our anger in a good way, just like Jesus did. We should never use it to hurt others or act out of control.

Instead, when we feel angry, we can learn from Jesus and use that anger to teach others about what is right and wrong. We can stand up for justice and fairness, just like Jesus did in the temple. We can speak up when we see something that is not right, and try to make a positive change.

So, remember, anger is not always bad. It's how we use it that matters. Let's learn from Jesus and use our anger to teach others about what is right and how to make the world a better place.

Managing Anger
Jesus Clears the Temple Courts

Jesus became angry when he went into the temple, a church, in Mark 11:15-18. If we were to map out how we are to handle our anger based upon Jesus' example in this verse, it is:

1. Recognizing Anger
2. Controlling Anger
3. Expressing Disapproval
4. Teaching and Guiding
5. Showing Compassion

Jesus' Lesson on Dealing with Anger

In the Bible, there are various instances where Jesus taught important life lessons through his actions. One such lesson is about dealing with anger is in Mark 11:15-18, in which Jesus demonstrates how to handle anger in a righteous and constructive manner.

Step 1: Recognizing Anger:

Jesus observed that people were using the temple courtyard for buying and selling instead of worshiping God. He saw this as disrespectful and became angry. Explain to the child that anger is a normal emotion, but it is essential to understand why we feel angry and how to express it appropriately.

Step 2: Controlling Anger:

Instead of reacting impulsively, Jesus controlled his anger. He didn't shout or get violent. He decided to handle the situation wisely. Discuss with the child that when we become angry, it's important to pause, take a deep breath, and calm ourselves down before responding.

Step 3: Expressing Disapproval:

Jesus expressed his disapproval by overturning the tables of the money changers and the seats of those selling doves. Explain to the child that Jesus wanted to show these people that what they were doing was wrong. However, emphasize that physical aggression is not the right approach for us. Instead, we can express our disagreement by using words or finding peaceful solutions.

Step 4: Teaching and Guiding:

After overturning the tables, Jesus began to teach the people about the proper use of the temple. He explained that the temple was a place of prayer, not a marketplace. Help the child understand that when we are angry, it's important to use that energy to educate and guide others towards what is right, just as Jesus did.

Step 5: Showing Compassion:

Despite being angry, Jesus didn't harm anyone. He didn't want to hurt people physically or emotionally. Instead, he healed the sick who came to him, demonstrating compassion and love. Teach the child that even when we are angry, it's crucial to treat others with kindness and empathy.

Conclusion:

By following Jesus' example in Mark 11:15-18, He teaches us that anger is a natural emotion, but it's important to control it and express our feelings in constructive ways. By recognizing anger, controlling it, expressing disapproval, teaching and guiding, and finally showing compassion despite being angry, Jesus teaches us that anger is just another emotion and when we use it the right way, we can educate and guide others towards what is right the way He did.

Mark 11:15-18 KJV, And they come to Jerusalem: and Jesus went into the temple, and began to cast out them that sold and bought in the temple, and overthrew the tables of the moneychangers, and the seats of them that sold doves; And would not suffer that any man should carry any vessel through the temple. And he taught, saying unto them, Is it not written, My house shall be called of all nations the house of prayer? but ye have made it a den of thieves. And the scribes and chief priests heard it, and sought how they might destroy him: for they feared him, because all the people was astonished at his doctrine.

Managing Anger
Jesus Heals on the Sabbath

In another example about anger in the Bible, in Mark 3:5, Jesus tells us about a man with a withered hand coming into a church or synagogue on the sabbath day. The sabbath day is Sunday, a day that is supposed to be a day for only rest and prayer.

When Jesus entered the synagogue, he saw a man with a hand that was not working properly. It made Jesus feel sad because he knew that the man wanted to use his hand just like everyone else.

Some of the religious leaders in the synagogue were watching Jesus very carefully. They did not like Jesus because they were jealous of his popularity and the love people had for him. They wanted to find a way to trick Jesus and make him look bad in front of the people.

Jesus looked at the religious leaders, and he felt something deep inside him – anger. But it was not an angry feeling like when we get mad at someone for being mean to us. It was a righteous anger, a feeling of deep concern and sadness for the hardness of their hearts.

Jesus knew that these religious leaders were more interested in following their rules and traditions rather than caring for people. He wanted to teach them and everyone else in the synagogue an important lesson about what was truly important to God.

So, Jesus called the man with the hand to come forward. He said to the people, "Is it lawful to do good on the Sabbath or to do evil? To save life or to kill?" Jesus was asking them if it was right to show kindness and heal someone on the Sabbath day, which was a day of rest and worship.

The religious leaders didn't answer because they knew that Jesus was right, but they were too stubborn to admit it. Jesus looked at them with love and sadness in his eyes, and then he healed the man's hand. The man's hand became completely well, just like it was supposed to be.

Jesus used his anger in that moment to teach everyone a lesson. He showed them that it's not wrong to feel angry when we see injustice or when people are being treated unfairly. Jesus wanted to show the religious leaders that love and compassion are more important than following strict rules.

Anger is a natural emotion that we all feel sometimes, but it's how we use that anger that matters. Jesus used his anger to stand up for what was right and to help the man that needed help even though it was on the Sabbath day and against the "rules" of the religious leaders.

Mark 3:5 ESV, Again he entered the synagogue, and a man was there with a withered hand. And they watched Jesus, to see whether he would heal him on the Sabbath, so that they might accuse him. And he said to the man with the withered hand, "Come here." And he said to them, "Is it lawful on the Sabbath to do good or to do harm, to save life or to kill?" But they were silent. And he looked around at them with anger, grieved at their hardness of heart, and said to the man, "Stretch out your hand." He stretched it out, and his hand was restored. The Pharisees went out and immediately held counsel with the Herodians against him, how to destroy him.

A CHILDREN'S GUIDE TO A GODLY WAY OF LIFE

Anger Without A Good Reason

Imagine you and your friend are playing together, having a great time. Suddenly, your friend accidentally breaks your favorite toy. How would you feel? You might feel angry, right? It's normal to feel angry when something bad happens, but it's important to remember what Jesus said about anger.

In Matthew 5:21-26, Jesus teaches us about anger. He says that if we get angry with someone without a good reason, it's like we are breaking an important rule. Jesus wants us to treat others with kindness, even when we're upset.

You see, Jesus knows that anger can hurt not just the person we're angry at but also ourselves. When we're angry, we might say or do things that we don't mean, and it can make the situation worse. Jesus wants us to find ways to resolve our conflicts peacefully, without hurting anyone's feelings.

He tells us that if we're ever angry with someone, we should try to make things right as soon as possible. If we don't, our anger can build up and make us feel unhappy and disconnected from others. Jesus wants us to make peace with others and mend our relationships, just like when we forgive our friend for accidentally breaking our toy.

So, when you feel angry, take a moment to calm down and think about why you're feeling that way. If it's for a good reason, like someone being mean or unfair, you can talk to a trusted adult about it and find a solution together. But if it's for a small mistake or accident, remember what Jesus said and try to forgive and make peace with that person.

By following Jesus' teachings, we can learn to control our anger, treat others with kindness, and build stronger relationships with the people around us.

This is what Jesus is talking about in Matthew 5:21-26 when He says "whoever is angry with his brother without cause". Jesus is teaching us that our thoughts and attitudes as well as our physical actions can be just as wrong. All of these things can all be wrong and hurtful.

Matthew 5:21-26 NKJV, But I say unto you, That whosoever is angry with his brother without a cause shall be in danger of the judgment: and whosoever shall say to his brother, Raca, shall be in danger of the council: but whosoever shall say, Thou fool, shall be in danger of hell fire. "You have heard that it was said to those of old, 'You shall not murder, and whoever murders will be in danger of the judgment.' But I say to you that whoever is angry with his brother without a cause shall be in danger of the judgment. And whoever says to his brother, 'Raca!' shall be in danger of the council. But whoever says, 'You fool!' shall be in danger of hell fire. Therefore if you bring your gift to the altar, and there remember that your brother has something against you, leave your gift there before the altar, and go your way. First be reconciled to your brother, and then come and offer your gift. Agree with your adversary quickly, while you are on the way with him, lest your adversary deliver you to the judge, the judge hand you over to the officer, and you be thrown into prison. Assuredly, I say to you, you will by no means get out of there till you have paid the last penny.

Controlling Our Anger
Knowing All The Facts

James 1:19-20 says, 'My dear brothers and sisters, take note of this: Everyone should be quick to listen, slow to speak, and slow to become angry, because human anger does not produce the righteousness that God desires.'"

Jesus is teaching us an important lesson here, and it's all about how we should behave towards others. He wants us to remember three things: listening, speaking carefully, and controlling our anger.

First, Jesus says be quick to listen. This means that when someone is talking to us, we should pay attention to what they are saying. We should listen carefully and try to understand their words, feelings, and thoughts. Listening is very important because it shows that we care about others and what they have to say.

Second, Jesus tells us to be slow to speak. This means we should think before we talk. We need to choose our words wisely and be careful with what we say. Sometimes, if we speak too quickly without thinking, we might say something hurtful or mean. But if we take our time and think about our words, we can use them to encourage and help others.

Lastly, Jesus wants us to be slow to become angry. Anger is a strong feeling we might have when something upsets or frustrates us. But Jesus tells us that getting angry doesn't help us or make things better. Instead, it can make things worse. So, we should try to control our anger and not let it take over us. This way, we can act in a kind and loving way, just like Jesus wants us to.

In summary, Jesus wants us to listen carefully, speak thoughtfully, and control our anger. By following these teachings, we can grow closer to God and treat others with kindness and love.

James 1:19-20 ESV, Know this, my beloved brothers: let every person be quick to hear, slow to speak, slow to anger; for the anger of man does not produce the righteousness of God.

A CHILDREN'S GUIDE TO A GODLY WAY OF LIFE

Animals

Jesus taught us many important lessons about animals and how we should treat them.

God's Love and Care For All Animals

Jesus reminds us of God's love and care for all animals in Matthew 6:26, He says, "Look at the birds of the air; they do not sow or reap or store away in barns, and yet your heavenly Father feeds them. Are you not much more valuable than they?"

God takes care of all creatures, including birds. He provides them with food and takes care of their needs. Jesus is telling us that if God cares for the birds, who are not as important as us, then surely He will take care of us because we are much more valuable to Him.

This means that we can learn to trust God just like the birds do. We don't need to worry about things like food and clothes because God promises to take care of us. He knows what we need and will provide for us, just like He does for the birds.

Jesus also wants us to appreciate and respect animals. When we see birds flying freely in the sky, we can remember that God created them and takes care of them. We can learn from their carefree nature and trust in God's provision.

Matthew 6:26 NIV Look at the birds of the air; they do not sow or reap or store away in barns, and yet your heavenly Father feeds them. Are you not much more valuable than they?

Compassion Towards Animals

Jesus teaches us to be compassionate towards animals. In Proverbs 12:10, it says, "The righteous care for the needs of their animals, but the kindest acts of the wicked are cruel." This verse reminds us that taking care of animals is a reflection of our character.

Jesus taught us to be kind and compassionate towards all living creatures, including animals. He wants us to take care of them and make sure they have everything they need to be happy and healthy.

When the Bible says "the righteous care for the needs of their animals," it means that good and kind-hearted people make sure their pets and other animals are well-fed, have a safe place to live, and receive love and attention. They treat animals with respect and compassion, just like Jesus would want us to.

On the other hand, the verse also talks about how even the kindest acts of the wicked can be cruel. This means that even if someone seems nice, if they treat animals badly or harm them, it shows that they are not truly kind-hearted.

So, Jesus teaches us to be loving and caring towards animals, just as we would be towards other people. We should always remember to treat them with kindness, respect their lives, and take care of them just as Jesus takes care of us.

Remember, animals are part of God's creation, and it is our responsibility to treat them with love and compassion.

Proverbs 12:10 NIV The righteous care for the needs of their animals, but the kindest acts of the wicked are cruel.

Responsibility As Caretakers

Jesus reminds us that we have a responsibility to care for God's creation. In Genesis 1:26, God gives humans dominion over the animals, which means we should protect and responsibly manage them.

God created humans in His own image, which means He made us special and unique. But it also tells us something important about animals. God gave us a responsibility to take care of them.

Jesus taught us many things about love, kindness, and compassion, and that includes how we should treat animals. He showed us that all living creatures, including animals, are part of God's creation and deserve our love and respect.

Just like we have feelings and emotions, animals also have their own feelings. They can feel happy, sad, or scared, just like us. Jesus wants us to be kind to animals, to take care of them, and to treat them with love and compassion.

We can show this by being gentle with animals, not hurting or being mean to them. We can help them when they are in need, like feeding a hungry bird or giving water to a thirsty animal. We can also protect them and their habitats, as it is our responsibility to be good stewards of God's creation.

Remember, Jesus taught us to love and care for all of God's creation, and that includes animals. So let's always try to be kind to them and treat them with love, just like Jesus taught us.

Genesis 1:26 NIV Then God said, "Let us make mankind in our image, in our likeness, so that they may rule over the fish in the sea and the birds in the sky, over the livestock and all the wild animals,[a] and over all the creatures that move along the ground."

Appreciating The Beauty Of Creation

Jesus often used nature and animals in his teachings to illustrate spiritual truths. For example, in Matthew 6:28-29, Jesus talks about how the lilies of the field and how they are clothed with beauty by God. This reminds us to appreciate and marvel at the beauty of God's creation, including animals.

Matthew 6:28-29 it talks about what Jesus taught us about animals. It says, "Consider the lilies of the field, how they grow: they neither toil nor spin, yet I tell you, even Solomon in all his glory was not arrayed like one of these."

Now, this might sound a little bit confusing at first, but let me explain it to you. Jesus wants us to look at the beautiful flowers in the field, called lilies. He tells us to notice how they grow without any worries or hard work. But even though they don't do any work, they are still very beautiful.

Jesus uses this example to teach us that just like the lilies, animals are also important and special in their own way. He wants us to appreciate and take care of them. Jesus wants us to learn from the simplicity and beauty of nature.

So, when Jesus taught us about animals, He wanted us to understand that they are a part of God's creation, just like we are. He wants us to show kindness and love towards animals, just as we would towards other people. We should take care of them, protect them, and treat them with respect, just like we would want to be treated.

Matthew 6:28-29 NIV And why do you worry about clothes? See how the flowers of the field grow. They do not labor or spin. Yet I tell you that not even Solomon in all his splendor was dressed like one of these.

A CHILDREN'S GUIDE TO A GODLY WAY OF LIFE

Asking

God's Rules for Asking: Ask in Jesus Name and God will do it, Ask having faith with no doubting, Ask for the Right Things, Ask According to His Will, Keep God's Commandments

God's Rules For Asking

Rules for Asking	
Ask In Jesus Name	John 14:14
Ask In Faith & With No Doubting	James 1:6-7
Ask for the Right Things and not spend it on our passions	James 4:3
Ask According to His Will	1 John 5:14-15
Keep His Commandments	1 John 3:22

God wants us to ask Him for everything; however God has rules for asking Him for anything. His rules are quite simple and straight forward but they are rules.

The basic rules are we ask Him "in Jesus name", as John 14:14 tells us to do, "ask in faith and with no doubting" as James 1:6-7 tells us to do, ask for the right things and not to "spend it on our passions" as James 4:3 tells us which simply means that we ask for the right things, "ask according to His will" as 1 John 5:14-15 tells us to do, and we "keep his commandments and do those things that are pleasing in his sight" as 1 John 3:22 has instructed us to do.

How do we know how do do these things? Let's take a look at each one.

John 14:14 ESV, If you ask me anything in my name, I will do it.

James 1:6-7 ESV, But let him ask in faith, with no doubting, for the one who doubts is like a wave of the sea that is driven and tossed by the wind. For that person must not suppose that he will receive anything from the Lord;

James 4:3 ESV, You ask and do not receive, because you ask wrongly, to spend it on your passions.

1 John 5:14-15 KJV, And this is the confidence that we have in him, that, if we ask any thing according to his will, he heareth us: and if we know that he hear us, whatsoever we ask, we know that we have the petitions that we desired of him.

1 John 3:22 KJV, And whatsoever we ask, we receive of him, because we keep his commandments, and do those things that are pleasing in his sight.

Ask In Jesus Name

How do we ask in Jesus name? We say "In Jesus name" either at the beginning or at the ending of whatever we are asking for. It's that simple.

Ask in Faith & Without Doubting

How do we "ask in Faith & Without Doubting"? Well, this one takes a little more time and understanding of God and Jesus. You know God, Jesus, our creator, can do anything, right? Yes, of course they can. God created everything we know, the earth, time, trees, animals, even us. Everything we know and even things we don't know about, God created. God can do anything.

Knowing God, our creator can do anything and everything, is there any doubt, He can do anything we could ever ask Him to do? No, there isn't is there. He can do everything. But will He do it? That is the real question, isn't it? We know he CAN do it. There is NO doubt he can do it.

Ask in Faith

The dictionary says faith is "complete trust or confidence in someone or something". See also chapter on Faith.

When we know God can do everything, our faith says, we believe He have faith God will do whatever He says He will do.

Faith is this believing God will do what He says He will do. Faith is what helps us believe and trust in God even when bad or scary things happen. Faith is what we use when we are not sure if things are going to turn out the way you we think they should or want them to turn out. With faith, we can pray and say, "Jesus, I do not know or understand why this is happening, but I am going to use my faith in You and trust that everything is going to be all right in my life." This is how faith helps us get through the bad times or scary times in our lives.

A Psalm is a song. We learn in Hebrews 1:11, which is a lyric from a song or Psalm 102:126-127, Faith is "confidence in what we hope for and assurance about what we do not see".

Hebrews 1:11 KJV "They shall perish; but thou remainest; and they all shall wax old as doth a garment;"

Psalm 102:126-127 KJV "They shall perish, but thou shalt endure: yea, all of them shall wax old like a garment; as a vesture shalt thou change them, and they shall be changed: "

Ask with How Much Faith?

You may be thinking, I have faith, but how much faith does it take Well, Jesus tells us just a tiny bit of faith. In Matthew 17:20, Jesus tell us that "if you have faith as a grain of mustard seed". A grain of mustard seed is about the size of a tiny dot or period at the end of a sentence. Maybe a little bit larger. Anyway, this isn't very much is it? Jesus tells us that is all we need for faith. If we just believe that much, we can do anything.

Matthew 17:20 KJV And Jesus said unto them, Because of your unbelief: for verily I say unto you, If ye have faith as a grain of mustard seed, ye shall say unto this mountain, Remove hence to yonder place; and it shall remove; and nothing shall be impossible unto you.

Faith as much as a tiny mustard seed, isn't very much, is it? We know God, Jesus, our creator can do anything right? He created the heavens, the earth and everything we know of and can every know about, so He can do anything. So having faith or believing He can do anything is easy to believe, isn't it? Having faith as much or more than a tiny mustard seed is easy , isn't it? Yes, it is! We know He can do everything so Asking Him without doubting is easy for us, isn't it? Yes, it is!

Ask having No Doubt

Doubt is basically not knowing something, not being sure about something.

In this form, a doubt is okay, because when you don't know something or you don't understand something, you ask questions in order to understand it. We asking questions to help us learn and feel more confident in our beliefs.

However, adults don't always have all the answers and our questions are hard even for adults to answer.

We do not need to have any doubts because 1 John 5:4 tells us every child of God can use Faith to overcome bad things. Isn't that amazing! I love when God takes such great care of us. Because we are His, a child of God. He gives us the ability to use our "faith" to overcome everything in this world.

No doubt about this one. God has taken all doubts away, hasn't He? If we have faith, we need not have any doubts.

1 John 5:4 KJV "For whatsoever is born of God overcometh the world: and this is the victory that overcometh the world, even our faith."

Ask in Faith & Without Doubt

When we don't get the answers we need because the adults don't always know how to answer all of our questions, we have our faith in God, our complete trust that God will do what he says He will do to helps us believe and know, that is to have trust in God even when things go bad.

This is what is meant by "Ask in Faith & Without Doubt" . It is knowing God will always do what He says. He will do what He has said He will do regardless of whatever else is going on in the world or in our lives. This is what gives us the confidence to believe in God and have the faith in Him.

We may not always see the bigger picture of everything that God sees to know all that is going on, but God does. We can trust that God has our best interests in place and He will keep His promises to us in everything He does.

Rules for Asking	
Ask In Jesus Name	John 14:14
Ask In Faith & With No Doubting	James 1:6-7
Ask for the Right Things and not spend it on our passions	James 4:3
Ask According to His Will	1 John 5:14-15
Keep His Commandments	1 John 3:22

John 14:14 ESV, If you ask me anything in my name, I will do it.

James 1:6-7 ESV, But let him ask in faith, with no doubting, for the one who doubts is like a wave of the sea that is driven and tossed by the wind. For that person must not suppose that he will receive anything from the Lord;

James 4:3 ESV, You ask and do not receive, because you ask wrongly, to spend it on your passions.

1 John 5:14-15 KJV, And this is the confidence that we have in him, that, if we ask any thing according to his will, he heareth us: and if we know that he hear us, whatsoever we ask, we know that we have the petitions that we desired of him.

1 John 3:22 KJV, And whatsoever we ask, we receive of him, because we keep his commandments, and do those things that are pleasing in his sight.

Ask For The Right Things

The next rule God has for asking Him is that we ask Him for the right things. In James 4:3, it tells us that if we ask but we do not receive anything it is because we have asked wrongly. We may have asked for something that only benefits us and no one else.

God wants us to ask Him for things that glorify Him. The Bible teaches us to glorify God is to mirror His image, which is to love and honor Him with praise or worship, and to love generously, as He does.

The way we we glorify God is by obeying His commands and following His will for our life. It also means using our time, talents, and resources to bless others.

If we ever wonder if we are inside our Creator's will when we ask God? God tells us that if we ask but our

If we ask and we don't receive what we ask for, it is either because, we had the wrong motives when we asked God. This means, we weren't in God's Will at the time when we asked and it was for your own pleasure. We need to rethink what you have asked and ask God again but in a way that is more suitable to A Godly purpose. Or the timing of our request isn't the right time for us right now.

Isn't that a great way for God to provide for us? God tells us to always ask Him. If we ask with the wrong motives or attitude, He will say No but we can ask again with the right motives or attitude. When we have the right real need to whatever we are asking, God will provide it to us because He loves us and wants to provide for our needs.

James 4:3, "When you ask, you do not receive, because you ask with wrong motives, that you may spend what you get on your pleasures".

Ask According to God's Will

God's will means to believe in Jesus, and to do things in line with God's plan and purpose.

1 John 5:14-15 KJV, And this is the confidence that we have in him, that, if we ask any thing according to his will, he heareth us: and if we know that he hear us, whatsoever we ask, we know that we have the petitions that we desired of him.

To ask within God's will means we ask for things that are in line with God's plan and purpose. To says this ever more simply, it is to ask for the things that God wants. God is straight forward in communicating the things He wants from us. For example, 1 Timothy 2:3-4, shares with us that God wants all people to be saved and to come to a knowledge of truth.

1 Timothy 2:3-4 – "This is good, and pleases God our Savior, who wants all people to be saved and to come to a knowledge of the truth."

God tells us all through the Bible the things that He wants from us and for us by saying He "wants" this. God will also say His will by saying God's "will" or God's "plan" for us is … in the scripture. Some examples of these are: Jeremiah 29:11, which talks about God's plans for us, to prosper us and not harm us, to give us hope and a future, 1 Thessalonians 5:18, which is God's will for us to give thanks in all circumstances, and 1 John 1:9, that says if we confess our sins, he is faithful and just and will forgive us our sins and purify us from all unrighteousness

Jeremiah 29:11 For I know the plans I have for you," declares the LORD, "plans to prosper you and not to harm you, plans to give you hope and a future

1 Thessalonians 5:18 give thanks in all circumstances; for this is God's will for you in Christ Jesus

1 John 1:9 If we confess our sins, he is faithful and just and will forgive us our sins and purify us from all unrighteousness

Ask Keeping God's Commandments

The last of God's most important rules for asking Him is that we keep his commandments in 1 John 3:22, that tells us that "whatsoever we ask, we keep his commandments".

1 John 3:22 KJV, And whatsoever we ask, we receive of him, because we keep his commandments, and do those things that are pleasing in his sight.

God's first and greatest commandment is in Matthew 22:37:39 which commands us "Thou shalt love the Lord thy God with all thy heart, and with all thy soul, and with all thy mind. This is the first and great commandment."

Matthew 22:37-39 KJV Jesus said unto him, Thou shalt love the Lord thy God with all thy heart, and with all thy soul, and with all thy mind. This is the first and great commandment.

God's commandments are throughout the Bible from the book of Genesis through the book of Revelation. See Chapter **Commandments** for a more comprehensive list of God's commandments.

Now we know and trust these 5 very important things we've learned about asking our creator for the things we want or need in our lives. We can feel confident asking God for these things, can't we? Yes, we can because we can ask faithfully without doubt or fear, can't we? Yes we can!

LADY KIMBERLY MOTES DOTY, AURORA BRAND & CONOR FINNEGAN

Attitude

Attitude is how we think, feel and act towards other people and things.

Our attitude is what we think, feel and how we act towards other people and things. Sometimes we can act one way towards people but think something very different about them in our minds.

Jesus taught what we think and feel, our attitude, is just as important to Him as how we act. What we really think about something should be the way we act towards it.

It is better to be nice to everyone even when we are angry. Even though I do agree with this, there is a right way and a not so right way to do this.

In this short story, we learn about what Jesus taught us about how our attitude, or how we think, feel or act towards other people and things affects us.

Once upon a time, there was a boy named Conor. Conor loved to play with his friends and have fun. One day, Conor woke up feeling grumpy. He didn't want to talk to anyone or do anything. Conor's friends tried to cheer him up, but he just kept frowning and saying mean things.

Conor's mom noticed his bad attitude and called him over to talk. She reminded him of something that Jesus taught us. In the Bible, in Luke 6:31, Jesus said, "Do to others as you would have them do to you". Conor's mom explained that this means we should treat others the way we want to be treated.

Conor started to understand. He realized that his grumpy attitude was making him feel even worse. He didn't like when his friends ignored him or said mean things, so he decided to change his attitude.

The next day, Conor woke up with a smile on his face. He greeted his friends with kindness and helped them when they needed it. And you know what? Conor felt so much happier! His friends started being nice to him too, and they all had a great time playing together.

Conor learned an important lesson that day. He learned that when we have a good attitude, it not only makes others feel good, but it also makes us feel good too. Jesus taught us that being kind and treating others with love is the best way to live.

So, remember children, always try to have a positive attitude and treat others the way you want to be treated. You'll be amazed at how it can make your life better!

Luke 6:31 NIV "Do to others as you would have them do to you."

Baptism

Baptism is a special ceremony that people do to show they believe in Jesus and want to follow Him.

Baptism is a special ceremony that people do to show that they believe in Jesus and want to follow Him. It's kind of like a way to say, "I love Jesus and I want to be part of His family!"

When someone gets baptized, they usually go into a pool of water or a special tub, and a pastor or a church leader will pour water over their head or dunk them underwater for a moment. This is a symbol of washing away their old life and starting fresh with Jesus.

In the Bible, Matthew 28:19 talks about baptism. In this verse, Jesus said this to His followers: "Go and make disciples of all nations, baptizing them in the name of the Father and of the Son and of the Holy Spirit."

This means that Jesus told His friends to go and tell people about Him and baptize them as a way of showing they want to be His followers. It's a special way to let everyone know that they believe in Jesus and want to live like Him.

So, if you ever see someone getting baptized or if you want to get baptized someday, remember that it's a way to show your love for Jesus and to start a new life with Him.

Matthew 28:19 NIV Therefore go and make disciples of all nations, baptizing them in the name of the Father and of the Son and of the Holy Spirit,

A CHILDREN'S GUIDE TO A GODLY WAY OF LIFE

Blasphemy

Blasphemy means saying something disrespectful or offensive about God or sacred things.

What Is Blasphemy

Blasphemy is when someone says or does something disrespectful or hurtful towards God. It's important to be respectful and kind when talking about God and our beliefs.

In a story from the Bible called Matthew 12:22-31, Jesus encounters some people who were saying bad things about him and the miracles he was doing. They were trying to say that Jesus was working with the devil, which was a very hurtful thing to say.

Jesus explained to them that this kind of thinking was wrong. He said that if they spoke against him, it could be forgiven, but if they spoke against the Holy Spirit, it would not be forgiven. This means that if people reject the love and goodness that comes from God, it is a very serious thing.

Jesus wanted us to understand that we should always respect God and not say mean things about Him or His ways. God loves us unconditionally, and Jesus taught us to show love and kindness to others as well. Blasphemy is like hurting God's feelings, and Jesus wanted us to avoid doing that because it can separate us from His love and forgiveness.

So, in simple words, Jesus taught us that we should never say or do anything that disrespects or hurts God. It's important to always remember to be kind, loving, and respectful towards God and others.

Mark 3:29 NIV, but whoever blasphemes against the Holy Spirit will never be forgiven; they are guilty of an eternal sin

Matthew 12:22–31 NIV Then they brought him a demon-possessed man who was blind and mute, and Jesus healed him, so that he could both talk and see. All the people were astonished and said, "Could this be the Son of David?" But when the Pharisees heard this, they said, "It is only by Beelzebul, the prince of demons, that this fellow drives out demons." Jesus knew their thoughts and said to them, "Every kingdom divided against itself will be ruined, and every city or household divided against itself will not stand. If Satan drives out Satan, he is divided against himself. How then can his kingdom stand? And if I drive out demons by Beelzebul, by whom do your people drive them out? So then, they will be your judges. But if it is by the Spirit of God that I drive out demons, then the kingdom of God has come upon you. "Or again, how can anyone enter a strong man's house and carry off his possessions unless he first ties up the strong man? Then he can plunder his house. "Whoever is not with me is against me, and whoever does not gather with me scatters. And so I tell you, every kind of sin and slander can be forgiven, but blasphemy against the Spirit will not be forgiven.

Luke 12:10 ESV, And everyone who speaks a word against the Son of Man will be forgiven, but the one who blasphemes against the Holy Spirit will not be forgiven.

Blasphemy Against The Holy Spirit

Blasphemy against the Holy Spirit is something much more serious.

The Holy Spirit is a part of God, and He helps us understand what is right and wrong. He is like a little voice inside our hearts that tells us to be kind, loving, and helpful. When we listen to the Holy Spirit, we make good choices and try to make the world a better place.

But blasphemy against the Holy Spirit means that someone is being really mean or disrespectful to God's Spirit. It's like ignoring that little voice in our hearts and doing the opposite of what it tells us. This is a very serious thing because it means refusing to listen to what is good and right.

The Bible verse Matthew 12:31 says, "So I tell you, every kind of sin and slander can be forgiven, but blasphemy against the Spirit will not be forgiven." This means that God is very forgiving and loving, and He can forgive us when we make mistakes or do wrong things. But when someone keeps on disrespecting and rejecting the Holy Spirit, refusing to change their ways, it becomes harder for them to ask for forgiveness.

It's important for us to remember that God loves us and wants us to do good. We should always listen to the Holy Spirit and try to be kind and loving to everyone. And if we ever make a mistake, we can ask God for forgiveness, and He will always forgive us.

Matthew 12:31 NIV And so I tell you, every kind of sin and slander can be forgiven, but blasphemy against the Spirit will not be forgiven.

LADY KIMBERLY MOTES DOTY, AURORA BRAND & CONOR FINNEGAN

Born Again

Being Born Again means having new beginning in our relationship with God.

Being born again means having a new beginning with God, accepting His love, and allowing Him to change us from the inside out. It's like starting a beautiful journey with Jesus, where we learn and grow in His teachings and become the best version of ourselves.

Just like a baby is born into a family and starts a new life, we can be born again into God's family and start a new life with Him. It's a special and important thing that Jesus talked about in the Bible.

In the Bible, in the book of John 3:3 Jesus said, "Truly, truly, I say to you, unless one is born again, he cannot see the kingdom of God."

Now, being born again doesn't mean physically being born out of our mother once more. It means experiencing a spiritual rebirth, a change that happens within our hearts and souls. Just like when we are born as a baby, we grow and learn new things, being born again means starting fresh and growing in our relationship with God.

You see, Jesus wants us to have a close relationship with God and be a part of His kingdom. He taught us that being born again is like having a fresh start, like becoming a new person. It means letting go of the things that keep us away from God's love and choosing to follow Him with all our hearts.

When we are born again, we become more like Jesus. We learn to love and forgive others, to be kind and compassionate, just like He was. Jesus wants us to have a heart that is full of love, joy, peace, patience, kindness, goodness, faithfulness, gentleness, and self-control.

John 3:3 ESV Jesus answered him, "Truly, truly, I say to you, unless one is born again he cannot see the kingdom of God."

LADY KIMBERLY MOTES DOTY, AURORA BRAND & CONOR FINNEGAN

Children

In the book of Matthew, 18:1 says, "At that time, the disciples came to Jesus and asked, 'Who is the greatest in the kingdom of heaven?'"

Now, the disciples were curious about who would be considered the greatest among them, just like children sometimes wonder who is the best at something. But Jesus, being wise and loving, responded in a special way. He called a little child to come close to him and said, "Truly I tell you, unless you change and become like little children, you will never enter the kingdom of heaven."

Jesus was trying to teach his disciples, and all of us, an important lesson. He wanted us to understand that we should be humble, innocent, and trusting, just like children. You see, children have pure hearts and minds. They believe without doubting and have a simple faith. They are not burdened by pride or selfishness.

Jesus wants us to be like children in our relationship with God, to trust Him completely and rely on Him for everything. He wants us to have a childlike faith, believing in His love and following His teachings with joy and obedience. Jesus also wants us to treat others with kindness and love, just as children often do naturally.

When we read this verse in the Bible, we learn that Jesus wants us to be like children in our hearts. He wants us to be humble, innocent, and full of trust, just like you. And when we do that, we can truly experience the love and blessings of God's kingdom.

Mathew 18:1 NIV "At that time, the disciples came to Jesus and asked, 'Who is the greatest in the kingdom of heaven?'"

Be Humble, Loving, Trusting

Also in the book of Matthew 18:2-4, Jesus called a little child and told his friends that they should become like that child if they want to enter God's kingdom. He said that we should humble ourselves and become like little children.

So, what does that mean? It means that Jesus wants us to have some special qualities that children often have. Children are usually very trusting and innocent. They believe in things without questioning too much. Jesus wants us to trust him and believe in him just like children do.

Children are also very dependent on their parents. They rely on them for everything. Jesus wants us to depend on him too, to trust that he will take care of us and guide us through life.

Children are also very curious and eager to learn. Jesus wants us to have that same eagerness to learn about God and his teachings. He wants us to ask questions and seek answers, just like children do.

Lastly, children are often very loving and forgiving. They don't hold grudges or stay angry for too long. Jesus wants us to be loving and forgiving towards others, just like children are.

So, when Jesus tells us to become like children, he wants us to have these special qualities - to trust him, depend on him, be curious, eager to learn, and to love and forgive others. By following these teachings, we can grow closer to God and experience the joy of his kingdom.

Matthew 18:2-4 NIV He called a little child to him, and placed the child among them. And he said: "Truly I tell you, unless you change and become like little children, you will never enter the kingdom of heaven. Therefore, whoever takes the lowly position of this child is the greatest in the kingdom of heaven.

Don't Harm Children

Continuing in Matthew 18:6, Jesus said, "But if anyone causes one of these little ones who believe in me to stumble, it would be better for them to have a large millstone hung around their neck and to be drowned in the depths of the sea."

Now, this might sound a bit serious, but let me explain what Jesus meant. He was telling us that children are very special to him and to God. He wants us to be protected and loved, just like how parents take care of their children.

Jesus was saying that if anyone tries to harm or hurt a child, it's a very serious thing. He wants us to understand that children are precious and should be treated with kindness, respect, and love.

Jesus wants us to have childlike qualities, such as being humble, trusting, and having faith. Children are often curious, full of wonder, and they believe in things with all their heart. Jesus wants us to have that same childlike faith in him and in God.

He also wants us to be humble, which means not being proud or thinking we are better than others. Children are usually very humble and don't boast about themselves. Jesus wants us to have that same attitude of kindness and humility.

Jesus taught us that children are precious and should be protected. He also wants us to have childlike qualities of faith, trust, and humility. Remember, Jesus loves you just as you are, and he wants you to grow up to be a kind and loving person.

Matthew 18:6 NIV "If anyone causes one of these little ones—those who believe in me—to stumble, it would be better for them to have a large millstone hung around their neck and to be drowned in the depths of the sea.

Be Kind To Children

In Matthew 10:42, Jesus says, "And if anyone gives even a cup of cold water to one of these little ones who is my disciple, truly I tell you, that person will certainly not lose their reward."

This means that Jesus wants us to show kindness and help other people, especially those who are younger or in need. It's important to care for each other just like how parents take care of their children.

Matthew 10:42 KJV, "And whosoever shall give to drink unto one of these little ones a cup of cold water only in the name of a disciple, verily I say unto you, he shall in no wise lose his reward."

Help Children

In Matthew 25:40, Jesus says, "Truly I tell you, whatever you did for one of the least of these brothers and sisters of mine, you did for me."

This means that when we help others, it's like we are helping Jesus Himself. Jesus wants us to treat everyone with love and respect, just like how children should be treated.

Matthew 25:40 KJV, "And the King shall answer and say unto them, Verily I say unto you, Inasmuch as ye have done it unto one of the least of these my brethren, ye have done it unto me."

Protect Children

In Matthew 18:10, Jesus says, "See that you do not despise one of these little ones. For I tell you that their angels in heaven always see the face of my Father in heaven."

This means that children are special to God. Jesus wants us to protect and take care of children, because they are important to God. We should never look down on or hurt them, but instead, we should show them kindness and love.

Matthew 18:10, ESV, "See that you do not despise one of these little ones. For I tell you that in heaven their angels always see the face of my Father who is in heaven.

So, in summary, Jesus taught us that being children means being kind, helping others, treating everyone with love and respect, and protecting and taking care of children. Jesus wants us to be like children in these ways, because it makes God happy.

Childlike Faith, Love & Trust

The next thing Jesus teaches us about children is also found in Matthew, Matthew 19:13-15, where he tells us that to enter the kingdom, "we must become like a child".

In Matthew 19:13-15, Mark 10:13-16, and Luke 18:15-18, it tells us about children who wanted to meet Jesus. When the disciples tried to stop the children from coming to Jesus, Jesus said, "Let the little children come to me, and do not hinder them, for the kingdom of heaven belongs to such as these."

What Jesus meant by this is that he wants us to be like children in certain ways. Children are innocent, trusting, and have a pure heart. They are not burdened with worries or pride like some grown-ups can be. Jesus is telling us that in order to enter heaven, we should have a childlike faith, love, and trust in God.

Children are also humble, which means they are not concerned about being the greatest or most important. Jesus wants us to be humble too, and not think we are better than others. Instead, we should love and care for everyone, just like children do.

So, when Jesus said we should be innocent like children, he meant that we should have a pure heart, trust in God, be humble, and love others without any selfishness. These qualities are important if we want to follow Jesus and enter the kingdom of heaven.

Matthew 19:13-15 ESV, Then children were brought to him that he might lay his hands on them and pray. The disciples rebuked the people, but Jesus said, "Let the little children come to me and do not hinder them, for to such belongs the kingdom of heaven." And he laid his hands on them and went away.

Mark 10:13-16 KJV, And they brought young children to him, that he should touch them: and his disciples rebuked those that brought them. But when Jesus saw it, he was much displeased, and said unto them, Suffer the little children to come unto me, and forbid them not: for of such is the kingdom of God. Verily I say unto you, Whosoever shall not receive the kingdom of God as a little child, he shall not enter therein. And he took them up in his arms, put his hands upon them, and blessed them.

Luke 18:15-18 KJV, And they brought unto him also infants, that he would touch them: but when his disciples saw it, they rebuked them. But Jesus called them unto him, and said, Suffer little children to come unto me, and forbid them not: for of such is the kingdom of God. Verily I say unto you, Whosoever shall not receive the kingdom of God as a little child shall in no wise enter therein. And a certain ruler asked him, saying, Good Master, what shall I do to inherit eternal life?

A CHILDREN'S GUIDE TO A GODLY WAY OF LIFE

Commandments

A commandment is like a rule that God gives us to help us live in a good and fair way that pleases God.

The Bible contains many commandments for the way God wants us to live our lives.

Love God With All Your Heart, Soul, Mind

Matthew 22:36-40 is a part of the Bible where Jesus is talking to some people. He is asked a question about which commandment is the most important, and Jesus gives a very special answer.

He says that the most important commandment is to love God with all our heart, soul, and mind. This means that we should love God with everything we have, like our feelings, our thoughts, and our whole being.

But Jesus doesn't stop there. He also tells us that there is another commandment that is just as important. He says that we should love our neighbors as ourselves. This means that we should treat other people with kindness and love, just like we would want to be treated.

Matthew 22:36-40 KJV Master, which is the great commandment in the law? Jesus said unto him, Thou shalt love the Lord thy God with all thy heart, and with all thy soul, and with all thy mind. This is the first and great commandment. And the second is like unto it, Thou shalt love thy neighbor as thyself. On these two commandments hang all the law and the prophets.

Honor Dad & Mom

In Ephesians 6:2, Paul says, "Honor your father and mother," which means that children should show respect and love to their parents. It's like saying that we should listen to our parents, be kind to them, and obey their rules.

Paul goes on to say that this commandment comes with a special promise. Can you guess what that promise might be? It's a promise that things will go well for us and that we'll live a long and happy life!

So, in simple words, Ephesians 6:2 is telling us that it's important for kids to honor and respect their parents. By doing so, we not only make our parents happy, but we also receive blessings and a good life in return.

Remember, our parents take care of us, love us, and want what's best for us. So, it's important to show them love and respect in return.

Ephesians 6:2 "Honor your father and mother"— which is the first commandment with a promise— "

A CHILDREN'S GUIDE TO A GODLY WAY OF LIFE

Rule Over Everything on Earth

It's a reminder for us to be responsible and make sure that we live in harmony with nature.

Take Care Of The Earth

Genesis 1:28 is a verse from the Bible that talks about a commandment given to humans. It says, "God blessed them and said to them, 'Be fruitful and increase in number; fill the earth and subdue it. Rule over the fish in the sea and the birds in the sky and over every living creature that moves on the ground.'"

Now, let's break it down in a way that's easy to understand. Imagine that you are playing in a big room with lots of toys. Your parents come in and tell you something important. They say, "We want you to take care of all the toys in this room and have fun with them, but make sure you don't break them. You can play with everything, but remember to be responsible."

Fill The Earth

Similarly, in Genesis 1:28, God is talking to the first humans, Adam and Eve. He is telling them that they have a special role on Earth. God wants them to take care of the planet and all the animals that live in it. He asks them to have babies and **make sure there are more people on Earth**. But it's not just about having lots of people; it's about being responsible and taking care of everything around them.

Take Care of All The Animals

God also tells them that they have the authority to rule over the fish in the sea, the birds in the sky, and all the animals that walk on land. This means that humans have a responsibility to look after and protect all the living creatures on Earth.

Genesis 1:28 is a commandment from God to take care of the Earth and all the animals in it. It's a reminder for us to be responsible and make sure that we live in harmony with nature.

Genesis 1:28 NIV God blessed them and said to them, "Be fruitful and increase in number; fill the earth and subdue it. Rule over the fish in the sea and the birds in the sky and over every living creature that moves on the ground."

The Ten Commandments

You shall have no other gods before me

Exodus 20:3 is one of the Ten Commandments given by God to the people of Israel. It says, "You shall have no other gods before me."

Now, let's imagine you have a very special toy that you love so much. You play with it every day and it brings you a lot of joy. But one day, someone comes to you and says, "Hey, I have a different toy that is even more amazing than the one you have. You should forget about your toy and play with this one instead."

Now, this commandment is like a rule from God that tells us that we should only worship and love Him. It means that we should not give our love and devotion to anything or anyone else before God. Just like you shouldn't forget about your special toy for another one, we should always remember that God is the most important and special in our lives.

God loves us so much that He wants us to have a close relationship with Him. He wants us to trust and rely on Him, and not to put anything else above Him. This commandment reminds us to always remember God's love and to keep Him as the number one in our hearts.

So, in simple words, Exodus 20:3 tells us that we should only have God as our most important and special one, and not put anything or anyone else before Him.

Exodus 20:3 KJV Thou shalt have no other gods before me.

Thou shalt not make yourself an idol

Exodus 20:4 is one of the commandments from the Bible. It says, "You shall not make for yourself an idol or worship any other gods besides me."

Imagine you have a very special toy that you love so much. You play with it all the time, and it makes you really happy. But then, one day, your parents tell you that you shouldn't become too obsessed with that toy and ignore everything else. They want you to remember that there are other important things in life, like spending time with your family, going to school, and being kind to others.

In a similar way, this commandment is like a rule from God. He wants us to remember that He is the most important and the only God we should worship. It means we shouldn't make statues or images of things and worship them, thinking they are gods. We should only worship and love God, who created everything in the world, including us.

This commandment reminds us that God wants us to give Him our love, trust, and respect, just like we give our love and attention to our family and friends. He wants us to focus on Him and follow His teachings, rather than following false gods or things that are not real.

So, the commandment in Exodus 20:4 is a reminder to put God first in our lives and not worship or make idols of other things. We should always remember that God is the most important and deserves our love and worship.

Exodus 20:4 KJV Thou shalt not make unto thee any graven image, or any likeness of any thing that is in heaven above, or that is in the earth beneath, or that is in the water under the earth.

Thou shalt not take the name of the Lord thy God in vain

Exodus 20:7 is one of the Ten Commandments that God gave to the people of Israel a long time ago. It says, "You shall not take the name of the Lord your God in vain." Now, let's try to understand what this means.

When we talk about someone's name, it's not just the word we use to call them, but it represents who they are. Like your name represents who you are, your identity. Similarly, God's name represents who He is, and it is very special.

So, when the commandment says "do not take the name of the Lord your God in vain," it means we should not use God's name carelessly or disrespectfully. We should always speak of God and use His name with honor, love, and respect.

Sometimes people use God's name in a way that doesn't show respect. They might say it when they are angry or frustrated, or use it as a bad word. This commandment reminds us that we should use God's name in a way that shows reverence and love towards Him.

Instead of using God's name in a disrespectful way, we should use it to pray, to worship, and to talk to God with love and gratitude. We should remember that God is our creator and protector, and He deserves our utmost respect.

So, as a commandment, it teaches us to always remember the importance of God's name and to use it with honor and reverence.

Remember the Sabbath day and keep it Holy

Exodus 20:8 is one of the Ten Commandments, which are rules that God gave to His people a long time ago. This specific commandment says, "Remember the Sabbath day, to keep it holy."

Now, you might be wondering what the Sabbath day is. Well, the Sabbath is a special day of the week that God wants us to set apart and make it holy. In the Bible, it says that God created the world in six days, and on the seventh day, He rested. So, God wants us to take a day off from our regular work and activities, just like He did.

By keeping the Sabbath day holy, it means that we should make it a special day to spend time with God and our families. We can use this day to go to church, read the Bible, pray, and learn about God's teachings. It's a time to rest, relax, and have fun with our loved ones.

Remembering to keep the Sabbath day holy is important because it helps us remember that God is our Creator and Provider. It also allows us to take a break from our busy lives and focus on our relationship with Him. It's like a gift from God, a day where we can recharge and connect with Him.

So, when you see Exodus 20:8, it's a reminder for us to set aside a special day each week to spend time with God and enjoy His blessings.

Honor your father and mother

Exodus 20:12 is one of the Ten Commandments, which are rules given by God to help us live a good and happy life. This specific commandment says, "Honor your father and mother."

Now, what does "honor" mean? It means to show respect, love, and appreciation to our parents. Our parents take care of us, feed us, and teach us many things. They work hard to provide us with a safe and comfortable home. So, it's important to be grateful for all that they do for us.

By obeying this commandment, we can show our parents that we love and appreciate them. We can listen to them, help them when they need it, and obey their rules. We can also say kind words to them and show them affection.

When we honor our parents, it not only makes them happy but also brings joy to our own lives. Our parents are like our guides, helping us grow and learn. So, by showing them respect and love, we can create a loving and harmonious family.

Remember, this commandment is not just for kids, but for everyone, because parents are important figures in our lives, and they deserve our honor and gratitude.

Exodus 20:12 KJV "Honor your father and your mother, that your days may be prolonged in the land which the LORD your God gives you."

Thou shalt not kill

Exodus 20:13 is a commandment given by God in the Bible. It says, "You shall not murder." Now, I know this might sound a little serious, but let me explain it in a way that makes sense to a child.

Do you know what it means to murder? Murder is when someone intentionally hurts or kills another person. But why would God give us this commandment? Well, God is all about love and kindness. He wants us to treat others with respect and care for their lives.

When we follow this commandment, it means we should never hurt or harm anyone on purpose. We should always try to solve our problems peacefully and not use violence. It teaches us to value and protect each other's lives.

Instead of hurting others, God wants us to show love, kindness, and forgiveness. He wants us to help others and treat them with respect. That way, we can live in peace and harmony with one another.

Remember, it's important to always treat others the way we would like to be treated. We should be kind and caring towards everyone, and that includes not hurting or taking someone's life.

So, the commandment "You shall not murder" is a way for God to remind us to value and protect life, to be loving and kind, and to live in peace with one another.

Exodus 20:13 KJV "Thou shalt not kill."

Thou shallot not commit adultery

Exodus 20:14 is one of the Ten Commandments from the Bible, which are rules given to us by God to help us live in a loving and respectful way. This commandment says, "You shall not commit adultery."

Now, I know that might be a big word for you, so let me break it down. Adultery means when someone who is married decides to be romantic or have a special relationship with someone who is not their husband or wife.

God wants us to have strong and happy families, and this commandment is there to remind us to always be faithful and loyal to our husbands or wives. It means that when we grow up and get married, we should only have romantic feelings and special relationships with our husband or wife.

This commandment teaches us about the importance of trust, honesty, and respect in our relationships. It's like a promise we make to our future husband or wife to always be loyal and cherish them.

Remember, God's commandments are meant to guide us towards a life filled with love and happiness. So, as we grow older, it's important to always remember and follow this commandment to show love and respect to our future partners.

Exodus 20:14 KJV Thou shalt not commit adultery.

Thou Shalt Not Steal

Exodus 20:15 is one of the commandments given by God to the people of Israel. It says, "You shall not steal." Now, let's imagine you and your friend have some toys. God wants us to be kind and respectful to others, so this commandment is like a reminder to be honest and not take something that doesn't belong to us.

Stealing means taking something that doesn't belong to you without asking or without permission. It could be taking a toy from a friend's house without telling them, or taking something from a store without paying for it. God wants us to treat others with love and respect, and stealing goes against that.

When we follow this commandment, it shows that we care about others' feelings and belongings. It's important to always ask permission and be honest when we want to use or take something that belongs to someone else. By doing this, we can create a world where everyone feels safe and respected.

Remember, God gives us commandments to help guide us in making good choices and treating others with kindness. So, let's always remember not to steal and show respect for other people's things.

Exodus 20:15 KJV Thou shalt not steal.

Thou shalt not bear false witness against thy neighbor

Exodus 20:16 is one of the Ten Commandments given to us by God. It says, "You shall not give false testimony against your neighbor."

Imagine you and your friend are playing a game, and you accidentally break something. Your friend didn't see what happened, so they ask you what happened. God wants us to always tell the truth, even when it's not easy. So, if you were to lie and say that you didn't break anything, you would be breaking this commandment.

God wants us to be honest and trustworthy. He wants us to treat others with respect and not say things about them that are not true. This commandment reminds us to always speak the truth and not to say things that could hurt others or cause trouble.

Remember, it's important to be honest and kind to others, just like God wants us to be.

Exodus 20:16 KJV Thou shalt not bear false whiteness against thy neighbor.

Thou shall not covet

Exodus 20:17 is one of the commandments given by God to the people of Israel. It says, "You shall not covet your neighbor's house. You shall not covet your neighbor's wife, or his male or female servant, his ox or donkey, or anything that belongs to your neighbor."

Now, let's break it down in a way that you can understand it better. To covet is to want or desire something that does not belong to you. So, this commandment is about not wanting or desiring things that belong to other people. It's normal to admire or like what someone else has, but this commandment is telling us not to let that turn into jealousy or wanting to take those things away from them.

For example, imagine if your friend has a really cool toy that you really want. It's okay to think it's neat and maybe even ask your friend if you can play with it, but it's not okay to feel jealous or try to take it away from them. This commandment reminds us to be happy for others and be content with what we have.

We should focus on being grateful for the things we have and not compare ourselves too much to others. It's important to remember that everyone has different things and we should respect that. Instead of feeling jealous, we can learn from others and appreciate the blessings we have in our own lives.

Exodus 20:17 KJV You shall not covet.

Repair or Replace Damaged Borrowed Items

Exodus 22:6 is a commandment from the Bible that tells us how we should take care of other people's things. It says, "If someone borrows something from their neighbor, like a bike or a toy, and it gets hurt or damaged, they have to fix it or replace it with a new one."

You see, this commandment teaches us about being responsible and respectful. When we borrow something from someone, it's like they are giving us a special trust to take care of what belongs to them. Just like we wouldn't want our things to get broken, we should treat other people's things with care and make sure we give them back in the same or even better condition.

If, by accident, something does happen to what we borrowed, this commandment reminds us to make it right by fixing or replacing it. It's all about showing kindness and being honest to others, just like we would want them to be kind and honest to us.

Remember, this commandment is a way to remind us to be responsible and thoughtful towards others, and it helps us build good relationships with our friends and neighbors.

Exodus 22:6 KJV If fire break out, and catch in thorns, so that the stacks of corn, or the standing corn, or the field, be consumed therewith; he that kindled the fire shall surely make restitution.

Right to Defend Yourself & Property

Exodus 22:8 has a commandment from God that gives us the right to defend ourselves and out property from a thief.

The commandment says, "If a thief is caught breaking in at night and is struck a fatal blow, the defender is not guilty of bloodshed."

Imagine you have a special treasure box in your room, and you want to keep it safe. One night, a thief tries to break into your room to steal your treasure. But luckily, you wake up and see the thief. In this situation, you may feel scared or want to protect yourself and your treasure.

Now, the commandment in Exodus 22:8 is saying that if you defend yourself or your property against the thief and something happens to the thief, you are not considered guilty for hurting them. It means you didn't do anything wrong because you were only protecting yourself and what is yours.

However, it's important to remember that this commandment doesn't mean we should go around hurting people. It is only talking about defending ourselves in certain situations when we are in danger.

So, the commandment is teaching us about the importance of self-defense and protecting what is ours. It reminds us that we have the right to keep ourselves safe, but we should also try to resolve conflicts peacefully whenever possible.

Exodus 22:8 KJV If the thief be not found, then the master of the house shall be brought unto the judges, to see whether he have put his hand unto his neighbor's goods.

A CHILDREN'S GUIDE TO A GODLY WAY OF LIFE

Breach of Trust

Exodus 22:9 is a verse from the Bible that talks about one of the commandments from God. In this verse, it says, "For every breach of trust, whether it is for an ox, for a donkey, for a sheep, for a cloak, or for any kind of lost thing, of which one says, 'This is it,' the case of both parties shall come before God. The one whom God condemns shall pay double to his neighbor."

Now, let's break it down to help you understand it better! Imagine you and your friend have something valuable, like a toy or a snack. If one of you loses or breaks the valuable thing, and then says, "This is it!" or "This is the one!" it means that's the thing that got lost or broken.

In this commandment, God is telling us that if someone loses or damages something that belongs to another person, they have to go to God to settle the matter. God will decide who is responsible for the loss or damage, and that person will have to pay the other person double the value of what was lost or broken.

This commandment teaches us to be careful with other people's belongings and to take responsibility for our actions. It reminds us to treat others fairly and to make things right if we make a mistake or cause harm to someone else's things.

Remember, God wants us to show love, respect, and fairness to one another, and this commandment helps us understand how to do that.

Exodus 22:9 KJV For every breach of trust, whether it is for an ox, for a donkey, for a sheep, for a cloak, or for any kind of lost thing, of which one says, 'This is it,' the case of both parties shall come before God. The one whom God condemns shall pay double to his neighbor.

Widows & Orphans
Don't Harm Widows or Orphans

Exodus 22:22-23 is a commandment from the Bible that says that we should not mistreat or harm people who are in vulnerable or difficult situations, like widows or orphans.

You see, in those times, widows and orphans didn't have anyone to take care of them or protect them. They could be lonely or sad because they didn't have a family anymore. So, this commandment is telling us to be kind and compassionate towards them.

God wants us to treat everyone with love and respect, especially those who are going through a tough time. He wants us to help and support people who may not have anyone else to turn to. It's like a reminder to be there for others and show them kindness, just like God shows us kindness.

So, this commandment is teaching us to have empathy and to reach out to those who may be feeling lonely or sad. It's a way for us to show God's love and care for all people, no matter their situation.

Exodus 22:22 KJV "Do not take advantage of the widow or the fatherless. If you do and they cry out to me, I will certainly hear their cry."

Don't Oppress Widows, Fatherless, Foreigner or Poor

Zechariah 7:9-10 is another commandment from the Bible that talks about how God wants us to treat widows and the fatherless. It says, "This is what the Lord Almighty said: 'Administer true justice; show mercy and compassion to one another. Do not oppress the widow or the fatherless, the foreigner or the poor. Do not plot evil against each other.'"

To understand this commandment better imagine you are playing with your friends, and one of them accidentally breaks your favorite toy. God tells us that instead of getting angry and seeking revenge, we should be fair and just. We should show kindness, mercy, and compassion to one another. This means forgiving your friend and understanding that accidents happen.

God also wants us to care for people who are in need or who may be feeling sad. We should not be mean or treat them poorly because they are different from us or because they don't have as much as we do. Instead, we should help and support them. We should treat everyone with love and respect, just as we would like to be treated ourselves.

Do you know what a widow or an orpha is? A widow is someone who has lost their spouse, their partner in life. They may feel sadness and loneliness, but they also have great strength and courage to carry on. They become an inspiration to others, showing that even in difficult times, they can find happiness and love again.

An orphan is a child who has lost their parents. It can be very tough for them, as they miss their mom and dad so much. However, they are incredibly resilient and brave. They learn to rely on themselves and find love and support from others around them. They teach us that family is not just about blood, but about the love and care we give one another.

Both a widow and an orphan show us that no matter what challenges life throws at us, we have the ability to keep going and find happiness. They remind us to be grateful for the love and support we have in our own lives, and to always be kind and compassionate towards others who may be going through difficult times.

Zechariah 7:9-10 NIV "This is what the Lord Almighty said: 'Administer true justice; show mercy and compassion to one another. Do not oppress the widow or the fatherless, the foreigner or the poor. Do not plot evil against each other.'

Don't Charge Interest To The Poor

Exodus 22:25 is a commandment from the Bible that teaches us how to be kind and fair to others, especially those who are not as fortunate as we are. It says, "If you lend money to any of my people with you who is poor, you shall not be like a moneylender to him, and you shall not exact interest from him."

Now, let's imagine you have a friend who needs some money because they are going through a difficult time and don't have enough. The commandment tells us that if we lend money to our friend who is poor, we should not ask for anything extra in return. We should be kind and not treat them like a bank, where we make them pay back more money than they borrowed.

It's important to remember that this commandment is about being fair and compassionate towards others, especially when they are in need. It teaches us to show love and generosity to those who may not have as much as we do. By following this commandment, we can make the world a better place by helping and supporting each other.

Exodus 22:25 KJV If thou lend money to any of my people that is poor by thee, thou shalt not be to him as an usurer, neither shalt thou lay upon him usury. 25 "If you lend money to any of my people with you who is poor, you shall not be like a moneylender to him, and you shall not exact interest from him.

A CHILDREN'S GUIDE TO A GODLY WAY OF LIFE

Don't Curse gods or Ruler of Your People

Exodus 22:28 is a verse from the Bible that contains a commandment which says, "You shall not curse the gods, nor curse the ruler of your people."

First, it says "You shall not curse the gods." This means that we should not use mean or disrespectful words towards any gods or deities that people believe in. Different people believe in different gods, and it is important to show respect for their beliefs. This does not mean we have to believe in other people's gods because God tells us to not put any gods before Him. This commandment is about being respectful of other people's beliefs. Having respect for other people is important and that is what God is talking about in this commandment.

Next, it says "nor curse the ruler of your people." This means that we should not use bad or hurtful words towards the leaders or people in authority in our community or country. It's important to treat them with respect and kindness, even if we may disagree with them sometimes.

So, this commandment is telling us to be respectful in our words and actions towards gods and leaders. It encourages us to be kind, considerate, and understanding towards others, even when we may have different beliefs or opinions.

Exodus 22:28 KJV Thou shalt not revile the gods, nor curse the ruler of thy people.

Be Honest & Don't Spread Rumors

Exodus 23:1 is a verse from the Bible that gives us a special commandment or rule to follow. It says, "Do not spread false reports. Do not help a guilty person by being a malicious witness."

Now, imagine that you have a friend who did something wrong, like breaking a toy. As a commandment, Exodus 23:1 is telling us not to tell lies about what happened or make up stories to get our friend in more trouble. We should always be honest and truthful.

Sometimes, people might try to say things that aren't true about someone else, like spreading rumors or gossip. But this commandment tells us not to do that. It reminds us to be kind and fair to others by not saying things that could hurt them or make them look bad.

So, in simpler terms, Exodus 23:1 teaches us that we should always be honest and not say or spread things that are not true about others. It encourages us to be good friends, treating everyone with fairness and kindness.

Exodus 23:1 KJV Thou shalt not raise a false report: put not thine hand with the wicked to be an unrighteous witness.

Don't Follow The Crowd

Exodus 23:2 is a verse from the Bible that contains a commandment about not following the crowd. The verse says, "Do not follow the crowd in doing wrong. When you give testimony in a lawsuit, do not pervert justice by siding with the crowd."

Now, what does this mean? Well, it's telling us that we should not do something wrong just because everyone else is doing it. Sometimes, when we see lots of people doing something, we might feel tempted to join in, even if we know it's not the right thing to do. But this commandment reminds us to stay true to what we know is right, even if others are doing something different.

The verse also talks about giving testimony in a lawsuit. "Testimony" means telling the truth about what happened. So, it's saying that when we are asked to tell what we know about something that happened, we should always tell the truth. We should never say something that isn't true, just because we want to please or agree with the crowd.

In simpler words, this commandment teaches us to be honest and to make our own choices based on what we know is right, even if it means going against what everyone else is doing. It reminds us to always stand up for what is true and just, even if it's not the popular or easy thing to do.

Exodus 23:2 KJV Thou shalt not follow a multitude to do evil; neither shalt thou speak in a cause to decline after many to wrest judgment:

Show Kindness Even To Enemies

Exodus 23:4-5 says, "If you see your enemy's donkey wandering off, be sure to return it." This is a commandment that teaches us to be kind and helpful, even to people we might not get along with.

Imagine if you had a friend who you didn't always get along with. One day, you see their donkey wandering away from their house. Even though you might not like your friend very much, this commandment tells us that we should still help them. So, you would go and bring back their donkey to them.

This commandment reminds us to treat others with kindness and to show compassion, even if they are not our friends. It's important to remember that being kind to others is always the right thing to do, no matter how we feel about them.

Exodus 23:4-5 KJV If thou meet thine enemy's ox or his ass going astray, thou shalt surely bring it back to him again. If thou see the ass of him that hateth thee lying under his burden, and wouldest forbear to help him, thou shalt surely help with him.

A CHILDREN'S GUIDE TO A GODLY WAY OF LIFE

Treat Everyone With Fairness and Kindness

Exodus 23:8 is a verse from the Bible, which is a book that teaches us about God and how we should live our lives. This verse is part of a commandment that God gave to the people of Israel a long time ago.

Now, let's imagine you have a big basket of delicious fruits. You love these fruits, and you want to share them with your friends. But there are some people who might be mean or unfair, and they might try to take advantage of you or your friends.

In Exodus 23:8, God tells us not to take sides or show favoritism. It means that we should treat everyone fairly and equally, no matter who they are or where they come from. Just like you would share your fruits with all your friends, you should treat everyone kindly, without choosing favorites or being unfair.

God wants us to be fair and just, just like He is. He loves all people, and He wants us to love and respect others too. So, if you remember this commandment, you will be a kind and fair person, just like God wants us to be.

Remember, it's important to treat everyone with fairness and kindness, just like you would want to be treated.

Exodus 23:8 KJV And thou shalt take no gift: for the gift blindeth the wise, and perverteth the words of the righteous.

Let Your Land Rest In The 7th Year

In Exodus 23:11, there is a commandment that says, "But the seventh year you shall let it rest and lie fallow, so that the poor of your people may eat; and what they leave, the beasts of the field may eat. You shall do likewise with your vineyard, and with your olive grove."

This commandment is about taking care of the land and helping others. It says that every seven years, the people should let the land rest and not grow any crops on it. This is called letting it lie fallow. When the land rests, it becomes healthier and can grow better crops later on.

By letting the land rest, it also helps the poor people in the community. They can go to the fields and gather the food that grows naturally during that year. It's like a special time for them to get food without having to work so hard.

The commandment also says that whatever is left after the poor people have taken what they need, the animals in the field can eat. So it's a way of making sure that everyone, including animals, can have enough to eat.

Basically, this commandment teaches us to be kind and fair to the land and to others. We should take care of the Earth by giving it a break sometimes, and we should share what we have with those who are in need.

Exodus 23:11 KJV But the seventh year thou shalt let it rest and lie still; that the poor of thy people may eat: and what they leave the beasts of the field shall eat. In like manner thou shalt deal with thy vineyard, and with thy oliveyard.

Rest on the 7th Day

Exodus 23:12 is a commandment that tells us to rest on a special day. It says, "Six days do your work, but on the seventh day do not work, so that your ox and your donkey may rest, and so that the slave born in your household and the foreigner living among you may be refreshed."

God wants us to work hard for six days, just like how we have school or chores to do. But on the seventh day, which is like a special day, God wants us to take a break and rest. He doesn't want us to do any work, so that even our animals like ox and donkey can have a day of rest too. It's also a time for everyone, even people who work for us or people from other places, to feel refreshed and have a day to relax.

So, this commandment is a reminder for us to take a day off, spend time with family and friends, and have some fun. It's like a gift from God to make sure we don't get too tired and have time to enjoy life.

Exodus 23:12 KJV Six days thou shalt do thy work, and on the seventh day thou shalt rest: that thine ox and thine ass may rest, and the son of thy handmaid, and the stranger, may be refreshed.

LADY KIMBERLY MOTES DOTY, AURORA BRAND & CONOR FINNEGAN

Do Not Invoke The Name Of Other gods

Exodus 23:13 is a verse from the Bible, and it's a commandment that God gave to the people. It says, "Do not invoke the names of other gods; do not let them be heard on your lips."

Now, imagine if you have a best friend, and you really like spending time with them. You wouldn't want to talk about other friends in a way that might hurt their feelings, right? In the same way, God wants us to only worship Him and not talk about or worship other gods.

God loves us so much, and He wants us to have a special relationship with Him. He wants us to trust Him and believe in Him. So, this commandment reminds us to be loyal to God and to only follow Him.

Exodus 23:13 KJV And in all things that I have said unto you be circumspect: and make no mention of the name of other gods, neither let it be heard out of thy mouth.

Worship & Love God & He Will Keep You Healthy

Exodus 23:25 says, "Worship the Lord your God, and his blessing will be on your food and water. I will take away sickness from among you."

So, what God is telling the people is that if they worship Him, which means showing love, respect, and devotion to Him, then He will bless their food and water. It means that they will have enough to eat and drink, and they will be healthy because God will take away sickness from them.

It's like when we do something good, like being kind or helpful, our parents might reward us with something nice, right? In the same way, God is saying that if the people worship Him and follow His commandments, He will give them good things and protect them from getting sick.

So, this commandment is a reminder for the people to always remember to worship and love God, and in return, God will take care of them and keep them healthy.

Exodus 23:25 KJV And ye shall serve the Lord your God, and he shall bless thy bread, and thy water; and I will take sickness away from the midst of thee.

Stay True to God & Don't Let Anything Lead You Away

Exodus 23:33 says, "Do not let them live in your land, or they will cause you to sin against me. If you worship their gods, it will be like putting a trap in front of you."

Imagine you have a special room in your house, and you want to keep it clean and safe. But sometimes, there are things that can make the room messy or dangerous. In Exodus 23:33, God is giving a commandment to the people, telling them not to let certain people live in their land.

Why would God say that? Well, those people might have different beliefs and worship different gods. God wants the people to stay faithful to Him and not start believing in other gods. It's like God is saying, "Don't let them into your special room, or they might make it messy and dangerous."

God wants to protect the people and keep them close to Him, just like parents want to protect their children. So, this commandment is a way for God to remind the people to stay true to Him and not let anything or anyone lead them away from Him.

Exodus 23:33 KJV They shall not dwell in thy land, lest they make thee sin against me: for if thou serve their gods, it will surely be a snare unto thee.

A CHILDREN'S GUIDE TO A GODLY WAY OF LIFE

If You Accidentally Take Something, Return it + Extra

Leviticus 6:3 is a commandment that was written a long time ago. It says that if someone accidentally takes something that doesn't belong to them, they need to give it back and also make up for it by giving a little bit extra.

Imagine if you borrowed your friend's toy without asking and then realized it wasn't right. According to this commandment, you would need to return the toy to your friend and also give them something extra to make up for taking it without permission.

This rule teaches us about being honest and taking responsibility for our actions. It reminds us to treat other people's things with respect and to make things right when we make a mistake.

Leviticus 6:3 KJV Or have found that which was lost, and lieth concerning it, and sweareth falsely; in any of all these that a man doeth, sinning therein:

Be Honest and Responsible For Your Actions

Leviticus 6:5 says if someone does something wrong, like tell a lie, or take something that doesn't belong to them, they need to go and tell the truth about what they did. It's like saying sorry for what they did and making things right again.

Just like when you accidentally break a toy or make a mess, it's important to own up to it and tell the truth. That way, you can learn from your mistake and make things better. It's a way of being honest and responsible for our actions. The commandment in Leviticus 6:5 reminds us to always be truthful and try to make things right when we do something wrong.

Leviticus 6:5 KJV Or all that about which he hath sworn falsely; he shall even restore it in the principal, and shall add the fifth part more thereto, and give it unto him to whom it appertaineth, in the day of his trespass offering.

A CHILDREN'S GUIDE TO A GODLY WAY OF LIFE

Be Pure, Good, & Righteous Like God Is

Leviticus 11:44 is a commandment where God is telling the people how they should live and what they should do. He says, "I am the Lord your God; consecrate yourselves and be holy because I am holy."

When God says "consecrate yourselves," it means that He wants the people to set themselves apart and be different from others. He wants them to live in a way that is special and dedicated to Him.

And when God says "be holy because I am holy," He wants the people to be pure, good, and righteous, just like He is. He wants them to try their best to be like Him in their words, actions, and thoughts.

So, this commandment is a reminder for the people to be good, kind, and loving, just like God. He wants them to live in a way that shows their love and respect for Him.

When we say, live the "way" Jesus lived, the "Godly Way", the divine way, this is what we mean. We are living our lives, doing the best we can, to be the best we can to follow God's commandments for being good people, good humans and taking care of each other and this earth to the best of our ability. We are being kind to ourselves, taking care of ourselves, we are taking care of those around us, the environment around us, and the animals around us

Leviticus 11:44 KJV For I am the Lord your God: ye shall therefore sanctify yourselves, and ye shall be holy; for I am holy: neither shall ye defile yourselves with any manner of creeping thing that creepeth upon the earth.

Respect & Honor Your Parents

Leviticus 19:3 is a commandment from the Bible that tells us to respect and honor our parents. It says that we should listen to them and follow their instructions.

This commandment is important because our parents take care of us, love us, and want what is best for us. When we listen to them and show them respect, it helps us to grow up to be good and loving people. So, it's like a rule that reminds us to be kind and obedient to our parents because they are very special and important in our lives.

Leviticus 19:3 KJV Ye shall fear every man his mother, and his father, and keep my sabbaths: I am the Lord your God.

Don't Worship Idols or Make Statues of Them

Imagine you have a favorite toy that you really, really love. You might want to play with it all the time and take care of it. But imagine if you started to think that the toy is super special and magical, and you started to pray to it or treat it like it's a real person. That's what worshiping idols means.

In the olden days, some people used to make statues of things they thought were important or powerful, like animals or gods. But this verse is saying that it's not right to worship or believe in those statues as if they are real and have special powers.

In a nutshell, Leviticus 19:4 is telling us that we shouldn't worship idols or make statues to worship them, but instead, we should focus on what is truly important and real.

Leviticus 19:4 Turn ye not unto idols, nor make to yourselves molten gods: I am the Lord your God.

Leave the Corners of Your Fields & Vineyards for the Poor

Leviticus 19:9 is a commandment that says when people are growing crops in their fields, they are supposed to leave some of the crops behind. They should not gather all of it. Instead, they should leave some of it for the poor and the needy.

So, this commandment is telling us that we should be kind and share with others who may not have enough food. It's important to remember that we should always help those in need and not be selfish.

Leviticus 19:9-10KJV And when ye reap the harvest of your land, thou shalt not wholly reap the corners of thy field, neither shalt thou gather the gleanings of thy harvest. And when ye reap the harvest of your land, thou shalt not wholly reap the corners of thy field, neither shalt thou gather the gleanings of thy harvest. And thou shalt not glean thy vineyard, neither shalt thou gather every grape of thy vineyard; thou shalt leave them for the poor and stranger: I am the Lord your God.

A CHILDREN'S GUIDE TO A GODLY WAY OF LIFE

Wait 3 Years to Harvest or Eat Fruit When You Plant New Trees

Leviticus 19:23 is a commandment that says, "When you come into the land and plant any kind of tree for food, then you shall regard its fruit as forbidden. For three years it shall be forbidden to you; it must not be eaten."

Now, let me explain it to you in a simpler way. Imagine you have a beautiful garden, and you decide to plant a tree that gives yummy fruits, like apples or oranges. This commandment says that when you plant that tree, you have to wait for three years before you can eat any of the fruits it produces.

You might wonder why it says that. Well, the reason is that during those three years, the tree needs time to grow strong and healthy. By not eating the fruits during that time, it helps the tree to become stronger and produce even more delicious fruits in the future.

So, this commandment teaches us to be patient and take care of nature. It reminds us that good things sometimes take time, and when we wait patiently, we can enjoy even better results in the end.

Leviticus 19:23 KJV "And when ye shall come into the land, and shall have planted all manner of trees for food, then ye shall count the fruit thereof as uncircumcised: three years shall it be as uncircumcised unto you: it shall not be eaten of."

Don't Make Cuts Or Tattoos On Your Body For The Dead

Leviticus 19:28 is a commandment says, "You shall not make any cuts on your body for the dead or tattoo yourselves: I am the Lord."

So, what this means is that in those times, people used to make cuts on their bodies or get tattoos as a way to show their sadness when someone died. It's a rule from God, who is called the Lord, that this is not allowed to show sadness.

But the main idea behind this commandment is to remind us to treat our bodies with care and respect, and to remember that God is looking out for us and wants us to be safe and healthy.

Leviticus 19:28 KJV "Ye shall not make any cuttings in your flesh for the dead, nor print any marks upon you: I am the Lord."

Respect & Honor Places of Worship

Leviticus 19:30 is a commandment in the Bible that tells us to respect and honor special places. It says, "You shall keep my Sabbaths and reverence my sanctuary: I am the Lord."

Now, let's break it down into simpler words.

"Keep my Sabbaths" means to set aside a special day, like Sunday, to rest and spend time with family and friends. It's like having a day off from school or work to relax and enjoy ourselves.

"Reverence my sanctuary" means to show respect for a holy place, like a church or a temple. It's like being quiet and well-behaved when we visit a special place, so we don't disturb others who are praying or trying to focus on their thoughts.

"I am the Lord" means that this commandment comes from God, who wants us to understand the importance of resting and respecting special places.

So, when we follow this commandment, we show gratitude to God for creating a day of rest and for giving us special places to worship and connect with our faith.

Leviticus 19:30 KJV "Ye shall keep my sabbaths, and reverence my sanctuary: I am the Lord."

Avoid People Who Pretend To Have Powers

Leviticus 19:31 is a commandment that says, "Do not turn to mediums or seek out spiritists, for you will be defiled by them. I am the Lord your God."

Imagine you have a really special toy that you love and take care of. You wouldn't want anything bad to happen to it, right? Well, in this commandment, God is telling us not to go to people who claim to talk to spirits or predict the future.

You see, there are some people who pretend to have special powers and say they can talk to people who have passed away or tell us what will happen in the future. God wants us to stay away from them because they can trick us or give us false information.

By following this commandment, we are showing respect to God and trusting that He will guide and protect us. It's like listening to our parents or guardians when they tell us not to do something that could be dangerous.

So, just like we take care of our special toy, we should listen to God and stay away from people who claim to talk to spirits or predict the future.

Leviticus 19:31 KJV "Regard not them that have familiar spirits, neither seek after wizards, to be defiled by them: I am the Lord your God."

Be Kind & Considerate To Older Generations

Leviticus 19:32 is a verse from the Bible that gives us a special commandment. It says, "Stand up in the presence of the elderly, and show respect for the aged. Fear your God. I am the Lord."

This means that we should treat older people with kindness and respect. We should listen to them and be polite when we talk to them. Just like we listen to our parents and teachers, we should also listen to older people because they have a lot of wisdom and experience.

This commandment reminds us to be kind and considerate to our grandparents, great-grandparents, and other elderly people we meet. We should help them when they need it and spend time with them. It's important to show love and respect to everyone, no matter how old they are.

Leviticus 19:32 KJV "Thou shalt rise up before the hoary head, and honor the face of the old man, and fear thy God: I am the Lord."

Be Fair & Honest

Leviticus 19:35 is a commandment from the Bible that tells us how we should act in a fair and honest way.

Imagine you have a bag of marbles, and someone asks you to give them 10 marbles. The verse says that when you give those marbles, you should make sure it's exactly 10 marbles, and not more or less. This is because being honest and fair is important.

The verse also tells us not to cheat or trick others in any way. It teaches us to use fair weights and measures, just like when you play a game with your friends, you want everyone to have the same chances to win.

So, Leviticus 19:35 reminds us to always be honest, fair, and kind to others, just as God wants us to be.

Leviticus 19:35 KJV "Ye shall do no unrighteousness in judgment, in meteyard, in weight, or in measure."

A CHILDREN'S GUIDE TO A GODLY WAY OF LIFE

Don't Do Wrong Things Because It's Customary

Leviticus 20:23 is a commandments that says "You must not live according to the customs of the nations I am going to drive out before you. Because they did all these things, I abhorred them."

Imagine you have a special toy that you really like, and you take good care of it. But one day, you see some other kids mistreating their toys. They throw them around, break them, and don't take care of them at all.

In Leviticus 20:23 it is a commandment where the people were told not to copy the actions of those who didn't take care of their toys. God was telling them not to do the same things as those people because He didn't like what they were doing.

It's kind of like a reminder to be good and kind, and not to do things that are wrong. God wanted the people to have good customs and do good things, just like taking care of our toys.

Leviticus 20:23 KJV "And ye shall not walk in the manners of the nation, which I cast out before you: for they committed all these things, and therefore I abhorred them."

The Lord Bless & Keep You

Numbers 6:24 is a special set of commandments from the Bible that says: "The Lord bless you and keep you."

The Lord Bless You With Good Things

Imagine that you have a really special friend who loves you very much. This friend is the Lord, and He wants to give you good things and protect you. So, when it says "The Lord bless you," it means that He wants to give you lots of good things in your life, like happiness, love, and success.

The Lord Keep You Safe

But it doesn't stop there! The verse also says, "The Lord keep you." This means that He wants to protect you and keep you safe from any harm. It's like having a guardian angel watching over you all the time.

So, when you hear this verse, remember that it's like a special message from the Lord to you. He wants to bless you with good things and keep you safe because He loves you very much. It's a beautiful commandment that reminds us of how much God cares for us.

Numbers 6:24 KJV "The Lord bless thee, and keep thee:"

Keep Your Promises

Numbers 30:2 is a commandment from the Bible that says that when someone makes a promise to God, they have to keep that promise and do what they said they would do. It's like when you make a promise to a friend, you have to keep your word and do what you promised. This commandment reminds us to be honest and responsible when we make promises to God or to others.

Keep Your Promises To God

Numbers 30:2 has two commandments, The first is to keep your promises to God. When you make a promise to God, you have to keep your promise to God. Numbers 30:20 says, "If a man vow a vow unto the Lord…; he shall not break his word"

Keep Your Promises to Everyone

The second commandment is "If a man … swear an oath to bind his soul with a bond; he shall not break his word". So it is just like a vow unto the Lord, you have to keep it.

Everything You Say Is A Promise

Where Numbers 30:2 says "he shall do according to all that proceedeth out of his mouth", this means that everything we say is considered a promise to God. Everything we say we will do, God expects us to do as if we said is as a promise. When we say we will clean our room, it is a promise we will clean our room, so we should do it.

Numbers 30:2 "If a man vow a vow unto the Lord, or swear an oath to bind his soul with a bond; he shall not break his word, he shall do according to all that proceedeth out of his mouth."

Create Cities of Refuge

Numbers 35:12 is a commandment that tells us to make cities of refuge. Now, imagine you have a big game of tag with your friends, and sometimes accidents happen where someone gets hurt unintentionally. This commandment is like a rule to help keep everyone safe.

God tells the people to make special cities called "cities of refuge" where someone who accidentally hurts another person can go to be safe. It's like a special place where they can go to be protected and not get in trouble for what happened. These cities were like a safe haven, where people could go and get fair treatment until everything was sorted out.

It's important to remember that this commandment teaches us to be understanding and forgiving, and to make sure that people who make mistakes are given a chance to be safe and receive fair judgment. It shows us that God cares about justice and wants us to be kind to one another.

Just like when you play tag, accidents can happen in life too. And this commandment reminds us to be understanding and create safe spaces for people, so they can feel protected and have a chance to make things right.

Numbers 35:12 KJV "And they shall be unto you cities for refuge from the avenger; that the manslayer die not, until he stand before the congregation in judgment."

Have Proof Before You Blame Someone

Numbers 35:30 is a commandment from the Bible which says if someone does something really wrong, like hurting or killing another person on purpose, they should be punished.

But the commandment also says that the punishment should only happen if there are enough witnesses who saw the bad thing happening. It's like when you play a game and someone says you did something wrong, but you have a group of friends who can tell the truth and say that you didn't do it.

So, this commandment is telling us that we should always have proof or evidence before we blame someone for doing something really bad. It's important to be fair and make sure we are only punishing people who are truly responsible for their actions.

Numbers 35:30 KJV "Whoso killeth any person, the murderer shall be put to death by the mouth of witnesses: but one witness shall not testify against any person to cause him to die."

Do Not Accept Ransom for the Life of a Murderer

Numbers 35:31 is a commandment from the Bible that says, "Do not accept a ransom for the life of a murderer, who deserves to die. They must surely be put to death."

Imagine you have a game with rules, just like how we have rules in life. In this game, there's a very important rule that says if someone does something really, really bad, like hurting or killing another person, they have to be punished.

Now, sometimes, when someone does something wrong, they might try to give something valuable or important to someone else to avoid getting in trouble. Giving this something valuable or important is what is known as a ransom. But this commandment says that we should not accept any kind of special gift or payment from someone who has hurt or killed someone else. Instead, they should be punished for what they did, because it's very serious and important to make sure people are safe and protected.

So, this commandment is telling us that when someone does something really bad, like hurting or killing someone, they can't just give something to make up for it. They have to face the consequences of their actions. It's about fairness and justice, making sure that everyone is accountable for what they do.

Remember, it's always important to treat others with kindness and respect, and to never hurt anyone.

Numbers 35:31 KJV "Moreover ye shall take no satisfaction for the life of a murderer, which is guilty of death: but he shall be surely put to death."

Listen Carefully to Live In Harmony

Deuteronomy 1:17 is a verse from the Bible that gives us a special commandment which says when people have a problem or a disagreement, we should all listen carefully to both sides of the story before making a decision.

Imagine you and your friend are arguing about something, like which game to play. If you both come to me for help, I would listen to what your friend has to say and then listen to your side too. It's important to hear both of you so that I can make a fair decision. This commandment teaches us to be fair and make wise choices by giving everyone a chance to be heard.

Just like in the Bible, this commandment helps us be fair and make good decisions in our everyday lives. It's important to listen to others and treat everyone kindly, so that we can live in harmony with one another.

Deuteronomy 1:17 KJV "Ye shall not respect persons in judgment; but ye shall hear the small as well as the great; ye shall not be afraid of the face of man; for the judgment is God's: and the cause that is too hard for you, bring it unto me, and I will hear it."

Be Kind and Caring Towards Animals

Deuteronomy 15:18-22 is a commandment from the Bible that talks about how to treat our animals. It says that when we have animals like sheep or cows, we should take good care of them and treat them kindly.

The Bible says that when we have a baby animal, like a lamb or a calf, we should let them stay with their mommy for a while. They need to be with their mommy so they can grow up healthy and strong. It's like how we need our parents to take care of us when we're little.

The Bible also tells us that we should not eat the mommy animal while the baby animal is still young. We should wait until the baby animal is older and then we can eat the mommy animal if we want to. This is because it's important to give the baby animal time with its mommy.

Deuteronomy 15:18-22 "It shall not seem hard unto thee, when thou sendest him away free from thee; for he hath been worth a double hired servant to thee, in serving thee six years: and the Lord thy God shall bless thee in all that thou doest. All the firstling males that come of thy herd and of thy flock thou shalt sanctify unto the Lord thy God: thou shalt do no work with the firstling of thy bullock, nor shear the firstling of thy sheep. Thou shalt eat it before the Lord thy God year by year in the place which the Lord shall choose, thou and thy household. And if there be any blemish therein, as if it be lame, or blind, or have any ill blemish, thou shalt not sacrifice it unto the Lord thy God. Thou shalt eat it within thy gates: the unclean and the clean person shall eat it alike, as the roebuck, and as the hart."

A CHILDREN'S GUIDE TO A GODLY WAY OF LIFE

The Lord our God is THE One Lord

Deuteronomy 6:4 is a special verse in the Bible that teaches us an important commandment. It says, "Hear, O Israel: The Lord our God, the Lord is one."

Now, let's break it down so it's easier for us to understand. "Hear, O Israel" means that God wants the people of Israel, and all of us, to listen carefully. The next part is, "The Lord our God." This means that God is our God, and He is very special to us. We should love and respect Him.

And finally, "The Lord is one" means that there is only one true God. It reminds us that we should not worship any other gods or idols, but only the one true God.

So, this commandment is telling us to always remember that God is our one and only God. We should listen to Him, love and respect Him, and not worship anything or anyone else as a god. It's a way for us to show our devotion and faith to God.

Deuteronomy 6:4 KJV "Hear, O Israel: The Lord our God is one Lord::

The Greatest Commandment

Deuteronomy 6:5 is a commandment from the Bible that says, "Love the Lord your God with all your heart, with all your soul, and with all your strength."

Love God With All Your Heart, Soul & Strength

Now, let's break it down. Imagine that your heart is like a special place inside you where you keep all your feelings. It means that you should have lots of love for God, similar to how you love your family and friends, but even more.

Your soul is like the very special part of you that makes you who you are. It's like your thoughts, your dreams, and your spirit. So, it means that you should love God with all those things too, by having faith in Him and believing in His love for you.

Lastly, your strength is like the power you have in your body. It means that you should use all your energy and effort to love and obey God. It's like giving your best, just like when you try your hardest in school or when you play your favorite game.

Love Your Neighbor As Yourself

So, when the Bible says, "Love the Lord your God with all your heart, with all your soul, and with all your strength," it's telling us that we should love God very much, with everything we have inside us – our feelings, our thoughts, and our effort.

Deuteronomy 6:5 KJV And thou shalt love the Lord thy God with all thine heart, and with all thy soul, and with all thy might.

Matthew 22:34-40 is another place in the Bible where Jesus tells us these commandments to "Love the Lord your God with all your heart, soul, and mind. This is the first and greatest commandment. And the second is like it: Love your neighbor as yourself."

Once again, we see in Matthew 22:34-40, Jesus telling us that the most important thing we can do is to love God with all our heart and soul. That means we should care about God and have a special connection with Him. And the second commandment is to love our neighbors, which means we should treat others with kindness and respect, just like we would want them to treat us.

Matthew 22:34-40 NIV Hearing that Jesus had silenced the Sadducees, the Pharisees got together. One of them, an expert in the law, tested him with this question: "Teacher, which is the greatest commandment in the Law?" Jesus replied: "'Love the Lord your God with all your heart and with all your soul and with all your mind.' This is the first and greatest commandment. And the second is like it: 'Love your neighbor as yourself.' All the Law and the Prophets hang on these two commandments."

Teach Important Things to Your Family

Deuteronomy 6:7 is a commandment in the Bible that tells us how we should learn and understand important things in life. It says, "You shall teach them diligently to your children, and shall talk of them when you sit in your house, and when you walk by the way, and when you lie down, and when you rise."

Imagine you have a special toy that you love very much. You would want to take good care of it and make sure it stays in good shape, right? Well, this commandment is like taking care of our minds and hearts. It tells us that we should learn and talk about important things with our family all the time, just like we take care of our special toy.

So, when you are at home with your family, when you are out walking or traveling, and even when you are going to bed or waking up, we should talk about things that are good and important. This can be things like being kind to others, helping those in need, and being grateful for the good things in our lives. It's like always having a conversation about what is right and good, just like taking care of our special toy.

By following this commandment, we can learn and grow in a positive way, and become better people. It helps us remember what is important in life and how we should treat others. Just like we take care of our special toy, this commandment tells us to take care of our hearts and minds by learning and talking about good things with our family.

Deuteronomy 6:7 KJV "And thou shalt teach them diligently unto thy children, and shalt talk of them when thou sittest in thine house, and when thou walkest by the way, and when thou liest down, and when thou risest up."

Do Good & Wise Things In Your Daily Lives

Deuteronomy 6:8 is a commandment from the Bible which says, "Tie them as symbols on your hands and bind them on your foreheads." Now, this might sound a little tricky, so allow me to explain it in a way you can understand it better.

Imagine you have a special bracelet that you really love. You wear it on your hand every day, and it reminds you of something important. Well, in the Bible, it tells us to do something similar. It says we should tie God's words and commandments around our hands and bind them on our foreheads.

But what does that mean? Well, it means we should always remember and follow what God teaches us. Just like you wear your special bracelet and it reminds you of something important, we should always keep God's teachings in our minds and live by them.

So, this commandment is telling us to remember to do good things and make wise choices in our daily lives. It's like a little reminder to always be kind, loving, and honest, just like God wants us to be. This commandment is a good reminder that thoughts are things so it is what we think about as well as what we talk about that determines how we behave every day.

Deuteronomy 6:8 KJV "And thou shalt bind them for a sign upon thine hand, and they shall be as frontlets between thine eyes."

Write Commandments Everywhere

Deuteronomy 6:9 is another commandment about remembering God's words which says, "Write these commandments on the doorposts of your houses and on your gates."

For this commandment, imagine you have a special list of rules that you really, really need to remember. The commandment is telling us that we should write those rules on the doors of our houses and on our gates, so that we see them every day.

Just like when we have an important test at school and we write notes to help us remember things, this verse is saying that we should write down these rules from the Bible to help us remember to follow them and be good people.

So, it's like a reminder that we should always try our best to follow these rules and make good choices in our lives. If we see the commandments in posters, paintings, or signs around our homes and rooms, it is a constant reminder to help us to better in our daily lives.

Deuteronomy 6:9 KJV "And thou shalt write them upon the posts of thy house, and on thy gates."

A CHILDREN'S GUIDE TO A GODLY WAY OF LIFE

Do Not Test God

Deuteronomy 6:16 is a commandment from the Bible which says, "Do not test the Lord your God."

To understand this commandment, imagine you have a really special toy that you love very much. Your mom tells you not to throw it or break it because it's important. That's similar to what this commandment is saying. It tells us not to test or try to challenge God's power or authority.

God is really powerful and knows what's best for us. So, it's important to trust Him and not try to do things that might make Him prove Himself. It's like knowing that your mom or dad can do amazing things, but you don't have to test them to see if it's true.

We should have faith and believe in God's love and guidance, and always respect and obey Him.

Deuteronomy 6:16 KJV "Ye shall not tempt the Lord your God, as ye tempted him in Massah."

Do Not Desire / Keep False Gods or Idol Items

Deuteronomy 7:25 is a commandment from the Bible that talks about a commandment given by God. It says that we should not desire or keep any things that are used in worshiping false gods or idols.

Now, you might be wondering, what are false gods or idols? Well, they are things that some people in the past used to believe were gods, but they are not the real God. They can be statues or objects that people would worship and give their attention to.

The commandment is telling us that we should stay away from these things. We should not have them in our homes or want them because they can distract us from the true God and they are not good for us. God wants us to focus on Him and love Him with all our hearts.

So, in simpler words, this commandment is saying that we should not have or desire things that people used to worship as gods because they are not real and can take us away from loving and worshiping the one true God.

Deuteronomy 7:25 KJV "The graven images of their gods shall ye burn with fire: thou shalt not desire the silver or gold that is on them, nor take it unto thee, lest thou be snared therin: for it is an abomination to the Lord thy God."

Do Not Bring Anything Bad Into Your Homes

Deuteronomy 7:26 is a commandment from the Bible which says that we should not bring anything that is bad or not good into our homes. It's like when you clean your room and you want to keep it neat and tidy. You wouldn't want to bring something dirty or broken into your room, right? That's the same idea here.

God wants us to keep our hearts and homes pure and good. He wants us to fill our lives with things that are kind, loving, and helpful. So, this verse is like a reminder for us to be careful about what we bring into our lives and our homes.

Remember, it's important to surround ourselves with good things, like love, kindness, and joy. By doing this, we can make our hearts and homes a happy place to be.

Deuteronomy 7:26 KJV "Neither shalt thou bring an abomination into thine house, lest thou be a cursed thing like it: but thou shalt utterly detest it, and thou shalt utterly abhor it; for it is a cursed thing."

Remember to Say Thank You to God

Deuteronomy 8:10 is a special Bible commandment that teaches us to be grateful and thankful for the good things we have in our lives. Just like when you receive a gift, it's important to say "thank you" to the person who gave it to you. This commandment reminds us to say "thank you" to God for all the wonderful things He gives us, like our family, friends, food, and home.

Imagine if you went to a friend's birthday party, and they gave you a really awesome present. How would you feel? You would probably be very happy and excited, right? Now, think about what you would say to your friend to show your gratitude. You would say "thank you" because you appreciate their kindness and the gift they gave you.

In the same way, Deuteronomy 8:10 tells us to always remember to say "thank you" to God for everything He blesses us with. It's like telling God, "Hey God, thank you so much for all the good things in my life!" When we have a grateful heart, it makes God happy too.

Remember, being thankful is an important part of our relationship with God. It helps us appreciate all the wonderful things He does for us, and it also reminds us to be kind and thankful to others. So, let's always remember to say "thank you" to God and show our gratitude for His love and blessings!

Deuteronomy 8:10 KJV "When thou hast eaten and art full, then thou shalt bless the Lord thy God for the good land which he hath given thee."

A CHILDREN'S GUIDE TO A GODLY WAY OF LIFE

Be Kind and Loving to New People

Deuteronomy 10:19 is a verse from the Bible that talks about how we should treat other people. It says, "Love the foreigners living among you, for you yourselves were foreigners in the land of Egypt."

Now, imagine if you went to a new school and didn't know anyone there. How would you feel? Probably a little scared and lonely, right? Well, this verse is telling us to be kind and loving to people who are new to our country or our community, just like how we would want to be treated if we were in their shoes.

You see, a long time ago, the people of Israel were once foreigners in a place called Egypt. They didn't have a home, and it was really hard for them. So, God wanted them to remember what it felt like, and to show compassion and love to others who might be feeling the same way.

So, this verse teaches us an important lesson: to be friendly, welcoming, and helpful to people who are new to our neighborhood or country. We should treat them with kindness, just like we would want to be treated. It's a commandment from the Bible that reminds us to be loving and caring towards everyone, no matter where they come from.

Deuteronomy 10:19 KJV "Love ye therefore the stranger: for ye were strangers in the land of Egypt."

Fear, Serve & Cleave To God

Deuteronomy 10:20 is a verse from the Bible that tells us about three important commandments. Let me explain them to you in a way that is easy to understand:

Love & Obey God

This means that we should show our love for God by listening to Him and doing what He says. Just like you listen and obey your parents, we should do the same with God because He loves us and wants the best for us.

Serve God With All Your Heart

Serving God means doing things that make Him happy and helping others. We can show our love for God by being kind, sharing, and being helpful to people around us. It's like being a good friend to others and being nice to them.

Keep God's Commandments

"To Swear by his name" means to Keep God's commandments.

Deuteronomy 10:20 KJV "Thou shalt fear the Lord thy God; him shalt thou serve, and to him shalt thou cleave, and swear by his name."

Share Your Blessings & Help Others In Need

Deuteronomy 12:4 is a commandment that tells us to share our blessings and help others who may not have as much as we do.

To help understand this commandment, imagine you have a very special toy that you love playing with. The commandment says that if you have this toy, you should not keep it to yourself and hide it away. Instead, you should share it with others, like your friends and family, so they can enjoy it too.

This commandment tells us that we should not keep all the good things we have just for themselves. Instead, we should share our blessings and help others who may not have as much. When we share, it makes us happy and it also makes the people around us happy. It's a way of showing love and kindness to others, just like God wants us to do.

Deuteronomy 12:4 KJV "Ye shall not do so unto the Lord your God."

Always Do What Is Right & Good

Deuteronomy 12:13 is a commandment from God to us to always do what is right and good in His eyes. He wants us to obey His rules and follow His ways.

Imagine if you have a list of rules at home, like cleaning your room, listening to your parents, and being kind to others. These are the rules that your parents set so that you can grow up to be a good person.

When Deuteronomy 12:13 says to always do what is right and good in God's eyes, it means that we should try our best to follow God's commandments and be good in His eyes. We should make choices that are kind, honest, and respectful, just like how our parents want us to make good choices.

Deuteronomy 12:13 KJV "Take heed to thyself that thou offer not thy burnt offerings in every place that thou seest:"

Do Not Alter God's Commandments

Deuteronomy 12:32 is a commandment from the Bible that says, "Do not add to what I command you and do not subtract from it, but keep the commands of the Lord your God that I give you."

Do Not Add To God's Commandments

Do Not Subtract From God's Commandments

Imagine if you had a special recipe that you really liked, and it had a list of ingredients and instructions on how to make it. The verse is telling us that we should not add any extra things to the recipe that are not in the instructions, and we should not take away any important parts from it.

Deuteronomy 12:32 KJV "What thing soever I command you, observe to do it: thou shalt not add thereto, nor diminish from it."

Walk After The Lord Your God

Only Worship God

Only Listen to God

Deuteronomy 13:4 is a commandment from God that says we should only worship and listen to God. It means that we should not believe or follow any other gods or people who say things that go against what God wants.

So, just like when your parents tell you what is right and wrong, God also tells us what is right and wrong through His commandments. And we should always listen to Him and follow His rules because He loves us and wants what is best for us.

Deuteronomy 13:4 KJV "Ye shall walk after the Lord your God, and fear him, and keep his commandments, and obey his voice, and ye shall serve him, and cleave unto him."

Don't Allow Anything To Lead You Away From God

In Deuteronomy 13:8 says that we should not listen to people who tell us to do bad things or to worship other gods. It's like when someone tries to convince you to do something you know is wrong, or to believe in something that goes against what you believe in.

God wants us to always be good and follow His teachings. He wants us to be loyal to Him and not get swayed by people who want to lead us away from what is right and true.

Remember, it's important to stay strong in what you believe and always do what is right in God's eyes. That's what this commandment is all about.

Deuteronomy 13:8 NIV "do not yield to them or listen to them. Show them no pity. Do not spare them or shield them."

Stay Faithful To God

Deuteronomy 13:16 is a commandment that says if there are people who are trying to lead you away from God or make you worship other gods, it is important to stay faithful to God and not listen to them.

This commandment also say if a city is doing things that are against God's rules, it might need to be destroyed. This might sound scary, but it is a way to show how serious it is to stay faithful to God and not let anything or anyone lead us away from Him.

As an 8-year-old, it's important to understand that the Bible has many different stories and lessons, and this verse is just one of them. It teaches us to always stay true to our beliefs and not let anyone or anything try to change them.

Deuteronomy 13:16 KJV "And thou shalt gather all the spoil of it into the midst of the street thereof, and shalt burn with fire the city, and all the spoil thereof every whit, for the Lord thy God: and it shall be an heap for ever; it shall not be built again."

Don't Do Things For The Dead

Deuteronomy 14:1 gives us two Bible commandments!

Respect & Honor God

The first commandment is to be children of God and to respect and honor Him. This means we should love and obey God with all our hearts, just like how we love and listen to our parents. We should always remember that God created us and cares for us, so we should be grateful and thankful to Him.

Do Not Cut Or Hurt Yourself For The Dead

The second commandment is about not hurting ourselves. It tells us that we shouldn't make cuts or marks on our bodies as a way of worshiping or showing sadness. God wants us to take care of ourselves and treat our bodies with love and care. We should be kind to ourselves and remember that we are special and valuable to God.

Deuteronomy 14:1 KJV "Ye are the children of the Lord your God: ye shall not cut yourselves, nor make any baldness between your eyes for the dead.

Take Care Of Yourself

Deuteronomy 14:3, says, "You shall not eat any detestable thing." Now, this might sound a little confusing, but let me break it down for you.

Do Not Eat Unhealthy Things

The first commandment we can learn from this verse is that we should not eat things that are considered detestable. Detestable means something that is really gross or disgusting. So, God is telling us to avoid eating things that are yucky or not good for us.

Eat Healthy Food

Now, the second commandment we can learn from this verse is that we should be careful about what we put into our bodies. God wants us to take care of ourselves and eat healthy food that is good for us. So, we should choose foods that are good for our bodies and avoid things that are bad for us.

Deuteronomy 14:3 KJV "Thou shalt not eat any abominable thing."

How To Know If Something Comes From God

In Deuteronomy 18:6-8, God gave special commandments and instructions to the people of Israel, and one of those instructions was about something called prophets. Prophets were people who would listen to God and then share His messages with others. They were like messengers from God.

Prophets Can Only Say Things That Come From God

Now, God wanted to make sure that the people listened to the true prophets, the ones who really heard His voice. So, He gave them some rules to know who were the real prophets and who were not.

One of the rules was that the prophets should only say things that came from God. They were not allowed to make up their own messages or pretend to know things that God didn't tell them. God wanted His people to trust the real prophets and not get confused by fake ones.

Prophets Can Only Speak In God's Name

Another rule was that the prophets should only speak in God's name. It means they had to say, "This is what God is saying," and not say things as if it was their own words. This way, the people could be sure that the messages were really from God and not just from the prophet's own thoughts.

God wanted His people to be safe and not be tricked by false prophets. So, He gave them these commandments to help them know who to trust and who to listen to. By following these rules, the people could stay close to God and understand His messages better.

Even though these commandments were given a long time ago, they can still teach us important lessons today. We learn that it's important to be careful and wise when we hear someone claiming to speak for God. We should always make sure that what they say matches with what the Bible tells us, and that their words are filled with love, truth, and kindness.

So, remember, just like the people of Israel, we should listen to God's true messengers and follow His teachings with all our hearts.

Deuteronomy 18:6-8 KJV "And if a Levite come from any of thy gates out of all Israel, where he sojourned, and come with all the desire of his mind unto the place which the Lord shall choose; Then he shall minister in the name of the Lord his God, as all his brethren the Levites do, which stand there before the Lord. They shall have like portions to eat, beside that which cometh of the sale of his patrimony."

Avoid Occult Practices

Deuteronomy 18:11 has 4 commandments from God about avoiding everything to do with occult practices. Occult practices involved trying to gain special powers or knowledge from things that were not from God.

You see, in the Bible, God wants us to trust and love Him with all our hearts. He wants us to talk to Him and ask for help when we need it. But some people didn't trust God, so they tried to find power or answers in other ways.

Occult practices could include things like trying to talk to spirits of people who have passed away, or using magic or spells to try and control things. These things might seem exciting or mysterious, but they are not what God wants for us.

God wants us to focus on Him and His love for us. He wants us to live in a way that is good and kind to others, and to always ask Him for help and guidance. That's why He asks us to stay away from occult practices.

Remember, it's important to always trust in God and know that He loves us and is always there for us. He is the one who can give us the best guidance and help we need. So let's keep our hearts and minds focused on Him!

Stay Away From Charmers

1. Commandment 1 from Deuteronomy 18:11: Stay away from charmers. Charmer refers to someone who tries to use magic or tricks to control or manipulate people. It's important to remember that we shouldn't try to control or manipulate others, but instead treat them with kindness and respect.

Stay Away From Mediums

2. Commandment 2 from Deuteronomy 18:11: Stay away from mediums. A medium is someone who claims to communicate with spirits or ghosts. We should always remember that it's not right to seek answers or guidance from the spirits of the dead. Instead, we should seek guidance from our family, friends, and most importantly, from God.

Stay Away From People Who Talk To The Dead

3. Commandment 3 from Deuteronomy 18:11: Stay away from necromancers. A necromancer is someone who tries to talk to or raise the dead. This is something that we should never attempt or be a part of, because it's not natural or safe. We should cherish and remember our loved ones who have passed away, but not try to bring them back or communicate with them.

Stay Away From People Who Inquire of The Dead

4. Commandment 4 from Deuteronomy 18:11: Stay away from those who inquire of the dead. This means we shouldn't ask questions or seek answers from people who claim to know things from the spirits or the dead. Instead, we should trust in God's guidance and seek wisdom from people who love and care for us.

Deuteronomy 18:11 KJV "Or a charmer, or a consulter with familiar spirits, or a wizard, or a necromancer."

A CHILDREN'S GUIDE TO A GODLY WAY OF LIFE

Have Clean & Pure Hearts

Deuteronomy 23:10 is a Bible commandment that talks about something called cleanliness. In this verse, God gives a commandment to the people, including children, to be clean and pure.

Imagine you have a beautiful garden. In order to keep it healthy and growing, you have to take care of it. You water the plants, remove the weeds, and make sure everything is clean. This is similar to what God wants us to do with our lives. He wants us to take care of ourselves and keep our hearts and minds clean.

Being clean means not doing things that are wrong or hurtful to others. It means being kind and respectful to everyone. Just like we clean our bodies by taking a bath or brushing our teeth, God wants us to clean our hearts by being good and honest.

So, when God says in Deuteronomy 23:10 to be clean, it's like He's reminding us to be good and make good choices. By doing this, we can have a happy and healthy life, just like a beautiful garden.

Deuteronomy 23:10 KJV "If there be among you any man, that is not clean by reason of uncleanness that chanceth him by night, then shall he go abroad out of the camp, he shall not come within the camp:"

Keep Your Promises

Deuteronomy 23:21 is a commandment from the Bible says, "If you make a promise to the Lord your God, don't be slow to keep it. The Lord your God will certainly hold you accountable for it, and you would be guilty of sin."

Now, let's imagine you promised to do something for someone, like helping your friend clean their room. This commandment tells us if we promise to do something, we should do our best to keep that promise. It's important because when we make a promise, it shows that we care about others and want to be trustworthy.

Sometimes, we might feel tempted to break a promise or forget about it, but this verse reminds us that God wants us to be responsible and true to our word. So, if we promise something, it's good to make sure we do our very best to keep that promise, just like God would want us to.

Deuteronomy 23:21 KJV "When thou shalt vow a vow unto the Lord thy God, thou shalt not slack to pay it: for the Lord thy God will surely require it of thee; and it would be sin in thee."

A CHILDREN'S GUIDE TO A GODLY WAY OF LIFE

Do What We Say We Will Do

Deuteronomy 23:23 is a commandment that says, "You shall be careful to do what has passed your lips, for you have voluntarily vowed to the Lord your God what you have promised with your mouth."

Always Keep Your Promises

Now, let's break it down to make it easier for you to understand. Imagine you promise to do something, like cleaning your room or helping your friend with their homework. The commandment from God is saying we should always keep our promises and do what we said we would do.

What We Say We Will Do Is A Promise To God

It's important to remember that when we make a promise, we are making it to God too. So, we should be careful to keep our word and not forget about our promises. This commandment teaches us to be responsible and trustworthy by following through with the things we say we'll do.

Deuteronomy 23:23 KJV "That which is gone out of thy lips thou shalt keep and perform; even a freewill offering, according as thou hast vowed unto the Lord thy God, which thou hast promised with thy mouth."

When Borrowing, Don't Take Necessities

Deuteronomy 24:6 is a commandment that tells us when someone borrows something from another person, they should not take something that the person really needs, like their special tools or their yummy food.

God wants us to be kind and considerate to others, and not to make their lives difficult. He wants us to treat others the way we would like to be treated. So, if you ever borrow something from someone, remember to return it nicely and not to take anything that is really important to them. That's what this verse tells us, and it's a good way to be a good friend and neighbor!"

Deuteronomy 24:6 KJV No man shall take the nether or the upper millstone to pledge: for he taketh a man's life to pledge.

Be Kind, Loyal & Loving To Others

Proverbs 3:3-4 gives us 3 commandments from God that are all about being kind, loyal, and loving to others. When you do that, people will think well of you, and God will be happy too!

The verse says, "Let love and faithfulness never leave you; bind them around your neck, write them on the tablet of your heart. Then you will win favor and a good name in the sight of God and man." Let's break it down so it's a little easier to understand.

Always Be Loving & Loyal

First, it says, "Let love and faithfulness never leave you." Love means being kind, caring, and showing affection towards others.

Faithfulness means being loyal and keeping your promises. So, it's important to always be loving and loyal to the people around you.

Always Be Loving & Faithful

Next, it says, "Bind them around your neck, write them on the tablet of your heart." This means that you should keep love and faithfulness close to you, like wearing a necklace or keeping them in your heart. It's like a reminder to always be kind and loyal.

Will Win Favor & Good Name With God & Man

And finally, it says, "Then you will win favor and a good name in the sight of God and man." This means that when you practice love and faithfulness, people will think highly of you and God will be pleased too. It's like when you do good things, people will like you and think you're a good person.

Proverbs 3:3-4 NIV "Let love and faithfulness never leave you; bind them around your neck, write them on the tablet of your heart. Then you will win favor and a good."

Obey your parents & pay attention to their teachings

Proverbs 6:20-21 commandment says, "My child, obey your father's commandment, and don't neglect your mother's teaching. Keep their words always in your heart. Tie them around your neck."

To understand this commandment, imagine you have a mom and dad who love you very much. They want to teach you good things so that you can grow up to be a kind and responsible person. In these commandment, God is saying that it's important to listen to your mom and dad and follow their rules. They have wisdom and knowledge that they want to share with you.

When it says "keep their words always in your heart" and "tie them around your neck," it means that you should remember and cherish the things your parents teach you. They want to guide you in making good choices and help you to become the best version of yourself.

By obeying your parents and paying attention to their teachings, you are also obeying God's commandments. He wants us to respect and honor our parents because they love us and want what's best for us. It's a way to show love and gratitude to both our parents and God.

Proverbs 6:20-21 "My son, keep thy father's commandment, and forsake not the law of thy mother: 21 Bind them continually upon thine heart, and tie them about thy neck"

Remember God's Commandments

In simple words, Proverbs 7:1-4 is telling us that we should remember God's teachings, follow His commandments, treasure His wisdom, and obey Him so that we can live a good and happy life.

Keep God's Words In Our Hearts

First, it says that we should keep God's words in our hearts. This means that we should remember and hold on to the things that God teaches us, like being kind, honest, and loving.

Follow God's Commandments

Next, it says that we should follow God's commandments. These are like rules that God gives us to help us live a good and happy life. Some of these commandments include things like respecting our parents, being honest, and not hurting others.

Treasure God's Wisdom

Then, it says that we should treasure God's wisdom. Wisdom is like having good knowledge and making smart choices. By listening to God's wisdom and learning from it, we can make good decisions and live a better life.

Obey God's Commandments

Lastly, it says that we should make sure to obey God's commandments so that we can live. This means that if we follow God's teachings, we can have a happy and fulfilling life.

Proverbs 7:1-4 KJV "My son, keep my words, and lay up my commandments with thee. Keep my commandments, and live; and my law as the apple of thine eye. Bind them upon thy."

Obey God's Words, Do His Words & Live Accordingly

Jeremiah 11:4 is a commandment from the Bible that says, "Obey my voice, and do them, according to all which I command you: so shall ye be my people, and I will be your God."

Obey God's Words & Teachings

When God says, "Obey my voice," it means that we should listen to His words and teachings. God's words and his teachings are His commandments and the other things He tells us are good for us to do.

Put God's Teachings Into Action

Live Our Lives According To His Teachings

And when God says, "do them," it means that we should actually put those teachings into action and live our lives according to them. By following God's commandments, we become closer to Him. It's like being part of a special family. God promises that if we choose to be His people by following His commandments, He will be our God and take care of us.

So, just like how we obey our parents' rules because we know they love us and want the best for us, we should also try our best to follow God's commandments because He loves us and wants us to have a happy and fulfilling life.

Jeremiah 11:4 KJV "Which I commanded your fathers in the day that I brought them forth out of the land of Egypt, from the iron furnace, saying, Obey my voice, and do."

Speak truth, Don't Plot Evil & Don't Swear False Judgements

In Zechariah 8:16-17, God's commandments are to Speak the Truth, to Not Plot Evil against each other, and to not swear falsely because God hates these things.

Tell The Truth

The first thing God says in Zechariah 8:16-17 is, "These are the things you must do: Speak the truth to each other, and make true and fair judgments in your courts." This means that God wants people to always tell the truth and be honest with each other. He also wants them to be fair when they have to make decisions in their courts or when judging others.

Do Not Plan or Do Evil Against Each Other

Do Not Swear Falsely

The second thing God says is, "Do not plot evil against each other, and don't love to swear falsely. I hate all these things." This means that God doesn't want people to plan or think of doing bad things to each other. He also doesn't want them to say lies or false promises. God really dislikes all these things because they hurt and harm others.

Instead, God wants people to love peace and truth. He says, "So, love truth and peace." This means that God wants people to value and cherish honesty and peace. He wants us to live in harmony with each other, being kind, and treating others the way we would like to be treated.

So, in summary, God is giving us some important guidelines to follow. He wants us to be honest, fair, and loving towards others. He dislikes when people plan bad things or lie to each other. Instead, He wants us to love peace and truth.

Zechariah 8:16-17 NIV These are the things you are to do: Speak the truth to each other, and render true and sound judgment in your courts; do not plot evil against each other, and do not love to swear falsely. I hate all this," declares the Lord.

A CHILDREN'S GUIDE TO A GODLY WAY OF LIFE

Let Your Light Shine Before Others

Matthew 5:16 is a commandment from the Bible that says, "Let your light shine before others, that they may see your good deeds and glorify your Father in heaven."

To help us understand this commandment, imagine you have a special light inside you, like a flashlight. This light represents all the good things you do in the world, like being kind to others, helping your friends, or being respectful to your parents.

Show Others The Good Things You Do

God wants us to let this light shine, which means He wants us to show others all the good things we do. When we do good deeds and people see them, they might feel happy or inspired. And when people see us being kind and helpful, they might think about God and how wonderful He is.

So, when Matthew 5:16 says, "glorify your Father in heaven," it means that by doing good things and letting our light shine, we are showing others how amazing and loving God is.

Matthew 5:16 KJV "Let your light so shine before men, that they may see your good works, and glorify your Father which is in heaven."

Commandments About Being Angry

In Matthew 5:22-24, Jesus is talking about some commandments from God. He says that if we get angry with someone, it's like breaking one of God's commandments. He wants us to try and solve our problems with love and kindness instead of getting angry.

Jesus also says that if we want to give a special gift to God, like at church, but we have a problem with someone, we should go and fix that problem first. It's important to make things right with others before we try to make things right with God.

The special commandments from Matthew 5:22-24 are:

Don't get angry with someone or say mean things

Make peace w/ others before doing something special for God

Be kind, forgive, and show love to everyone

Basically, Jesus is telling us that it's important to be kind to others and to try and make things right when we have problems with them. He wants us to love and forgive each other just like God loves and forgives us.

Matthew 5:22-24 But I say unto you, That whosoever is angry with his brother without a cause shall be in danger of the judgment: and whosoever shall say to his brother, Raca, shall be in danger of the council: but whosoever shall say, Thou fool, shall be in danger of hell fire. Therefore if thou bring thy gift to the altar, and there rememberest that thy brother hath ought against thee; Leave there thy gift before the altar, and go thy way; first be reconciled to thy brother, and then come and offer thy gift.

Treating People With Respect & Kindness

Matthew 5:27-48 gives us a large listing of commandments to help us live a life that God is happy with with regard to treating people with respect and kindness.

Treat Everyone With Respect and Kindness

Don't just look at people in a bad way or with bad thoughts, but treat everyone with respect and kindness. It's important to have a good heart towards others.

Solve Problems In A Peaceful And Calm Way

Try not to get angry or mean with others. Instead, try to solve problems in a peaceful and calm way. It's better to be friends and show love to one another.

Keep Your Word

When you make a promise or say you will do something, always keep your word. It's important to be honest and trustworthy.

Don't Take Revenge

Don't try to take revenge when someone hurts you. Instead, forgive them and show them love. It's better to be kind and compassionate.

Treat Everyone The Way You Want To Be Treated

Love everyone, even those who may not be nice to you. Treat others the way you would want to be treated. It's important to be kind and caring to everyone.

Be Generous & Help Those In Need

Be generous and share what you have with others. Help those in need, whether it's your toys, food, or even your time. It's important to be selfless and help others.

Love Your Enemies & Pray For Them

Love your enemies and pray for them. Even if someone is mean to you, try to show them kindness and pray for them to have a change of heart. It's important to be forgiving and understanding.

Matthew 5:27-48 KJV **27** *Ye have heard that it was said by them of old time, Thou shalt not commit adultery: But I say unto you, That whosoever looketh on a woman to lust after her hath committed adultery with her already in his heart. And if thy right eye offend thee, pluck it out, and cast it from thee: for it is profitable for thee that one of thy members should perish, and not that thy whole body should be cast into hell. And if thy right hand offend thee, cut it off, and cast it from thee: for it is profitable for thee that one of thy members should perish, and not that thy whole body should be cast into hell. It hath been said, Whosoever shall put away his wife, let him give her a writing of divorcement: But I say unto you, That whosoever shall put away his wife, saving for the cause of fornication, causeth her to commit adultery: and whosoever shall marry her that is divorced committeth adultery. Again, ye have heard that it hath been said by them of old time, Thou shalt not forswear thyself, but shalt perform unto the Lord thine oaths: But I say unto you, Swear not at all; neither by heaven; for it is God's throne: Nor by the earth; for it is his footstool: neither by Jerusalem; for it is the city of the great King. Neither shalt thou swear by thy head, because thou canst not make one hair white or black. But let your communication be, Yea, yea; Nay, nay: for whatsoever is more than these cometh of evil. Ye have heard that it hath been said, An eye for an eye, and a tooth for a* *tooth: But I say unto you, That ye resist not evil: but whosoever shall smite thee on thy right cheek, turn to him the other also. And if any man will sue thee at the law, and take away thy coat, let him have thy cloak also. And whosoever shall compel thee to go a mile, go with him twain. Give to him that asketh thee, and from him that would borrow of thee turn not thou away. Ye have heard that it hath been said, Thou shalt love thy neighbour, and hate thine enemy. But I say unto you, Love your enemies, bless them that curse you, do good to them that hate you, and pray for them which despitefully use you, and persecute you; That ye may be the children of your Father which is in heaven: for he maketh his sun to rise on the evil and on the good, and sendeth rain on the just and on the unjust. For if ye love them which love you, what reward have ye? do not even the publicans the same? And if ye salute your brethren only, what do ye more than others? do not even the publicans so? Be ye therefore perfect, even as your Father which is in heaven is perfect*

A CHILDREN'S GUIDE TO A GODLY WAY OF LIFE

Do Not Judge Or Criticize Others

In Matthew 7:1-5 Jesus is teaching us commandments about judgement.

Imagine you and your friends are playing a game, and sometimes you might get upset if your friend does something you don't like. But in this commandment in Matthew, Jesus is telling us that we shouldn't be quick to judge or criticize others. He wants us to be kind and understanding towards everyone.

Jesus says that before we point out the mistakes of others, we need to look at ourselves and see if we have made any mistakes too. It's like looking in a mirror and seeing our own reflection. We need to remember that nobody is perfect, and we all make mistakes sometimes.

Jesus also tells us that instead of judging others, we should try to help them and be kind to them. If we want others to be kind to us, we need to show kindness to them first.

So, the commandment from God in this verse is to treat others with kindness, not to judge or criticize them, and to remember that we also make mistakes.

Matthew 7:1-5 KJV Judge not, that ye be not judged. For with what judgment ye judge, ye shall be judged: and with what measure ye mete, it shall be measured to you again. And why beholdest thou the mote that is in thy brother's eye, but considerest not the beam that is in thine own eye? Or how wilt thou say to thy brother, Let me pull out the mote out of thine eye; and, behold, a beam is in thine own eye? Thou hypocrite, first cast out the beam out of thine own eye; and then shalt thou see clearly to cast out the mote out of thy brother's eye.

Be Loving & Forgiving To Everyone

The commandments in Luke 6:27-36 are where Jesus is teaching us to be kind, loving, and forgiving to everyone, no matter how they treat us. Jesus says that we should love our enemies and do good things for them. This means that even if someone is mean to us or hurts our feelings, we should still be nice to them.

Love Your Enemies

1. Love your enemies: Jesus tells us to love even those who are mean or unkind to us. It means we should try to be kind to everyone, even if they are not kind to us.

Do Good To Those Who Hate You

2. Do good to those who hate you: When someone doesn't like us or treats us badly, Jesus wants us to do good things for them. We can help them, be nice to them, or even forgive them.

Bless Those Who Curse You

3. Bless those who curse you: Sometimes people say mean things to us, but Jesus wants us to respond with kind words instead. We can say nice things back or wish good things for them.

Pray For Those Who Mistreat You

4. Pray for those who mistreat you: If someone mistreats us or does something unkind, Jesus tells us to pray for them. We can ask God to help them be kinder and happier.

Turn The Other Cheek

5. Turn the other cheek: If someone hurts us physically or does something mean, Jesus wants us to respond with peace and not fight back. It means we should try to find peaceful solutions instead of being mean or violent.

Give To Everyone Who Asks

6. Give to everyone who asks: Jesus wants us to be generous and share what we have with others. If someone asks for help or needs something, we should try to give what we can and help them.

Treat Others As You Want To Be Treated

7. Treat others as you want to be treated: This commandment is often called the Golden Rule. It means we should treat others the way we would like to be treated. If we want others to be kind to us, we should be kind to them too.

Love Your Enemies

8. Love your enemies: Jesus repeats this commandment to remind us how important it is. He wants us to show love, kindness, and forgiveness to everyone, even if they are not our friends.

Luke 6:27-36 KJV But I say unto you which hear, Love your enemies, do good to them which hate you, Bless them that curse you, and pray for them which despitefully use you. And unto him that smiteth thee on the one cheek offer also the other; and him that taketh away thy cloak forbid not to take thy coat also. Give to every man that asketh of thee; and of him that taketh away thy goods ask them not again. And as ye would that men should do to you, do ye also to them likewise. For if ye love them which love you, what thank have ye? for sinners also love those that love them. And if ye do good to them which do good to you, what thank have ye? for sinners also do even the same. And if ye lend to them of whom ye hope to receive, what thank have ye? for sinners also lend to sinners, to receive as much again. But love ye your enemies, and do good, and lend, hoping for nothing again; and your reward shall be great, and ye shall be the children of the Highest: for he is kind unto the unthankful and to the evil. Be ye therefore merciful, as your Father also is merciful.

Love Your Enemies

In Luke 6:31-35, gave us commandments about loving your enemies which tell us to treat others the way we want to be treated, to love everyone, to not judge others, to be generous and to share with others.

Treat Others The Way You Want To Be Treated

The first commandment that Jesus tells us is "Do to others as you would have them do to you." This means that we should treat other people the way we want them to treat us. If we want others to be nice to us, then we should be nice to them too.

Love Your Enemies and Pray For Them

The second commandment is about loving others, even if they are not nice to us. Jesus says that we should love our enemies and pray for them. It might be hard to understand, but Jesus wants us to show love and kindness to everyone, even if they are mean to us.

Don't Judge or Criticize Others

Jesus also teaches us about not judging others. He says that we should not criticize or say mean things about other people. We should try to understand them and forgive them if they make mistakes.

Give To Everyone Who Asks

Lastly, Jesus tells us that if we give, then we will receive. He encourages us to be generous and share with others. This means that if we have something that someone else needs, we should share it with them and help them.

Luke 6:31-35 KJV And as ye would that men should do to you, do ye also to them likewise. For if ye love them which love you, what thank have ye? for sinners also love those that love them. And if ye do good to them which do good to you, what thank have ye? for sinners also do even the same. And if ye lend to them of whom ye hope to receive, what thank have ye? for sinners also lend to sinners, to receive as much again. But love ye your enemies, and do good, and lend, hoping for nothing again; and your reward shall be great, and ye shall be the children of the Highest: for he is kind unto the unthankful and to the evil.

The Golden Rule

In Matthew 7:6-14 Jesus also talks about something called "the Golden Rule" in which He says "So in everything, do to others what you would have them do to you." This means that we should treat other people the way we want to be treated. We should be kind, loving, and helpful to others, just like we would want them to be kind, loving, and helpful to us.

Choose Path That Leads To Happiness & Eternal Life

Jesus also talks about two paths - a wide one and a narrow one. He says that the wide path is easy and many people choose to walk on it, but it doesn't lead to good things. The narrow path, on the other hand, is a bit harder, but it leads to happiness and eternal life with God.

Be Careful Who We Trust

Jesus tells us that we need to be careful about who we listen to and follow. Some people might pretend to be good, but they might actually want to harm us or trick us. He says that we need to be wise and use our judgment to know who is good and who is not.

Look For People Who Do Good Things

Jesus also talks about how we can know if someone is truly following God's commandments. He says that a good tree will produce good fruit, and a bad tree will produce bad fruit. This means that if someone is following God's commandments, they will show it by doing good things and being kind to others.

So, in simple words, in the commandments in Matthew 7:6-14, Jesus is teaching us to be kind to others, to choose the path that leads to happiness and eternal life, to be careful about who we trust, and to look for people who do good things as a sign that they are following God's commandments.

Matthew 7:6-14 KJV Give not that which is holy unto the dogs, neither cast ye your pearls before swine, lest they trample them under their feet, and turn again and rend you. Ask, and it shall be given you; seek, and ye shall find; knock, and it shall be opened unto you: For every one that asketh receiveth; and he that seeketh findeth; and to him that knocketh it shall be opened. Or what man is there of you, whom if his son ask bread, will he give him a stone? Or if he ask a fish, will he give him a serpent? If ye then, being evil, know how to give good gifts unto your children, how much more shall your Father which is in heaven give good things to them that ask him? Therefore all things whatsoever ye would that men should do to you, do ye even so to them: for this is the law and the prophets. Enter ye in at the strait gate: for wide is the gate, and broad is the way, that leadeth to destruction, and many there be which go in thereat: Because strait is the gate, and narrow is the way, which leadeth unto life, and few there be that find it.

A CHILDREN'S GUIDE TO A GODLY WAY OF LIFE

Build A Solid Foundation

In Matthew 7:15-29 Jesus tells a story about two types of people. He compares them to two different houses. One house is built on a strong and sturdy foundation, like a rock, while the other house is built on a weak foundation, like sand.

False Prophets

Jesus says that some people might pretend to follow God's commandments and act like they are good, but inside they are not. He calls these people "false prophets" because they pretend to be good, but they don't really love and obey God's commandments.

He warns us to be careful and to look out for these false prophets because they can lead us in the wrong direction. He says that we can know if someone is a true follower of God by looking at the fruits of their actions. If they do good things and show love and kindness to others, then they are following God's commandments.

Obey & Do What Jesus Teaches

Jesus also says that it's not enough just to listen to what he says, but we should also obey and do what he teaches. It's like building a strong house on a strong foundation. When we hear God's words and obey them, it's like building our lives on a strong foundation.

Listen To Jesus' Words & Put Them Into Practice

At the end of the story, Jesus says that those who listen to his words and put them into practice are like the person who built their house on the strong foundation. When storms or troubles come, their house will not fall apart because it is built on something strong. But those who don't listen to his words and don't follow God's commandments are like the person who built their house on a weak foundation. When storms or troubles come, their house will fall apart because it is not built on something strong.

So, the lesson Jesus wants us to learn is that it's important to listen to his teachings and follow God's commandments. When we do that, our lives will be strong and we will be able to handle any troubles that come our way.

Matthew 7:15-29 KJV Beware of false prophets, which come to you in sheep's clothing, but inwardly they are ravening wolves. Ye shall know them by their fruits. Do men gather grapes of thorns, or figs of thistles? Even so every good tree bringeth forth good fruit; but a corrupt tree bringeth forth evil fruit. A good tree cannot bring forth evil fruit, neither can a corrupt tree bring forth good fruit. Every tree that bringeth not forth good fruit is hewn down, and cast into the fire. Wherefore by their fruits ye shall know them. Not every one that saith unto me, Lord, Lord, shall enter into the kingdom of heaven; but he that doeth the will of my Father which is in heaven. Many will say to me in that day, Lord, Lord, have we not prophesied in thy name? and in thy name have cast out devils? and in thy name done many wonderful works? And then will I profess unto them, I never knew you: depart from me, ye that work iniquity. Therefore whosoever heareth these sayings of mine, and doeth them, I will liken him unto a wise man, which built his house upon a rock. And the rain descended, and the floods came, and the winds blew, and beat upon that house; and it fell not: for it was founded upon a rock. And every one that heareth these sayings of mine, and doeth them not, shall be likened unto a foolish man, which built his house upon the sand: And the rain descended, and the floods came, and the winds blew, and beat upon that house; and it fell: and great was the fall of it. And it came to pass, when Jesus had ended these sayings, the people were astonished at his doctrine: For he taught them as one having authority, and not as the scribes.

Following Jesus

Matthew 16:24 is a commandment from the Bible where Jesus says, "If anyone wants to be my follower, he must deny himself, take up his cross, and follow me."

Now, let's break this down to make it easier to understand. Jesus is saying that if we want to be his followers, we need to do a few things. First, we should deny ourselves. To deny ourselves means we should not always think about what we want or what makes us happy, but instead, think about what Jesus would want us to do. It's like putting others before ourselves.

Be Willing To Face Any Challenge

Next, Jesus says we should take up our cross. Now, this doesn't mean we have to carry a real cross like Jesus did. It means that we should be willing to face any challenges or difficulties that come along the way while following Jesus. We should be strong and not give up, even if things get tough.

Live our lives in a way that Jesus taught us

Finally, Jesus tells us to follow him. This means that we should try our best to live our lives the way Jesus taught us. We should be kind to others, help those in need, and show love and compassion to everyone around us.

Matthew 16:24 is a reminder from Jesus to his followers that if we want to be like him, we should deny ourselves, be ready to face challenges, and live our lives in a way that makes him proud.

Mark 8:34 is another version of this same commandment.

Matthew 16:24 KJV Then said Jesus unto his disciples, If any man will come after me, let him deny himself, and take up his cross, and follow me.

Mark 8:34 NIV Then he called the crowd to him along with his disciples and said: "Whoever wants to be my disciple must deny themselves and take up their cross and follow me.

Don't Do Wrong Or Hurtful Things

In Matthew 18:8-10, Jesus was telling his friends that they should be very careful not to do things that are wrong or hurtful to themselves or others. He said that if their hand or foot causes them to do bad things, they should cut it off or get rid of it. But we don't have to worry because Jesus didn't mean that they should really cut off their body parts! He was just saying that it's better to stop doing bad things and be kind to others.

Focus On Good and Positive Things

Jesus also said that if their eyes make them look at bad things, they should close their eyes or look away. He wanted his friends to understand that it's important to focus on good and positive things.

Children Are Very Special To God

God's Angels Are Always Watching & Taking Care of Children

Then, Jesus talked about children. He said that children are very special to God and that God's angels are always watching and taking care of them. Jesus wanted his friends to know that God loves children and wants them to be safe and happy.

So, in these verses, Jesus was giving his friends some important rules to live by. He wanted them to be good, kind, and to take care of themselves and others. He also wanted them to remember that God loves children and is always looking out for them.

Matthew 18:8-10 KJV Wherefore if thy hand or thy foot offend thee, cut them off, and cast them from thee: it is better for thee to enter into life halt or maimed, rather than having two hands or two feet to be cast into everlasting fire. And if thine eye offend thee, pluck it out, and cast it from thee: it is better for thee to enter into life with one eye, rather than having two eyes to be cast into hell fire. Take heed that ye despise not one of these little ones; for I say unto you, That in heaven their angels do always behold the face of my Father which is in heaven.

How To Solve Problems With Others

In Matthew 18:15-17 Jesus is sharing commandments about how to solve problems and disagreements with others.

Solve Problems Peacefully with Love

Jesus said, "If your friend does something that makes you unhappy or hurts your feelings, it's important to talk to them about it. But first, you should go and talk to them privately, just between the two of you. You can tell them how you feel and try to work things out together."

Now, if talking to them alone doesn't solve the problem, Jesus says, "Take one or two other people with you, so they can help you listen and understand each other better. They can also give their opinions and help find a solution."

But if even with the help of others, the problem is still not resolved, Jesus tells us to "tell it to the church," which means sharing the issue with the leaders or people who can guide and help everyone involved.

Forgive Each Other

You see, Jesus wants us to try our best to solve our problems peacefully and with love. He wants us to forgive each other and find a way to get along. It's important to remember that Jesus loves and cares for all of us, and He wants us to treat each other with kindness and respect. So, if there is ever a problem or disagreement, we should try to follow these steps that Jesus taught us.

Matthew 18:15-17 KJV Moreover if thy brother shall trespass against thee, go and tell him his fault between thee and him alone: if he shall hear thee, thou hast gained thy brother. But if he will not hear thee, then take with thee one or two more, that in the mouth of two or three witnesses every word may be established. And if he shall neglect to hear them, tell it unto the church: but if he neglect to hear the church, let him be unto thee as an heathen man and a publican.

A CHILDREN'S GUIDE TO A GODLY WAY OF LIFE

Forgive Someone Endlessly

Matthew 18:21-22 is a commandment from Jesus about forgiveness. Jesus tells us that if someone does something wrong to us, we should forgive them. A man named Peter asked Jesus how many times he should forgive someone, and Jesus said not just seven times, but seventy-seven times!

Jesus wants us to understand that forgiveness is really important. He wants us to be kind and forgiving towards others, even if they make mistakes. Just like how we want others to forgive us when we do something wrong, Jesus wants us to forgive others too. It can be hard sometimes, but it helps us have peace in our hearts and make the world a better place.

Matthew 18:21-22 KJV Then came Peter to him, and said, Lord, how oft shall my brother sin against me, and I forgive him? till seven times? Jesus saith unto him, I say not unto thee, Until seven times: but, Until seventy times seven.

Love of Money

In Matthew 19:16-26 and Mark 10:17-29 Jesus tells a story about a rich man. In this story, a man comes to Jesus and asks Him what he needs to do to have eternal life. Jesus tells him to follow the commandments. The man tells Jesus that he has been following all these commandments since he was a little boy. But Jesus knows that the man loves his money a lot. So, Jesus says something interesting.

Love & Care For Others More Than You Love Money

Jesus tells the man to sell all his belongings and give the money to the poor because Jesus knows that sometimes, people care too much about their things instead of caring for others.

When the man hears this, he feels sad because he doesn't want to give away his money. You see, his money was very important to him. Then, Jesus says something that can be a little hard to understand. He says that it is easier for a camel to go through the eye of a needle than for a rich person to enter the kingdom of God.

This means that sometimes, when we have a lot of things, it can be hard for us to think about others and do what is right. Jesus wants us to understand that it's not bad to have things, but it's important to share and be kind to others too.

Be Kind & Help Those In Need

So, the lesson from this story is that Jesus wants us to love and care for others more than we love our things. He wants us to be kind, help those who need it, and follow His commandments. And when we do this, we can have eternal life with Him.

Matthew 19:16-26 KJV And, behold, one came and said unto him, Good Master, what good thing shall I do, that I may have eternal life? And he said unto him, Why callest thou me good? there is none good but one, that is, God: but if thou wilt enter into life, keep the commandments. He saith unto him, Which? Jesus said, Thou shalt do no murder, Thou shalt not commit adultery, Thou shalt not steal, Thou shalt not bear false witness, Honour thy father and thy mother: and, Thou shalt love thy neighbour as thyself. The young man saith unto him, All these things have I kept from my youth up: what lack I yet? Jesus said unto him, If thou wilt be perfect, go and sell that thou hast, and give to the poor, and thou shalt have treasure in heaven: and come and follow me. But when the young man heard that saying, he went away sorrowful: for he had great possessions. Then said Jesus unto his disciples, Verily I say unto you, That a rich man shall hardly enter into the kingdom of heaven. And again I say unto you, It is easier for a camel to go through the eye of a needle, than for a rich man to enter into the kingdom of God. When his disciples heard it, they were exceedingly amazed, saying, Who then can be saved? But Jesus beheld them, and said unto them, With men this is impossible; but with God all things are possible.

Mark 10:17-29 NIV As Jesus started on his way, a man ran up to him and fell on his knees before him. "Good teacher," he asked, "what must I do to inherit eternal life?" "Why do you call me good?" Jesus answered. "No one is good—except God alone. You know the commandments: 'You shall not murder, you shall not commit adultery, you shall not steal, you shall not give false testimony, you shall not defraud, honor your father and mother.' "Teacher," he declared, "all these I have kept since I was a boy." Jesus looked at him and loved him. "One thing you lack," he said. "Go, sell everything you have and give to the poor, and you will have treasure in heaven. Then come, follow me." At this the man's face fell. He went away sad, because he had great wealth. Jesus looked around and said to his disciples, "How hard it is for the rich to enter the kingdom of God!" The disciples were amazed at his words. But Jesus said again, "Children, how hard it is[e] to enter the kingdom of God! It is easier for a camel to go through the eye of a needle than for someone who is rich to enter the kingdom of God." The disciples were even more amazed, and said to each other, "Who then can be saved?" Jesus looked at them and said, "With man this is impossible, but not with God; all things are possible with God." Then Peter spoke up, "We have left everything to follow you!" "Truly I tell you," Jesus replied, "no one who has left home or brothers or sisters or mother or father or children or fields for me and the gospel 30 will fail to receive a hundred times as much in this present age: homes, brothers, sisters, mothers, children and fields—along with persecutions—and in the age to come eternal life. But many who are first will be last, and the last first."

Wise & Faithful Servant

In Matthew 24:42-51 Jesus tells a story about a wise and faithful servant. He says that this servant is like a good worker who takes care of his boss's house while the boss is away. The servant is very responsible and does everything he is supposed to do, even when the boss is not there to see him.

Be A Good Servant & Be Ready For His Return

Jesus then says that it's important for all of his followers to be like that good servant. He wants us to always be ready and prepared for his return, just like the servant is always ready for his boss to come back.

Be Kind & Loving Towards Others

Jesus also talks about how we should be kind and loving towards others. He says that when he comes back, he will reward those who have been good and loving to others. But he will be unhappy with those who have been mean or selfish.

So, the important commandments from Jesus in these verses are to always be ready for his return, to be responsible and faithful in doing what we should do, and to be kind and loving towards others. By following these commandments, we can make Jesus happy and be ready for his return.

Matthew 24:42-51 NIV "Therefore keep watch, because you do not know on what day your Lord will come. But understand this: If the owner of the house had known at what time of night the thief was coming, he would have kept watch and would not have let his house be broken into. So you also must be ready, because the Son of Man will come at an hour when you do not expect him. "Who then is the faithful and wise servant, whom the master has put in charge of the servants in his household to give them their food at the proper time? It will be good for that servant whose master finds him doing so when he returns. Truly I tell you, he will put him in charge of all his possessions. But suppose that servant is wicked and says to himself, 'My master is staying away a long time,' and he then begins to beat his fellow servants and to eat and drink with drunkards. The master of that servant will come on a day when he does not expect him and at an hour he is not aware of. He will cut him to pieces and assign him a place with the hypocrites, where there will be weeping and gnashing of teeth.

LADY KIMBERLY MOTES DOTY, AURORA BRAND & CONOR FINNEGAN

To Be In Charge, Serve With a Loving Heart

In Matthew 20:25-28 and Mark 9:35 Jesus is talking to His disciples, who were His close friends and followers. He wanted to teach them an important lesson about how to treat others.

Jesus said, "You know that the rulers of the world like to be in charge and have power over others. But it should not be the same for you. If you want to be great, you must be like a servant."

He meant that instead of trying to be the boss and have authority over people, we should be kind and helpful to them, just like a servant. Jesus showed this by example when He washed His disciples' feet, which was a job typically done by servants.

Jesus also said, "I came not to be served, but to serve others and give my life for them." He wanted His friends to understand that the most important thing in life is to love and care for others, just like He did.

So, the commandment from Jesus is to be humble, kind, and to put others before ourselves. He wants us to treat everyone with love and respect, just as He did.

Matthew 20:25-28 NIV Jesus called them together and said, "You know that the rulers of the Gentiles lord it over them, and their high officials exercise authority over them. Not so with you. Instead, whoever wants to become great among you must be your servant, and whoever wants to be first must be your slave just as the Son of Man did not come to be served, but to serve, and to give his life as a ransom for many."

Mark 9:35 KJV "And he sat down, and called the twelve, and saith unto them, If any man desire to be first, the same shall be last of all, and servant of all."

LADY KIMBERLY MOTES DOTY, AURORA BRAND & CONOR FINNEGAN

Helping People In Need Is Helping Jesus

Matthew 25:34-46 is where Jesus tells us the commandments about when we help other people who are in need, it's like we are helping him.

Jesus said that we should give food to those who are hungry, give water to those who are thirsty, and take care of people who don't have a place to stay.

Jesus also said that when we visit people who are sick or in prison, it's like we are visiting him. He wants us to not only take care of the food and water needs of people's body but their emotional needs of their hearts too, because people get lonely when they are sick and alone at home or in the hospital or they are alone away from their families in prison, or even just away from their families to go to college or traveling for work. He wants us to be kind and show love to everyone, because when we do that, we are doing it for him too.

Jesus told us that when we do all these things with love and kindness, we are following his commandments. He said that when we help others, it makes him very happy, and we will be blessed.

Matthew 25:34-46 NIV "Then the King will say to those on his right, 'Come, you who are blessed by my Father; take your inheritance, the kingdom prepared for you since the creation of the world. For I was hungry and you gave me something to eat, I was thirsty and you gave me something to drink, I was a stranger and you invited me in, I needed clothes and you clothed me, I was sick and you looked after me, I was in prison and you came to visit me.' "Then the righteous will answer him, 'Lord, when did we see you hungry and feed you, or thirsty and give you something to drink? When did we see you a stranger and invite you in, or needing clothes and clothe you? When did we see you sick or in prison and go to visit you?' "The King will reply, 'Truly I tell you, whatever you did for one of the least of these brothers and sisters of mine, you did for me.' "Then he will say to those on his left, 'Depart from me, you who are cursed, into the eternal fire prepared for the devil and his angels. For I was hungry and you gave me nothing to eat, I was thirsty and you gave me nothing to drink, I was a stranger and you did not invite me in, I needed clothes and you did not clothe me, I was sick and in prison and you did not look after me.' "They also will answer, 'Lord, when did we see you hungry or thirsty or a stranger or needing clothes or sick or in prison, and did not help you?' "He will reply, 'Truly I tell you, whatever you did not do for one of the least of these, you did not do for me.' "Then they will go away to eternal punishment, but the righteous to eternal life."

Having A Good Heart

In Matthew 15:2-20 Jesus is talking to some people who were following him wondering why his disciples didn't follow a certain tradition that the religious leaders of that time thought was very important.

Jesus replied to them by saying that what comes from our hearts is more important than following certain rules or traditions. He explained that it's not just about following rules on the outside, but having a good heart on the inside.

He gave an example:

Imagine you have a cup, and you want to make sure it's clean. You wouldn't just clean the outside of the cup, right? You would also clean the inside because that's where the dirt really is.

In the same way, Jesus wanted people to understand that having a clean heart and being kind to others is more important than just following rules.

He told them that it's not what we eat that makes us unclean, but the bad things that come out of our hearts, like being mean to others or not being truthful. He said that we should treat others with love and kindness, and that's what really matters to God.

So, Jesus was teaching us that it's not just about doing certain things because we have to, but it's about having a good heart and treating others with kindness and love.

Matthew 15:2-20 NIV "Why do your disciples break the tradition of the elders? They don't wash their hands before they eat!" Jesus replied, "And why do you break the command of God for the sake of your tradition? For God said, 'Honor your father and mother' and 'Anyone who curses their father or mother is to be put to death.' But you say that if anyone declares that what might have been used to help their father or mother is 'devoted to God,' they are not to 'honor their father or mother' with it. Thus you nullify the word of God for the sake of your tradition. You hypocrites! Isaiah was right when he prophesied about you: "'These people honor me with their lips, but their hearts are far from me. They worship me in vain; their teachings are merely human rules.'" Jesus called the crowd to him and said, "Listen and understand. 11 What goes into someone's mouth does not defile them, but what comes out of their mouth, that is what defiles them." Then the disciples came to him and asked, "Do you know that the Pharisees were offended when they heard this?" He replied, "Every plant that my heavenly Father has not planted will be pulled up by the roots. 14 Leave them; they are blind guides.[d] If the blind lead the blind, both will fall into a pit." Peter said, "Explain the parable to us." "Are you still so dull?" Jesus asked them. "Don't you see that whatever enters the mouth goes into the stomach and then out of the body? But the things that come out of a person's mouth come from the heart, and these defile them. For out of the heart come evil thoughts—murder, adultery, sexual immorality, theft, false testimony, slander. These are what defile a person; but eating with unwashed hands does not defile them."

God 1st & He Will Always Take Care Of You

In Luke 12:12-31, Jesus is talking to his followers and he wants to teach them that they don't need to worry too much about things like food, clothes, or other stuff. He tells them that God loves them very much and will always take care of them.

Jesus also tells them not to worry about what they will say when they need to talk about God or when they are in trouble. He says that God will give them the right words to say and will help them in difficult times.

Jesus then tells a story about birds and flowers. He says that if God takes care of these little things, then surely God will take care of us, who are even more important to Him. Jesus reminds his followers that worrying too much is not good because it doesn't change anything. Instead, he encourages them to trust in God and His love.

Jesus ends by saying that instead of worrying, his followers should seek God's kingdom and do what is right. He says that when they do this, God will give them everything they need.

So, to summarize, Jesus is telling his followers that they don't need to worry about basic things like food or clothes because God will always take care of them. He also says that when they trust in God and seek to do what is right, God will provide everything they need.

Luke 12:12-31 KJV For the Holy Ghost shall teach you in the same hour what ye ought to say. And one of the company said unto him, Master, speak to my brother, that he divide the inheritance with me. And he said unto him, Man, who made me a judge or a divider over you? And he said unto them, Take heed, and beware of covetousness: for a man's life consisteth not in the abundance of the things which he possesseth. And he spake a parable unto them, saying, The ground of a certain rich man brought forth plentifully: And he thought within himself, saying, What shall I do, because I have no room where to bestow my fruits? And he said, This will I do: I will pull down my barns, and build greater; and there will I bestow all my fruits and my goods. And I will say to my soul, Soul, thou hast much goods laid up for many years; take thine ease, eat, drink, and be merry. But God said unto him, Thou fool, this night thy soul shall be required of thee: then whose shall those things be, which thou hast provided? So is he that layeth up treasure for himself, and is not rich toward God. And he said unto his disciples, Therefore I say unto you, Take no thought for your life, what ye shall eat; neither for the body, what ye shall put on. The life is more than meat, and the body is more than raiment. Consider the ravens: for they neither sow nor reap; which neither have storehouse nor barn; and God feedeth them: how much more are ye better than the fowls? And which of you with taking thought can add to his stature one cubit? If ye then be not able to do that thing which is least, why take ye thought for the rest? Consider the lilies how they grow: they toil not, they spin not; and yet I say unto you, that Solomon in all his glory was not arrayed like one of these. If then God so clothe the grass, which is to day in the field, and to morrow is cast into the oven; how much more will he clothe you, O ye of little faith? And seek not ye what ye shall eat, or what ye shall drink, neither be ye of doubtful mind. For all these things do the nations of the world seek after: and your Father knoweth that ye have need of these things. But rather seek ye the kingdom of God; and all these things shall be added unto you.*

Judging Others

Luke 6:37-42 tells us about some important commandments from God about Judging Others.

Do Not Judge & You Will Not Be Judged

The first commandment says, "Do not judge, and you will not be judged." This means that we should not be quick to make judgments about other people. We should not think we are better than them or be mean to them because everyone makes mistakes sometimes. Instead, we should show kindness and understanding.

Don't Condemn & You Won't Be Condemned

The second commandment says, "Do not condemn, and you will not be condemned." This means that we should not be too harsh on others when they do something wrong. We should forgive them and try to help them learn from their mistakes, just like how we would like to be forgiven when we make mistakes.

Forgive & You Will Be Forgiven

The third commandment says, "Forgive, and you will be forgiven." This means that when someone says sorry for hurting us or doing something wrong, we should be willing to forgive them. Forgiving means letting go of any anger or grudges we may have towards them. It is important to remember that God forgives us when we make mistakes, so we should also forgive others.

Give & It Will Be Given To You

The fourth commandment is about being generous and kind. It says, "Give, and it will be given to you." This means that we should share what we have with others, like our toys, snacks, or time. When we are kind and generous to others, they will also be kind and generous to us.

Give Love & Kindness & Get Back Even More

Lastly, the fifth commandment says, "A good measure, pressed down, shaken together, running over, will be put into your lap; for the measure you give will be the measure you get back." This means that when we give love, kindness, and help to others, it will come back to us in even bigger and better ways. So it is important to always be loving and kind to others.

Luke 6:37-42 KJV Judge not, and ye shall not be judged: condemn not, and ye shall not be condemned: forgive, and ye shall be forgiven: Give, and it shall be given unto you; good measure, pressed down, and shaken together, and running over, shall men give into your bosom. For with the same measure that ye mete withal it shall be measured to you again. And he spake a parable unto them, Can the blind lead the blind? shall they not both fall into the ditch? The disciple is not above his master: but every one that is perfect shall be as his master. And why beholdest thou the mote that is in thy brother's eye, but perceivest not the beam that is in thine own eye? Either how canst thou say to thy brother, Brother, let me pull out the mote that is in thine eye, when thou thyself beholdest not the beam that is in thine own eye? Thou hypocrite, cast out first the beam out of thine own eye, and then shalt thou see clearly to pull out the mote that is in thy brother's eye.

A CHILDREN'S GUIDE TO A GODLY WAY OF LIFE

The Parable of the Good Samaritan

Luke 10:28-37, tells us commandments from Jesus to love God with all our heart and to love our neighbors as ourselves using The Parable of the Good Samaritan.

In these Bible verses, there was a man who asked Jesus, "Teacher, what must I do to inherit eternal life?" Jesus replied, "What does the law say?" The man answered, "Love the Lord your God with all your heart, soul, strength, and mind, and love your neighbor as yourself."

Then Jesus told a story:

There was a man traveling from one city to another. On the way, some robbers attacked him, took his clothes, and hurt him very badly. They left him on the side of the road, all alone and in pain.

Soon, a priest came walking by. He saw the hurt man but decided to ignore him and keep walking on the other side of the road. Then, a helper from the church came along, but he also chose to ignore the hurt man and walked by on the other side.

But then, a Samaritan man came by. He saw the hurt man and immediately felt sorry for him. He bandaged his wounds, poured oil and wine on them to help them heal, and then took him to an inn. The Samaritan took care of him all night and even paid the innkeeper to continue taking care of him.

Jesus asked the man who had questioned Him, "Which of these three men was a neighbor to the man who was hurt?" The man replied, "The one who showed him mercy." Jesus said, "Go and do likewise."

Love God With All Your Heart
Love Our Neighbors As Ourselves

So, the commandment from Jesus is to love God with all our heart and love our neighbors as ourselves. It means that we should be kind and helpful to others, just like the Samaritan man in the story.

Luke 10:28-37 KJV, And he said unto him, Thou hast answered right: this do, and thou shalt live.But he, willing to justify himself, said unto Jesus, And who is my neighbor And Jesus answering said, A certain man went down from Jerusalem to Jericho, and fell among thieves, which stripped him of his raiment, and wounded him, and departed, leaving him half dead. And by chance there came down a certain priest that way: and when he saw him, he passed by on the other side. And likewise a Levite, when he was at the place, came and looked on him, and passed by on the other side. But a certain Samaritan, as he journeyed, came where he was: and when he saw him, he had compassion on him, And went to him, and bound up his wounds, pouring in oil and wine, and set him on his own beast, and brought him to an inn, and took care of him. And on the morrow when he departed, he took out two pence, and gave them to the host, and said unto him, Take care of him; and whatsoever thou spendest more, when I come again, I will repay thee. Which now of these three, thinkest thou, was neighbour unto him that fell among the thieves? And he said, He that shewed mercy on him. Then said Jesus unto him, Go, and do thou likewise.

Married People Stay Together

In Mark 10:9, in the Bible, Jesus said something really important about marriage. He said, "What God has joined together, let no one separate." This means that when two people get married, they should stay together and not break apart.

It's like when you build something with Lego blocks, you don't want anyone to take it apart because it's meant to stay together. Jesus wants married people to love and support each other, and to stay committed to their marriage forever. So remember, if you see two people who are married, it's important to respect and encourage their love for each other.

Mark 10:9 NKJV "Therefore what God has joined together, let not man separate."

Don't Judge By What You See

In John 7:24 says, Jesus tells us this commandment to "Stop judging by mere appearances, but instead judge correctly!"

This means that we shouldn't judge people just by how they look on the outside or by what we think about them. Jesus wants us to look deeper and try to understand them better before making judgments.

Sometimes, we might see someone who looks different or acts differently than us, but we shouldn't make quick judgments about them. Instead, we should try to get to know them and understand them better. Jesus wants us to treat everyone with kindness and not judge them based on how they appear.

So, the commandment from Jesus in John 7:24 is to not judge others by their appearances, but to judge them correctly by getting to know them better.

John 7:24 NKJV "Do not judge according to appearance, but judge with righteous judgment."

Love Others The Way Jesus Loves Us

In the Bible verse John 13:34-35, Jesus tells us, "I have a special rule for you to follow. Love one another just as I have loved you."

You know how we love our family and friends? Jesus wants us to love everyone, even people we don't know too well or who many not like us very well. It means being kind, helpful, and caring towards others.

He said that when we love each other, people will know that we are Jesus' followers. It's like wearing a special badge of love that shows we belong to Him.

So, remember, love others the way Jesus loves us, and that will show the world how special and kind He is.

John 13:34-35 "A new command I give you: Love one another. As I have loved you, so you must love one another. By this everyone will know that you are my disciples, if you love one another."

Keep God's Commandments If We Love Jesus

In John 14:15 Jesus tells us, 'If you love me, you will do what I command.'

This means that if we truly love Jesus, we listen to and follow what He tells us to do. It's like when you have a best friend, and you want to make them happy, so you do things that they ask you to do. Jesus is our best friend, and he wants us to love him by doing what he asks."

John 14:15 NIV "If you love me, keep my commands."

John 14:23-24 (NIV) also tells us again that Jesus said, "Anyone who loves me will obey my teaching. My Father will love them, and we will come to them and make our home with them. Anyone who does not love me will not obey my teaching. These words you hear are not my own; they belong to the Father who sent me."

Jesus tells us that if we love Him, we should listen to and follow His teachings. When we do that, God, who is Jesus' Father, will love us and always be with us. But if we don't love Jesus, we won't follow His teachings. Jesus wants us to know that the words He speaks are not His own, but they come from God, who sent Him to teach us.

John 14:23-24 NIV Jesus replied, "Anyone who loves me will obey my teaching. My Father will love them, and we will come to them and make our home with them. Anyone who does not love me will not obey my teaching. These words you hear are not my own; they belong to the Father who sent me.

Remain Close To Jesus He Will Help Us Grow

Jesus tells us in John 15:4-5, 'Remain in me, and I will remain in you. A branch cannot bear fruit by itself; it must remain in the vine. Neither can you bear fruit unless you remain in me. I am the vine; you are the branches. If you remain in me and I in you, you will bear much fruit; apart from me, you can do nothing.'

Jesus wants us to stay connected to Him, just like branches are connected to a vine. When we believe in Him and have a close relationship with Him, He will stay with us and help us grow.

Imagine you have a tree with branches and fruits. The branches need to stay connected to the tree, or they won't be able to grow any fruits. In the same way, we need to stay connected to Jesus, or we won't be able to grow and do good things.

When we stay connected to Jesus, we can be kind, loving, and helpful to others. This is like bearing fruit because it brings joy and goodness to the world. But if we try to be good on our own, without Jesus, it will be difficult. Jesus says we can't do anything good without Him!

So, let's remember to stay close to Jesus, like branches to a vine. When we do that, He will help us grow and do amazing things that bring joy to ourselves and others."

John 15:4-5 NIV Remain in me, as I also remain in you. No branch can bear fruit by itself; it must remain in the vine. Neither can you bear fruit unless you remain in me. "I am the vine; you are the branches. If you remain in me and I in you, you will bear much fruit; apart from me you can do nothing."

Stay Close To Jesus & He Will Give You Your Needs

In John 15:7-12, Jesus tells us, 'If you stay close to me and follow my words, you can ask for anything you need, and it will be given to you. When you do these things, it pleases my Father in heaven.

Just like a branch gets its life from the tree it is attached to, we get our life from Jesus. If we don't stay connected to Him, we can't grow and be happy. But if we stay close to Him, we will grow and bear good fruit.

Jesus also told us to love one another, just as He loves us. We should always be kind, caring, and treat others with love. Jesus said that this is the greatest way to show that we are His followers.

John 15:7-12 NIV If you remain in me and my words remain in you, ask whatever you wish, and it will be done for you. This is to my Father's glory, that you bear much fruit, showing yourselves to be my disciples. "As the Father has loved me, so have I loved you. Now remain in my love. If you keep my commands, you will remain in my love, just as I have kept my Father's commands and remain in his love. I have told you this so that my joy may be in you and that your joy may be complete. My command is this: Love each other as I have loved you.

Do What Jesus Tells Us To Do To Be Close Him

In John 15:14, Jesus said, "You are my friends if you do what I command you."

This means that Jesus wants us to be his friends, but it comes with a condition. The condition is that we need to do what he tells us to do.

Just like when you have a best friend, you want to make them happy and do things that they ask, right? It's the same with Jesus. He wants us to obey him and follow his teachings. When we have a friend, we are close to them, aren't we, so To Be Jesus friend is to be close to Jesus, isn't it? Yes it is.

Jesus loves us so much that he wants to be our friend. And being a good friend to Jesus means listening to him and doing what he asks us to do. It's like following the rules your parents give you because they love you and want the best for you.

So, the commandment from Jesus in John 15:14 is to be a good friend to him, to be close to Him, we do what he commands us.

John 15:14 NIV You are my friends if you do what I command.

Be Kind & Caring Towards Everyone

In John 15:17, Jesus said, "Love each other."

This means that we should be kind and caring towards everyone we meet. We should treat others the way we want to be treated. When we love others, we make the world a better place.

So, let's remember to love one another just like Jesus taught us.

John 15:17 NIV This is my command: Love each other.

Following Jesus Might Not Be Easy

In the Bible, John 15:20-22, Jesus says, "If people were mean to me, they might also be mean to you. But don't be sad or scared because of that. Remember, I am with you, and I will help you."

Jesus wanted his friends to know that following him might not always be easy. Some people may not like them or be nice to them, just like some people were not nice to Jesus. But Jesus wanted them to be strong and not worry because he would always be there to help and protect them.

He also said that if someone doesn't know about him or his teachings, it's not their fault if they do wrong things. Jesus understands that not everyone knows about him, and he wants us to show kindness and love to others, even if they don't know him yet.

So, the important thing Jesus wanted his friends to remember is to stay strong and not be afraid even if people are mean sometimes. And to always be kind to others, even if they don't know about

Jesus yet. Because Jesus is always there to help and guide us, no matter what.

In John 15:20-22, Jesus gave us these important commandments:

Love Jesus

1. Love Jesus: Jesus is a very special person who loves us a lot. He wants us to love Him back and believe in Him.

Listen To Jesus

2. Listen to Jesus: When Jesus tells us something, it's important to pay attention and do what He says. He knows what's best for us.

Be Kind To Others

3. Be kind to others: Jesus wants us to be friendly and nice to everyone we meet. He wants us to treat others the way we want to be treated.

Don't Be Afraid

4. Don't be afraid: Sometimes, people might not like us or be mean to us because we love Jesus. But Jesus tells us not to worry or be scared. He will always be with us and take care of us.

Don't Do Bad Things

5. Don't do bad things: Jesus wants us to stay away from doing things that are wrong. He wants us to be honest, not lie, and not hurt others.

John 15:20-22 NIV Remember what I told you: 'A servant is not greater than his master.' If they persecuted me, they will persecute you also. If they obeyed my teaching, they will obey yours also. They will treat you this way because of my name, for they do not know the one who sent me. If I had not come and spoken to them, they would not be guilty of sin; but now they have no excuse for their sin.

Taking Care Of Ourselves

Romans 12:1-3 tells us three important commandments that we should follow about taking care of ourselves and giving ourselves self love. Romans 12:1-3 is the essence of Self Love which we will talk about later in a chapter entitled Self Love.

Take Care Of Your Body

1. The first commandment says, "Offer your bodies as a living sacrifice." Now, I know that sounds a bit strange, but it means that we should take care of our bodies and use them for doing good things. We don't want to harm ourselves or others but instead use our bodies to help people and make the world a better place.

Make Good Choices

2. The second commandment tells us, "Do not be conformed to this world." This one is a bit tricky, but it means that we shouldn't just follow what everyone else is doing if it's not right. We should think for ourselves and choose the right path, even if it's not the popular one.

Keep Learning & Growing To Become Better

3. The third commandment says, "Be transformed by the renewing of your mind." This means that we should always try to learn new things, be open to new ideas, and think in a positive way. We should try to be better and change for the good, just like a caterpillar transforms into a beautiful butterfly.

So, to help remember these three commandments from Romans 12:1-3:
- Take care of your body and use it for good things
- Make good choices, even if others are doing something wrong
- Keep learning and growing to become a better person

Romans 12:1-3 NIV Therefore, I urge you, brothers and sisters, in view of God's mercy, to offer your bodies as a living sacrifice, holy and pleasing to God—this is your true and proper worship. Do not conform to the pattern of this world, but be transformed by the renewing of your mind. Then you will be able to test and approve what God's will is—his good, pleasing and perfect will. For by the grace given me I say to every one of you: Do not think of yourself more highly than you ought, but rather think of yourself with sober judgment, in accordance with the faith God has distributed to each of you.

Love In Action

Jesus gave us quite a few commandments in Romans 12:6-21 about love in action.

Love & Be Kind To Everyone

1. Love and Be Kind: God wants us to love and be kind to everyone around us. Treat others with love and respect, just like the way Jesus loves us.

Use Your Talents

2. Use Your Talents: God has given each of us special talents and abilities. Use them to help others and make the world a better place.

Be Happy and Hopeful

3. Be Happy and Hopeful: Always be happy and have hope, even when things are tough. Trust in God's plan for your life.

Pray & Talk To God

4. Pray and Talk to God: Take time to pray and talk to God every day. He is always listening and wants to hear from you.

Help & Share

5. Help and Share: When you see someone in need, help them out. Share what you have with others and be generous.

Be Nice To Those Who Are Mean

6. Be Nice to Those Who Are Mean: Even if someone is mean to you, try to be kind to them. Show them love and forgiveness.

Don't Try To Get Even

7. Don't Try to Get Even: If someone does something wrong to you, don't try to get back at them. Let God handle it and focus on being kind.

Live In Peace

8. Live in Peace: Try your best to live in peace with everyone. Avoid fighting and arguing, and instead, be a peacemaker.

Don't Seek Revenge

9. Don't Seek Revenge: If someone hurts you, don't seek revenge. Leave it to God and trust that He will take care of it.

Overcome Evil With Good

10. Overcome Evil with Good: Instead of doing bad things, choose to do good. Show love and kindness even when others are being mean.

Romans 12:6-21 NIV We have different gifts, according to the grace given to each of us. If your gift is prophesying, then prophesy in accordance with your faith; if it is serving, then serve; if it is teaching, then teach; if it is to encourage, then give encouragement; if it is giving, then give generously; if it is to lead, do it diligently; if it is to show mercy, do it cheerfully. Love must be sincere. Hate what is evil; cling to what is good. Be devoted to one another in love. Honor one another above yourselves. Never be lacking in zeal, but keep your spiritual fervor, serving the Lord. Be joyful in hope, patient in affliction, faithful in prayer. Share with the Lord's people who are in need. Practice hospitality. Bless those who persecute you; bless and do not curse. Rejoice with those who rejoice; mourn with those who mourn. Live in harmony with one another. Do not be proud, but be willing to associate with people of low position. Do not be conceited. Do not repay anyone evil for evil. Be careful to do what is right in the eyes of everyone. If it is possible, as far as it depends on you, live at peace with everyone. Do not take revenge, my dear friends, but leave room for God's wrath, for it is written: "It is mine to avenge; I will repay," says the Lord. On the contrary: "If your enemy is hungry, feed him; if he is thirsty, give him something to drink. In doing this, you will heap burning coals on his head." Do not be overcome by evil, but overcome evil with good.

Love Fulfills The Law

In Romans 13:8-14, Jesus gave us seven commandments about how Love Fulfills The Law.

Love Others

1. Love others: God says we should love everyone around us. Treat others with kindness and respect, just like Jesus did.

Be Honest

2. Be honest: God wants us to always tell the truth. We should never lie or cheat because it hurts others and makes God sad.

Do Not Steal

3. Do not steal: Taking things that belong to someone else is wrong. We should be content with what we have and not take things that are not ours.

Respect Your Parents

4. Respect your parents: God wants us to listen to our parents and show them love and respect. They take care of us and teach us important things.

Be Good To Everyone

5. Be good to everyone: We should be kind to everyone we meet, whether they are our friends or strangers. God wants us to treat others the way we want to be treated.

Do Not Be Jealous

6. Do not be jealous: God says we should not be jealous of what other people have. Instead, we should be happy for them and be thankful for the things we have.

Stay Away From Bad Things

7. Stay away from bad things: God wants us to stay away from things that can hurt us or make us do wrong things. We should make good choices and always try to do what is right.

Remember these important commandments to always love others, be honest, don't steal, respect your parents, be good to everyone, don't be jealous, and stay away from bad things.

Romans 13:8-14 NIV Let no debt remain outstanding, except the continuing debt to love one another, for whoever loves others has fulfilled the law. The commandments, "You shall not commit adultery," "You shall not murder," "You shall not steal," "You shall not covet,"[a] and whatever other command there may be, are summed up in this one command: "Love your neighbor as yourself." Love does no harm to a neighbor. Therefore love is the fulfillment of the law. And do this, understanding the present time: The hour has already come for you to wake up from your slumber, because our salvation is nearer now than when we first believed. The night is nearly over; the day is almost here. So let us put aside the deeds of darkness and put on the armor of light. Let us behave decently, as in the daytime, not in carousing and drunkenness, not in sexual immorality and debauchery, not in dissension and jealousy. Rather, clothe yourselves with the Lord Jesus Christ, and do not think about how to gratify the desires of the flesh.

A CHILDREN'S GUIDE TO A GODLY WAY OF LIFE

Those Stronger In Faith

The commandments Jesus gave us from Romans 15:1-2 say:

"We who are strong in faith should help those who are weak. We should do things that help them grow stronger in faith. 2 Each of us should think about pleasing our neighbors. We should do things that help them grow stronger in faith." Now, let's break down these commandments so you can understand them better:

Strong In Faith Help Those With Weaker Faith

1. The first commandment tells us that if we have a strong faith in God, we should help those who have a weaker faith. It means we should be kind and patient with others, especially when they are struggling or feeling down. Just like when you help your little brother or sister with something they find difficult.

Strong in Faith Help Others Grow Stronger In Their Faith

2. The second commandment tells us that we should think about making our neighbors happy and helping them grow stronger in their faith. Neighbors can be anyone we know or meet, like our friends, family, or even people we don't know very well. We should be friendly and caring towards others, just like when you share your toys or help someone who is feeling sad.

Romans 15:1-2 NIV We who are strong ought to bear with the failings of the weak and not to please ourselves. Each of us should please our neighbors for their good, to build them up.

Do Not Indulge In Revelry

The commandments Jesus gives us in 1 Corinthians 10:7-10 say:

Do Not Worship Idols

1. Do not worship idols: It means we should not pray or give importance to statues or things that are not God. We should love and respect God above everything else.

Do Not Do Bad Things

2. Do not do bad things: This means we should not do things that we know are wrong, like lying, stealing, or hurting others. We should always try to be kind and do good things.

Do Not Complain

3. Do not complain: Complaining means always finding faults and being unhappy about things. Instead, we should try to be thankful and appreciate the good things we have.

Remember Stories & Teachings From Bible

4. Learn from the past: It means we should remember the stories and teachings from the Bible and try to learn from them. We can learn how to be better people and make good choices.

1 Corinthians 10:7-10 NIV Do not be idolaters, as some of them were; as it is written: "The people sat down to eat and drink and got up to indulge in revelry." We should not commit sexual immorality, as some of them did—and in one day twenty-three thousand of them died. We should not test Christ, as some of them did—and were killed by snakes. And do not grumble, as some of them did—and were killed by the destroying angel.

The Good Of Others

In 1 Corinthians 10:24 we see more of the commandments Jesus gave to us. As with everything we learn, Jesus repeated many of them saying them in different ways to ensure that we understood them and would remember them.

Love Others

1. Love Others: God wants us to always think about other people and not just ourselves. It's important to care about others and show kindness. When we do this, it makes God really happy!

Look Out For Others

2. Look Out for Others: Sometimes, we may want to do things that make us happy, but we need to think about how our actions might affect others. It's like putting ourselves in their shoes and asking, "Will this hurt someone or make them sad?" If it does, we should choose something else.

Do Good Things

3. Do Good Things: God wants us to make good choices and do things that help others. We should try to be helpful, generous, and honest. When we do good things, it brings joy to God's heart.

Think Of Others First

4. Think of Others First: Instead of always thinking about what we want, God wants us to think about what others need. It's like being a good friend and caring about their feelings. When we do this, it shows that we love and respect them.

1 Corinthians 10:24 NIV No one should seek their own good, but the good of others.

Eat or Drink - Do All For Glory Of God

In 1 Corinthians 10:28-32, Jesus gives us four commandments in these verses, "So whether you eat or drink or whatever you do, do it all for the glory of God."

Love & Thank God For The Food and Drink

1. Love and thank God for the food and drink: Whenever you have your meals, remember to be grateful to God for providing you with delicious food and refreshing drinks. It's important to appreciate and enjoy what you have, knowing that it comes from God.

Don't Hurt Others' Feelings Regarding Food

2. Don't hurt others' feelings: When you're eating with other people, be considerate of their beliefs and feelings. If someone tells you that they don't eat certain foods for religious or personal reasons, it's important to respect their choices and not make them feel bad about it.

Be A Good Example

3. Be a good example: In everything you do, remember that you represent God. So, whether you're eating, drinking, or playing, make sure to behave in a way that shows kindness, respect, and love towards others. People should be able to see God's goodness in you.

Don't Do Things That Go Against Your Beliefs

4. Don't do things that go against your beliefs: If you believe that something is wrong or against what God teaches, don't do it. Always listen to your conscience and follow what you know is right. This means avoiding things that are harmful or go against God's commandments.

1 Corinthians 10:28-32 NIV "But if someone says to you, "This has been offered in sacrifice," then do not eat it, both for the sake of the one who told you and for the sake of conscience. I am referring to the other person's conscience, not yours. For why is my freedom being judged by another's conscience? If I take part in the meal with thankfulness, why am I denounced because of something I thank God for? So whether you eat or drink or whatever you do, do it all for the glory of God. Do not cause anyone to stumble, whether Jews, Greeks or the church of God—"

A CHILDREN'S GUIDE TO A GODLY WAY OF LIFE

Don't Think Like Children

In the Bible, in 1 Corinthians 14:20 Jesus says, "Brothers and sisters, don't think like children. Be like babies when it comes to evil, but be grown up in your thinking."

This verse means that it's important for us to grow up and think like mature adults, especially when it comes to knowing what's right and wrong. I know in a book written for children, this is a difficult concept so let me explain this a little bit further.

Make The Best Decision Based Upon Our Maturity

1. Don't think like children: As we grow older, we should try to understand things better, just like how we learn new things at school. It means we shouldn't act or think in a childish way, but rather, we should try to be more responsible and make wise choices to the best of our ability. As we mature, the more mature our decisions will be. That is what this is telling us to do. Make decisions to the best of our maturity level.

Avoid From Evil

2. Be like babies when it comes to evil: Babies are innocent and don't know about bad things yet. So, this part means we should try to stay away from doing wrong things, just like babies don't know about them. It's important to be pure and good-hearted.

Make Smart Choices

3. Be grown up in your thinking: This part says that we should use our brains and think carefully about what we do. We should

make smart choices and consider the consequences of our actions. It's like being mature and responsible.

So, the verse is telling us to grow up, avoid doing bad things, and think like wise adults. This way, we can make good choices and live a better life.

Remember, it's always helpful to talk to your parents, teachers, or other trusted adults if you have any questions or need help understanding things.

1 Corinthians 14:20 NIV "Brothers and sisters, stop thinking like children. In regard to evil be infants, but in your thinking be adults."

Love Is The Most Important

Jesus gave us 4 commandments in 1 Corinthians 16:13-14 about love being the most important thing in the world.

Be Strong and Brave

1. Be strong and brave: Remember to stay strong and courageous in everything you do. Don't let fear stop you from being bold and doing the right thing.

Stay Firm In Your Faith

2. Stand firm in your faith: Always believe in God and trust Him. Don't let anyone or anything shake your trust in Him.

Be Loving And Kind

3. Be loving and kind: Show love and kindness to everyone you meet. Treat others the way you want to be treated, with gentle words and actions.

Do Everything In Love

4. Do everything in love: Whatever you do, do it with love in your heart. Love is the most important thing in the world, and it should guide all your actions.

1 Corinthians 16:13-14 NIV Be on your guard; stand firm in the faith; be courageous; be strong. Do everything in love.

Jesus Has Set Us Free

Galatians 5:1 says, "It is for freedom that Christ has set us free. Stand firm, then, and do not let yourselves be burdened again by a yoke of slavery."

This Bible verse means that Jesus has set us free, just like when you're playing a game and you're finally allowed to go wherever you want. It feels good to be free, right? So, the verse tells us to stand strong and not let anyone make us feel like we are not free anymore.

Now, let's look at how we can apply this verse in our lives by following some commandments:

Love God

1. Love God: Always remember to love and believe in God, who has set us free.

Be Kind

2. Be kind: Treat others with kindness and respect, just as Jesus did.

Share

3. Share: Share your toys, snacks, and love with others, because Jesus wants us to be generous.

Be Honest

4. Be honest: Always tell the truth and be honest with yourself and others.

Be Patient

5. Be patient: Sometimes things don't go the way we want, but it's important to be patient and stay calm.

Be Gentle

6. Be gentle: Use your words and actions gently, without hurting others.

Have Self Control

7. Have self-control: Make good choices and control yourself, like not eating all the candies at once.

Remember, these commandments help us to live freely, just like Jesus wants us to.

Galatians 5:1 NIV "It is for freedom that Christ has set us free. Stand firm, then, and do not let yourselves be burdened again by a yoke of slavery."

Do What Is Right & Make Good Choices

Galatians 5:16 Bible Verse: "But I say, walk by the Spirit, and you will not gratify the desires of the flesh." What does that mean for us? Let me explain in a way that you can understand!

Imagine you have two friends: one is called the Spirit, and the other is called the Flesh. The Spirit is like the voice inside you that tells you what is right and good. It wants you to be kind, helpful, and loving. The Flesh, on the other hand, is like your selfish desires. It wants you to do things that might not be good for you or others, like being mean or taking things that aren't yours.

So, when the Bible says, "walk by the Spirit," it means that we should listen to the good voice inside us. We should try to be like the Spirit and do what is right. When we do that, we won't give in to the desires of the Flesh, like being selfish or mean.

It's not always easy to do what is right, but with God's help and the Spirit's guidance, we can make good choices. So, remember, listen to the Spirit, be kind, and do what is right. That's what the commandment from Galatians 5:16 is all about!

Galatians 5:16 NIV So I say, walk by the Spirit, and you will not gratify the desires of the flesh.

If Someone Is Caught Up In Sin

Jesus gave us two additional commandments in Galatians 6:1-2 for if someone is caught up in sin.

Be Kind and Help Others

1. Be Kind and Help Others: The first commandment is to be kind and helpful to people around us. It's like when someone falls down and gets hurt, we should be there to pick them up and make sure they're okay. We should also help our friends when they are feeling sad or need someone to talk to.

Share Each Other's Burdens

2. Share Each Other's Burdens: The second commandment is about sharing. Sometimes, people have problems or worries that feel really heavy, like carrying a big backpack full of rocks. We should try to help them by listening to their worries and offering our support. It's like sharing the weight of their backpack so it doesn't feel as heavy.

Galatians 6:1-2 NIV Brothers and sisters, if someone is caught in a sin, you who live by the Spirit should restore that person gently. But watch yourselves, or you also may be tempted. Carry each other's burdens, and in this way you will fulfill the law of Christ.

Live a Life Worthy of the Calling

Ephesians 4:1-3 provides some additional commandments for us to follow as a follower of God.

Be A Good Friend

1. Be a good friend: The Bible says that we should walk in a way that is worthy of our calling. This means we should try our best to be kind to others, just like Jesus was. We should be friendly, helpful, and treat others the way we want to be treated.

Be Patient and Peaceful

2. Be patient and peaceful: It's important to be patient with our friends and family when they make mistakes or when things don't go our way. We should try not to get angry easily and instead, have a calm heart. This helps us to get along with others and bring peace to our relationships.

Stick Together

3. Stick together: The Bible tells us to make every effort to keep the unity of the Spirit through the bond of peace. This means we should try our best to stay united with our friends and family, even when we have disagreements. We should forgive each other and work things out, so that we can stay close and have a loving relationship.

Ephesians 4:1-3 NIV As a prisoner for the Lord, then, I urge you to live a life worthy of the calling you have received. Be completely humble and gentle; be patient, bearing with one another in love. Make every effort to keep the unity of the Spirit through the bond of peace.

Do Not Sin In YOur Anger

Jesus gave us an additional six commandments about not sinning when we are angry in Ephesians 4:26-32.

Don't Get Mad Easily & Be Kind To Others

1. Be kind to others and don't get mad easily. It's okay to feel angry sometimes, but try not to let it control you. (Ephesians 4:26)

When In Disagreement, Solve It Peacefully

2. When you have a disagreement or an argument with someone, try to solve it peacefully. Don't let it turn into a big fight. (Ephesians 4:26)

Don't Steal

3. Don't steal or take things that don't belong to you. Always respect other people's belongings. (Ephesians 4:28)

Say Nice Things & Encourage Others

4. Use your words to say nice things and encourage others. Never use your words to hurt people or say mean things. (Ephesians 4:29)

Be Forgiving & Understanding

5. Be forgiving and understanding. If someone says sorry for something they did wrong, try to forgive them and give them another chance. (Ephesians 4:32)

Always Be Kind & Caring Towards Others

6. Always be kind and caring towards others. Help them when they need it and be a good friend. (Ephesians 4:32)

Ephesians 4:26-32 NIV "In your anger do not sin": Do not let the sun go down while you are still angry, and do not give the devil a foothold. Anyone who has been stealing must steal no longer, but must work, doing something useful with their own hands, that they may have something to share with those in need. Do not let any unwholesome talk come out of your mouths, but only what is helpful for building others up according to their needs, that it may benefit those who listen. And do not grieve the Holy Spirit of God, with whom you were sealed for the day of redemption. Get rid of all bitterness, rage and anger, brawling and slander, along with every form of malice. Be kind and compassionate to one another, forgiving each other, just as in Christ God forgave you.

Follow God's Example

We know God loves us very much and He wants us to be like Him. In Ephesians 5:1-6, Jesus gives us even more commandments to help us be more like Him.

Be Kind & Loving to Everyone

1. Be kind and loving to everyone, just like Jesus loved us and gave Himself for us. We should treat others with kindness and love, just like how we want to be treated.

Don't Say Or Do Mean or Hurtful Things To Others

2. We should not say or do things that are mean or hurtful to others. Instead, we should always try to say and do things that make people happy and encourage them.

Don't Use Bad Or Rude Language

3. God wants us to be careful with our words and not use bad or rude language. We should use our words to say nice things and build others up.

Don't Listen To Or Be Influenced By Bad Things

4. We should not listen or be influenced by people who say or do bad things. We should choose to follow what is right and good, even if others are doing wrong things.

Always Show Gratitude To God

5. Always show gratitude to God for all the good things He has given us. We should thank Him for our family, friends, and all the blessings we have in our lives.

God Dislikes People Who Do Bad Things & Disobey Him

6. God dislikes people who do bad things and disobey Him. We should try our best to do what is right and please God in everything we do.

Ephesians 5:1-6 NIV Follow God's example, therefore, as dearly loved children and walk in the way of love, just as Christ loved us and gave himself up for us as a fragrant offering and sacrifice to God. But among you there must not be even a hint of sexual immorality, or of any kind of impurity, or of greed, because these are improper for God's holy people. Nor should there be obscenity, foolish talk or coarse joking, which are out of place, but rather thanksgiving. For of this you can be sure: No immoral, impure or greedy person—such a person is an idolater—has any inheritance in the kingdom of Christ and of God. Let no one deceive you with empty words, for because of such things God's wrath comes on those who are disobedient.

Stay Away From Doing Bad Things

Ephesians 5:11 says, "Have nothing to do with the fruitless deeds of darkness, but rather expose them."

Avoid Doing Bad Things

This verse is telling us that we should stay away from doing bad things and not get involved with people who do bad things. It's like when your parents tell you not to play with something dangerous or not to go near something that could hurt you. They want to keep you safe and away from harm.

Try To Show Others What Is Right And Good

So, in the same way, God wants us to stay away from things that are not good. We should not do things that hurt others or make them sad. Instead, we should be kind, helpful, and loving towards everyone.

If we see someone doing something wrong, we shouldn't be afraid to speak up and tell them it's not right. We can help them understand and make better choices. This will make the world a better place and please God too.

Remember, always try to do what is good, and if you see something bad happening, don't be afraid to stand up for what is right and good.

Ephesians 5:11 NIV Have nothing to do with the fruitless deeds of darkness, but rather expose them.

Be Careful How You Live

In Ephesians 5:15-21 says "Be very careful, then, how you live —not as unwise but as wise, making the most of every opportunity, because the days are evil. Therefore do not be foolish, but understand what the Lord's will is. Do not get drunk on wine, which leads to debauchery. Instead, be filled with the Spirit, speaking to one another with psalms, hymns, and songs from the Spirit. Sing and make music from your heart to the Lord, always giving thanks to God the Father for everything, in the name of our Lord Jesus Christ."

Let's learn about the commandments in these verses that tell us how to be careful how we live.

Be Careful How You Act

1. Be careful how you act: This means we should think before doing something and always try to make good choices. We should be kind to others and not do things that can hurt them or ourselves.

Use Your Time Wisely

2. Use your time wisely: Time is precious, so we should try not to waste it. We can spend time doing things that are helpful, like learning, playing, and helping others.

Understand What God Wants

3. Understand what God wants: We should try to understand what makes God happy and do our best to please Him. We can learn this by reading the Bible, listening to our parents and teachers, and praying.

Don't Be Silly Or Rude

4. Don't be silly or rude: It's important to be respectful to others and not say or do things that can hurt their feelings. We should use our words and actions to show kindness and love.

Be Thankful

5. Be thankful: We should always be grateful for the good things we have, like our family, friends, and the blessings God gives us. We can show our gratitude by saying thank you and appreciating what we have.

Sing & Praise God

6. Sing and praise God: We can show our love for God by singing songs and praising Him. This makes Him happy and brings joy to our hearts too.

Be Kind To Each Other

7. Be kind to each other: It's important to be kind to everyone around us, whether it's our family, friends, or even people we don't know. We should treat others with love, respect, and help them when they need it.

Ephesians 5:15-21 NIV "Be very careful, then, how you live—not as unwise but as wise, making the most of every opportunity, because the days are evil. Therefore do not be foolish, but understand what the Lord's will is. Do not get drunk on wine, which leads to debauchery. Instead, be filled with the Spirit, speaking to one another with psalms, hymns, and songs from the Spirit. Sing and make music from your heart to the Lord, always giving thanks to God the Father for everything, in the name of our Lord Jesus Christ."

Be Strong In The Lord & In His Mighty Power

In Ephesians 6:10-11, these commandments are to help us be strong where He tells us, "Finally, be strong in the Lord and in his mighty power. Put on the full armor of God, so that you can take your stand against the devil's evil tricks."

"God wants you to be strong and brave!
So, put on His special armor to behave!"

Here's what it means:

Be Strong

1. Be strong: God wants you to be strong, not just physically, but also in your heart. He wants you to be brave and not be afraid.

Put On God's Armor

2. Put on God's armor: Just like soldiers wear special armor to protect themselves in battle, God gives us special armor to protect us from bad things. This armor includes things like truth, righteousness, faith, and salvation.

Ephesians 6:10-11 NIV Finally, be strong in the Lord and in his mighty power. Put on the full armor of God, so that you can take your stand against the devil's schemes.

Superhero Armor

In Ephesians 6:13-18 and again in 1 Thessalonians 5:8 God wants us to be strong and brave, just like superheroes! He gives us commandments to follow to help us be understand what He expects from us in order to be good and make Him happy. Let's learn about them:

The Armor Of Truth, Righteousness, & Peace

6.Always put on your superhero armor: God wants us to wear the armor of truth, righteousness, and peace. It protects us from bad things.

Ephesians Verse: "Therefore put on the full armor of God, so that when the day of evil comes, you may be able to stand your ground, and after you have done everything, to stand."

Ephesians Verse: "Stand firm then, with the belt of truth buckled around your waist, with the breastplate of righteousness in place."

Explanation of the the belt of truth: The belt of truth is like being honest and always telling the truth. The breastplate of righteousness means doing what is right and making good choices.

Ephesians Verse: "And with your feet fitted with the readiness that comes from the gospel of peace."

Explanation of feet fitted with the readiness that comes with the gospel of peace: God wants us to be ready to spread His message of peace and love to others. So, our feet should be ready to go and tell people about God's love.

God wants us to be strong and ready for any difficult or bad situations that may come our way. He wants us to be brave and stand up for what is right, even if it's hard.

The Armor of Faith

7. Use your superhero shield: We have a special shield called faith. It helps us trust in God, even when things are tough.

Ephesians Verse: "In addition to all this, take up the shield of faith, with which you can extinguish all the flaming arrows of the evil one."

Faith is like a shield that protects us from bad things. It helps us trust in God and keep away from things that can hurt us.

Helmet Protects Our Minds

8. Wear your superhero helmet: God wants us to protect our minds by learning about Him and thinking good thoughts.

Ephesians Verse: "Take the helmet of salvation and the sword of the Spirit, which is the word of God."

Explanation of helmet of salvation: The helmet of salvation means that we believe in Jesus and His love for us. The sword of the Spirit is like the Bible, which is God's word. It helps us know what is right and wrong.

Sword Fights Against Evil

9. Hold your superhero sword: The sword is God's word, the Bible. It teaches us how to live and fight against evil.

Ephesians Verse: "Take the helmet of salvation and the sword of the Spirit, which is the word of God."

Explanation of helmet of salvation & sword of the Spirit: The helmet of salvation means that we believe in Jesus and His love for us. The sword of the Spirit is like the Bible, which is God's word. It helps us know what is right and wrong.

Prayer to Talk to God & Give Thanks

10. Pray like a superhero: Talk to God and tell Him your worries, hopes, and thanks. He listens and helps us.

Ephesians Verse: "And pray in the Spirit on all occasions with all kinds of prayers and requests."

Explanation of Pray in Spirit: God loves when we talk to Him through prayer. We can pray to Him anytime and about anything. He is always listening and wants to help us.

Ephesians Verse: "With this in mind, be alert and always keep on praying for all the Lord's people."

Explanation of keep praying for all the Lord's people: We should always be watchful and aware of what is happening around us

Ephesians 6:13-18 NIV Therefore put on the full armor of God, so that when the day of evil comes, you may be able to stand your ground, and after you have done everything, to stand. Stand firm then, with the belt of truth buckled around your waist, with the breastplate of righteousness in place, and with your feet fitted with the readiness that comes from the gospel of peace. In addition to all this, take up the shield of faith, with which you can extinguish all the flaming arrows of the evil one. Take the helmet of salvation and the sword of the Spirit, which is the word of God. And pray in the Spirit on all occasions with all kinds of prayers and requests. With this in mind, be alert and always keep on praying for all the Lord's people.

1 Thessalonians 5:8 NIV But since we belong to the day, let us be sober, putting on faith and love as a breastplate, and the hope of salvation as a helmet.

Conduct Yourselves Worthy Of Christ

Philippians 1:27-28 gives us some more commandments about the manner of our life being worthy of the gospel of Christ. Let's take a look at these in a way that's easy for you to understand:

Love Jesus

1. Love Jesus: Always remember to love and believe in Jesus. He is our best friend and Savior, and He wants us to have a special relationship with Him.

Be United

2. Be united: It means we should work together and be friends with everyone. We should treat others kindly and help them when they need it. We are like a team, and we should support and encourage each other.

Be Brave

3. Be brave: Sometimes people may not like us because we believe in Jesus. But don't be scared! Stand up for what is right and don't be afraid to talk about Jesus and His love for us.

Don't Be Worried

4. Don't be worried: It's normal to feel scared or worried sometimes, but remember that God is always with us. Trust Him and pray to Him when you feel afraid. He will give you peace and strength.

Philippians 1:27-28 says, "Whatever happens, conduct yourselves in a manner worthy of the gospel of Christ. Then, whether I come and see you or only hear about you in my absence, I will know that you stand firm in the one Spirit, striving together as one for the faith of the gospel without being frightened in any way by those who oppose you."

Continue To Work Out Your Salvation

Philippians 2:12-16 provides additional commandments about how we are to live our lives to continue to work out our salvation for God.

Work Hard & Be Good

1. Work hard and be good. God wants us to always try our best and do the right thing. Just like when you do your homework or help your parents, you are being obedient to this commandment.

Be Happy & Don't Complain

2. Be happy and don't complain. God wants us to have a happy heart and not grumble or whine about things. Instead, we should be thankful for what we have and appreciate the good stuff in our lives.

Shine Like A Star

3. Shine like a star. Have you ever seen the stars in the sky? They are so bright and beautiful. God wants us to shine too, but not with light. He wants us to shine by being kind, loving, and doing good things for others. When we do that, we show everyone how amazing God is!

Philippians 2:12-16 NIV Therefore, my dear friends, as you have always obeyed—not only in my presence, but now much more in my absence—continue to work out your salvation with fear and trembling, for it is God who works in you to will and to act in order to fulfill his good purpose. Do everything without grumbling or arguing, so that you may become blameless and pure, "children of God without fault in a warped and crooked generation." Then you will shine among them like stars in the sky as you hold firmly to the word of life. And then I will be able to boast on the day of Christ that I did not run or labor in vain.

Rejoice In The Lord Always

Philippians 4:4-6 continues with more commandments to Rejoice in the Lord always.

Always Be Happy And Joyful

1. Always be happy and joyful. No matter what happens, try to find something good and be happy about it. God loves to see us smiling!

Be Kind And Gentle To Everyone

2. Be kind and gentle to everyone. It's important to treat others with love and respect, just like Jesus did. Share your toys and help your friends when they need it.

Don't Worry About Anything

3. Don't worry about anything. When you feel scared or nervous, remember that God is with you. Talk to Him and ask Him for help. He will take care of you.

Instead Of Worrying, Pray To God

4. Instead of worrying, pray to God. Tell Him about your fears and worries. Thank Him for all the good things He has given you. He always listens to our prayers and wants to help us.

Say Thank You To God

5. Don't forget to say "thank you" to God. He is always watching over us and blessing us. Show your gratitude by saying thanks for all the wonderful things in your life.

Philippians 4:4-6 - "Rejoice in the Lord always. I will say it again: Rejoice! Let your gentleness be evident to all. The Lord is near. Do not be anxious about anything, but in every situation, by prayer and petition, with thanksgiving, present your requests to God."

A CHILDREN'S GUIDE TO A GODLY WAY OF LIFE

The God Of Peace Will Be With You

Philippians 4:8-9 is commandments about whatever is true, noble, right, pure, lovely, admirable, the God of peace will be with you.

Think About Good Things

1. Think about good things: This means we should fill our minds with thoughts that make us happy and bring us closer to God. We should think about things that are true, noble, right, pure, lovely, and admirable.

Be Kind To Others

2. Be kind to others: We should always treat others with kindness and love. This means being nice, sharing, and helping our friends and family.

Don't Worry, Pray Instead

3. Don't worry, pray instead: When we feel worried or scared, we can talk to God through prayer. God is always there to listen to us and help us feel better.

Thank God For Everything

4. Thank God for everything: It's important to be thankful for all the good things in our lives. We should say "Thank you, God" for our family, friends, toys, and everything that makes us happy.

Practice What Is Right

5. Practice what is right: We should try to do the things that are good and right. This means being honest, obeying our parents, and making good choices.

God's Peace Is With You

6. God's peace is with you: When we follow these commandments, we can feel God's peace in our hearts. It's a special feeling of calmness and happiness that God gives us when we do what is right.

Philippians 4:8-9 NIV "Finally, brothers and sisters, whatever is true, whatever is noble, whatever is right, whatever is pure, whatever is lovely, whatever is admirable—if anything is excellent or praiseworthy—think about such things. Whatever you have learned or received or heard from me, or seen in me—put it into practice. And the God of peace will be with you."

Live Your Lives In Christ Jesus

Colossians 2:6: "So then, just as you received Christ Jesus as Lord, continue to live your lives in him."

Love & Follow Jesus

1. Love and Follow Jesus: When we say we received Christ Jesus as Lord, it means we love Him and want to follow Him. Just like having a best friend, we should stick with Jesus and let Him guide our lives.

Trust & Believe In Jesus

2. Trust and Believe in Jesus: The verse also says, 'continue to live your lives in him.' This means that once we believe in Jesus, we should try to live our lives following his teachings. We can do this by being kind to others, helping those in need, and being honest. We trust Him and believe in Him. We can talk to Him through prayer and ask for help whenever we feel sad, scared, or confused. Jesus will always be there for us.

So, in simple words, the commandments from Colossians 2:6 are about loving Jesus and trying to live like him.

Colossians 2:6 NIV "So then, just as you received Christ Jesus as Lord, continue to live your lives in him,"

Take Off Your Old Self

Colossians 3:8-9 gives us commandments about Taking off your old self. Let's take a closer look at these to understand them better.

No More Lying

1. No More Lying: It's important to always tell the truth and not make up stories. Lying can hurt others and make them sad. So, promise to be honest and say what is true!

No More Anger

2. No More Anger: Sometimes, we feel angry or mad, but it's not good to let that anger control us. Instead, let's try to be kind and patient with others, even when we're upset.

No More Mean Words

3. No More Mean Words: Using mean or hurtful words can make others feel really bad. It's better to use our words to encourage and help others. So, let's always speak in a nice and friendly way!

No More Gossiping

4. No More Gossiping: Gossiping means talking about other people's secrets or spreading rumors. This can make others feel sad or embarrassed. Let's choose to keep secrets and only say nice things about others.

No More Bad Attitude

5. No More Bad Attitude: Our attitude is how we feel inside and how we act towards others. We should try to be happy, thankful, and respectful to everyone we meet. Being kind is always the best choice!

Colossians 3:8-9 NIV "But now you must also rid yourselves of all such things as these: anger, rage, malice, slander, and filthy language from your lips. Do not lie to each other, since you have taken off your old self with its practices"

Bear With Each Other & Forgive One Another

Colossians 3:12-17 says "Therefore, as God's chosen people, holy and dearly loved, clothe yourselves with compassion, kindness, humility, gentleness and patience. Bear with each other and forgive one another if any of you has a grievance against someone. Forgive as the Lord forgave you. And over all these virtues put on love, which binds them all together in perfect unity. Let the peace of Christ rule in your hearts, since as members of one body you were called to peace. And be thankful. Let the message of Christ dwell among you richly as you teach and admonish one another with all wisdom through psalms, hymns, and songs from the Spirit, singing to God with gratitude in your hearts. And whatever you do, whether in word or deed, do it all in the name of the Lord Jesus, giving thanks to God the Father through him."

This verse contains many commandments about being kind, patient, forgiving, loving, peaceful, thankful and teaching others about God's love. Let's take a closer look at these commandments to help understand them better.

Be Kind & Gentle To Others

1. Be kind and gentle to others, just like how you would like them to be kind and gentle to you. (Colossians 3:12)

Be Patient & Wait Calmly

2. Always be patient and wait calmly, even when things don't go your way or you have to wait for something you want. (Colossians 3:12)

Forgive Others For Their Mistakes

3. Try to forgive others when they make mistakes or do something that hurts you. Remember, we all make mistakes sometimes. (Colossians 3:13)

Love Others With All Your Heart

4. Above all, love others with all your heart. Love should be like a special coat you wear every day. (Colossians 3:14)

Let Peace Be In Charge Of Your Heart & Mind

5. Let peace be in charge of your heart and mind. Try to get along with everyone and avoid fighting or arguing. (Colossians 3:15)

Be Thankful For All The Good In Your Life

6. Remember to always be thankful for all the good things in your life, like your family, friends, and the things you have. (Colossians 3:15)

Teach Others About God's Love & Be Happy To Share Jesus

7. Teach others about God's love and be happy to share what you know about Jesus with them. (Colossians 3:16)

Do Everything With All Your Heart To Please God

8. Whatever you do, do it with all your heart and make sure it pleases God. Sing songs, pray, and thank God every day for everything. (Colossians 3:17)

Colossians 3:12-17 NIV "Therefore, as God's chosen people, holy and dearly loved, clothe yourselves with compassion, kindness, humility, gentleness and patience. Bear with each other and forgive one another if any of you has a grievance against someone. Forgive as the Lord forgave you. And over all these virtues put on love, which binds them all together in perfect unity. Let the peace of Christ rule in your hearts, since as members of one body you were called to peace. And be thankful. Let the message of Christ dwell among you richly as you teach and admonish one another with all wisdom through psalms, hymns, and songs from the Spirit, singing to God with gratitude in your hearts. And whatever you do, whether in word or deed, do it all in the name of the Lord Jesus, giving thanks to God the Father through him."

A CHILDREN'S GUIDE TO A GODLY WAY OF LIFE

Always Do Your Best

Colossians 3:23 says that whatever you do, do it with all your heart, as if you are doing it for God, not just for people.

This means that when you have a task to do, like cleaning your room or doing your homework, you should try your best and put in a lot of effort. You should remember that God sees everything you do and wants you to do your best, just like when you do things for your parents or teachers. So, always work hard and do your best, because it makes God happy!

Colossians 3:23 NIV "Whatever you do, work at it with all your heart, as working for the Lord, not for human masters,"

Be Kind & Love One Another Just As Jesus Loves Us

In 1 Thessalonians 3:12 Jesus says, "May the Lord make your love increase and overflow for each other and for everyone else, just as ours does for you."

What this means is that we are to be kind and love one another, just as Jesus loves us. We are to treat others with respect and be friendly. Share your toys and help those in need. Listen to your parents and teachers, and always be honest. Remember, God wants us to be good and show love to everyone!"

1 Thessalonians 3:12 (NIV) - "May the Lord make your love increase and overflow for each other and for everyone else, just as ours does for you."

Please God
Live In Order To Please God

1 Thessalonians 4:1 says, "As for other matters, brothers and sisters, we instructed you how to live in order to please God, as in fact you are living. Now we ask you and urge you in the Lord Jesus to do this more and more."

Be Kind, Helpful & Good

The first rule is to please God. It means we should try to make God happy by doing things that are kind, helpful, and good. We can do this by being obedient to our parents, being nice to others, and doing our best in everything we do.

Be Pure & Good Hearted

The second rule is about living a holy life. Being holy means being pure and good-hearted. We should try to avoid doing things that are wrong or hurtful. Instead, we should focus on being loving, forgiving, and treating others with respect.

Don't Give In To Bad Desires

The third rule is about not giving in to bad desires. Sometimes we might feel like doing things that we know are wrong, like being mean to someone or stealing something. But God wants us to control those feelings and choose to do what is right instead. This helps us grow and become better people.

These rules from 1 Thessalonians 4:1 are a way for us to show our love and respect for God and others. By following them, we can make the world a happier and more peaceful place to live.

1 Thessalonians 4:1 NIV "As for other matters, brothers and sisters, we instructed you how to live in order to please God, as in fact you are living. Now we ask you and urge you in the Lord Jesus to do this more and more."

Control Your Body In A Holy & Honorable Way

1 Thessalonians 4:4-6 says "Each of you should learn to control your own body in a way that is holy and honorable, not in passionate lust like the pagans, who do not know God; and that in this matter no one should wrong or take advantage of a brother or sister. The Lord will punish all those who commit such sins, as we told you and warned you before."

God wants us to treat others with kindness and respect. In the Bible, in 1 Thessalonians 4:4-6, it says that we should control our bodies and not do anything that hurts others. We should love and care for each other, and not take away someone else's happiness. God wants us to be good and make sure we don't do anything that makes others sad or upset.

Treat Our Bodies With Respect To Please God

This verse is telling us that we should take care of our bodies and treat them with respect. We shouldn't do things that are wrong or make us feel bad. It's important to control our actions and not do things just because we want to. We should think about what is right and what God would want us to do.

Don't Hurt Or Take Advantage Of Others

The verse also says that we shouldn't hurt or take advantage of other people. We should treat others with kindness and love. If we do the wrong things or hurt others, God will be unhappy with us. So, it's important to remember these commandments and try our best to follow them.

1 Thessalonians 4:4-6 - "Each of you should learn to control your own body in a way that is holy and honorable, not in the passion of lust like the Gentiles who do not know God; that no one transgress and wrong his brother in this matter, because the Lord is an avenger in all these things, as we told you beforehand and solemnly warned you."

Lead A Quiet Life

Thessalonians 4:9-12 says "Now about your love for one another we do not need to write to you, for you yourselves have been taught by God to love each other. And in fact, you do love all of God's family throughout Macedonia. Yet we urge you, brothers and sisters, to do so more and more, and to make it your ambition to lead a quiet life: You should mind your own business and work with your hands, just as we told you, so that your daily life may win the respect of outsiders and so that you will not be dependent on anybody."

These verse have commandments about leading a quiet life, minding your own business, and working with your hands.

Love One Another

1. Love one another: God wants us to show love to everyone around us. We should be kind, caring, and treat others the way we want to be treated.

Work Hard & Mind Your Own Business

2. Work hard and mind your own business: God wants us to be responsible and put effort into our tasks. We shouldn't be lazy and always try to do our best. We should also focus on our own work instead of meddling in other people's affairs.

Live A Peaceful Life

3. Live a peaceful life: God wants us to live in harmony with others. We should try to solve conflicts peacefully and avoid arguments or fights. Being peaceful means being calm and friendly, even when things get tough.

Mind Your Manners

4. Mind your manners: God wants us to be polite and respectful. We should use our words kindly, say "please" and "thank you," and be considerate of others' feelings.

Depend On God

5. Depend on God: God wants us to trust Him and believe in His plan for our lives. We can pray to Him, ask for help, and have faith that He will guide and take care of us.

Remember, commandments are not meant to be hard or scary, but to help us live a good and happy life.

1 Thessalonians 4:9-12 NIV "Now about your love for one another we do not need to write to you, for you yourselves have been taught by God to love each other. And in fact, you do love all of God's family throughout Macedonia. Yet we urge you, brothers and sisters, to do so more and more, and to make it your ambition to lead a quiet life: You should mind your own business and work with your hands, just as we told you, so that your daily life may win the respect of outsiders and so that you will not be dependent on anybody."

Do The Right Things

In the Bible, 1 Thessalonians 5:6 tells us that we should always be awake and alert. This means we need to pay attention and be aware of what is happening around us.

So, why is it important to be awake and alert? Well, it's like being ready for whatever comes our way. God wants us to be prepared and not miss out on anything good. He wants us to be aware of His love and guidance, and also be aware of things that could be harmful or wrong.

Being awake and alert means we should try our best to do the right things, like being kind to others, helping those in need, and being honest. It also means being careful not to do things that could hurt ourselves or others, like lying or being mean.

By following these commandments, we can make God happy and live a life full of love and goodness. So, let's remember to be awake and alert, and always try to do what's right!"

1 Thessalonians 5:6 "So then, let us not be like others, who are asleep, but let us be awake and sober."

Hold In The Highest Regard Those Who Work Hard

1 Thessalonians 5:12-22, says "Now we ask you, brothers and sisters, to acknowledge those who work hard among you, who care for you in the Lord and who admonish you. Hold them in the highest regard in love because of their work. Live in peace with each other. And we urge you, brothers and sisters, warn those who are idle and disruptive, encourage the disheartened, help the weak, be patient with everyone. Make sure that nobody pays back wrong for wrong, but always strive to do what is good for each other and for everyone else. Rejoice always, pray continually, give thanks in all circumstances; for this is God's will for you in Christ Jesus. Do not quench the Spirit. Do not treat prophecies with contempt but test them all; hold on to what is good, reject every kind of evil".

These verses give us commandments about holding those who work hard among you in the highest regard. Lets beak it down and make it easier to understand.

Listen & Respect Your Leaders

1. Listen and respect your leaders: This means you should pay attention and be kind to your teachers, parents, and other grown-ups who take care of you.

Be Peaceful & Kind To Everyone

2. Be peaceful and kind to everyone: Treat others with love and kindness, just like how you want to be treated. Avoid fighting and try to solve problems peacefully.

Encourage & Help Others

3. Encourage and help others: Give your friends and family members nice words and support when they need it. Share and be helpful whenever you can.

Respect & Appreciate God's Message

4. Respect and appreciate God's message: Listen to stories from the Bible and learn from them. Show gratitude to God for all the good things in your life.

Always Be Joyful & Happy

5. Always be joyful and happy: Try to find happiness in everyday things. Be positive and have a cheerful attitude.

Pray To God & Talk To Hm

6. Pray to God and talk to Him: Take time to talk to God through prayer. Share your thoughts, feelings, and ask for help when you need it.

Give Thank To God For Everything

7. Give thanks to God for everything: Say "thank you" to God for your family, friends, and blessings in your life. Remember to be grateful.

A CHILDREN'S GUIDE TO A GODLY WAY OF LIFE

Don't Ignore God's Teachings

8. Don't ignore God's teachings: Follow the rules and guidance given in the Bible. Try your best to live a good and righteous life.

Test & Hold On To What Is Good

9. Test and hold on to what is good: Always choose what is right and true. Don't believe in things that are wrong or harmful.

Stay Away From Evil & Bad Things

10. Stay away from evil and bad things: Avoid things that can hurt you or others. Be good and make choices that bring happiness and love.

1 Thessalonians 5:12-22 NIV "Now we ask you, brothers and sisters, to acknowledge those who work hard among you, who care for you in the Lord and who admonish you. Hold them in the highest regard in love because of their work. Live in peace with each other. And we urge you, brothers and sisters, warn those who are idle and disruptive, encourage the disheartened, help the weak, be patient with everyone. Make sure that nobody pays back wrong for wrong, but always strive to do what is good for each other and for everyone else. Rejoice always, pray continually, give thanks in all circumstances; for this is God's will for you in Christ Jesus. Do not quench the Spirit. Do not treat prophecies with contempt but test them all; hold on to what is good, reject every kind of evil."

A Warning Against Idleness & Laziness

2 Thessalonians 3:6-15 is a warning against idleness. Idleness is being lazy, inactive and without motion, in the state of being superficial, pointless and purpose-less, which is something that God hates for us to be. 2 Thessalonians gives us commandments to keep us busy.

Always Listen & Follow Jesus Teachings

1. Always listen to and follow the teachings of Jesus.

Stay Away From People Who Don't Work or Aren't Helpful

2. Stay away from people who don't want to work or be helpful.

Work Hard & Take Care Of Yourself & Others

3. Remember, hard work is important and helps us take care of ourselves and others.

Be Responsible & Help Your Family & Community

4. Be responsible and do your part in helping your family and community.

Be Patient & Kind

5. Be patient and kind to everyone, even if they are not always nice to you.

Do The Right Things & Make Good Choices

6. Always try to do the right thing and make good choices.

Keep Busy With Helpful Activities

7. Don't get bored or lazy, but keep yourself busy with helpful activities.

Share With Those In Need

8. Remember to share what you have with others who are in need.

Treat Everyone With Respect & Fairness

9. Treat everyone with respect and fairness, regardless of who they are.

Be Kind, Loving & Helpful To Everyone

10. Finally, be kind, loving, and helpful to everyone, just like Jesus taught us.

2 Thessalonians 3:6-15 NIV "In the name of the Lord Jesus Christ, we command you, brothers and sisters, to keep away from every believer who is idle and disruptive and does not live according to the teaching you received from us. For you yourselves know how you ought to follow our example. We were not idle when we were with you, nor did we eat anyone's food without paying for it. On the contrary, we worked night and day, laboring and toiling so that we would not be a burden to any of you. We did this, not because we do not have the right to such help, but in order to offer ourselves as a model for you to imitate. For even when we were with you, we gave you this rule: "The one who is unwilling to work shall not eat."We hear that some among you are idle and disruptive. They are not busy; they are busybodies. Such people we command and urge in the Lord Jesus Christ to settle down and earn the food they eat. And as for you, brothers and sisters, never tire of doing what is good. Take special note of anyone who does not obey our instruction in this letter. Do not associate with them, in order that they may feel ashamed. Yet do not regard them as an enemy, but warn them as you would a fellow believer."

Oppose False Teachers

1 Timothy 1:4 is commandments about opposing false teachers. False teachers are those who teach things that are the opposite of what God or Jesus tell us is the truth. They mislead us away from God and Jesus. The best way to prevent this from happening is to know what the Bible says about God and Jesus so we know the truth.

Love & Be Kind

1. Love and be kind to others: Treat everyone with love and respect, just like you would want them to treat you. (1 Timothy 1:4)

Be Honest

2. Be honest: Always tell the truth, even if it's hard. Honesty is important because it helps build trust. (1 Timothy 1:4)

Be Thankful

3. Be thankful: Remember to say "thank you" to God for all the good things in your life. It's important to appreciate what you have. (1 Timothy 1:4)

Listen To Your Parents & Teachers

4. Listen to your parents and teachers: They care about you and want what's best for you. So, it's important to listen to their guidance and follow their instructions. (1 Timothy 1:4)

Share & Be Generous

5. Share and be generous: Sharing your toys, snacks, and time with others is a way to show kindness and make others happy. (1 Timothy 1:4)

Forgive Others

6. Forgive others: When someone says sorry, try to forgive them and let go of any anger or hurt feelings. Forgiveness is important for peace and happiness. (1 Timothy 1:4)

Be Patient

7. Be patient: Sometimes things don't happen right away, but it's important to wait calmly and not get upset. Patience helps us learn and grow. (1 Timothy 1:4)

Be Brave & Stand Up For What Is Right

8. Be brave and stand up for what is right: If you see someone being treated unfairly or see something wrong happening, have the courage to speak up and help make things better. (1 Timothy 1:4)

1 Timothy 1:4 NIV "or to devote themselves to myths and endless genealogies. Such things promote controversial speculations rather than advancing God's work—which is by faith."

Instructions For Prayer

1 Timothy 2:1-2 contains commandments for instructions for prayer.

Pray For Everyone

1. The first commandment is to pray for everyone. Praying means talking to God and asking Him to take care of all people, including our leaders and those in charge.

Be Thankful

2. The second commandment is to be thankful. It means showing gratitude for the things we have and the people who help us. When we say 'thank you,' it makes others feel happy and appreciated.

These commandments remind us to be caring and considerate towards others by praying for them. It's a way of showing love, respect, and wanting the best for everyone. Remember, prayer is like talking to God and asking Him to help and bless others, including our leaders."

1 Timothy 2:1-2 (NIV) "I urge, then, first of all, that petitions, prayers, intercession, and thanksgiving be made for all people— for kings and all those in authority, that we may live peaceful and quiet lives in all godliness and holiness."

Train Yourself To Be Godly

1 Timothy 4:1-7 is commandments to help you train yourself to be Godly.

Don't Believe Everything

Some people might tell you things that are not true or are meant to confuse you. Always check with your parents or trusted adults if you are unsure.

Stay Away From Wrong Or Harmful Things

Just like you avoid touching a hot stove, it's important to avoid things that can hurt your heart or mind.

Spend Time With God & Pray

Just like you talk to your parents or friends when you need help or want to share something, God wants you to talk to Him too. He's always there for you!

Treat Everyone With Kindness & Love

It's important to be nice to everyone, just like you would want them to be nice to you. Sharing, helping, and being friendly are all ways to show love to others.

Learn about God and the Teachings of Jesus

Just like you learn about different subjects in school, it's important to learn about God and Jesus too. Reading the Bible and going to church can help you understand more about them.

User Your Gifts To Help

Everyone has special skills or things they are good at. Using those talents to help others is a wonderful way to show God's love.

Take Care of Yourself

Just like you eat healthy food and exercise to keep your body strong, it's important to take care of your spiritual health too. Reading the Bible and spending time with God can help you grow strong in your faith.

Be A Good Example

When you act in a way that makes others happy and proud, it can inspire them to do the same. Being a good example means showing kindness, respect, and making good choices.

1 Timothy 4:1-7 NIV "The Spirit clearly says that in later times some will abandon the faith and follow deceiving spirits and things taught by demons. Such teachings come through hypocritical liars, whose consciences have been seared as with a hot iron. They forbid people to marry and order them to abstain from certain foods, which God created to be received with thanksgiving by those who believe and who know the truth. For everything God created is good, and nothing is to be rejected if it is received with thanksgiving, because it is consecrated by the word of God and prayer. If you point these things out to the brothers and sisters, you will be a good minister of Christ Jesus, nourished on the truths of the faith and of the good teaching that you have followed. Have nothing to do with godless myths and old wives' tales; rather, train yourself to be godly."

Be Kind & Respectful To Those Who Support You

1 Timothy 5:16-21 is commandments that help us be kind and respectful to those who teach and support us in our daily lives such as teachers, pastors, parents and grandparents,

Be Kind & Respectful To Older People

1. Be kind and respectful to everyone, especially older people who need help. (1 Timothy 5:16)

Show Love & Support Of Your Parents & Grandparents

2. Take good care of your family, especially your parents and grandparents. Show them love and support. (1 Timothy 5:16)

Treat Others The Way You Want To Be Treated

3. Always do what is right and fair, and treat others the way you want to be treated. (1 Timothy 5:17)

Listen & Obey To Wise Adults

4. Listen and obey your parents, teachers, and other wise adults who can guide you. (1 Timothy 5:17)

Be Grateful & Thankful For What You Have

5. Be grateful and thankful for what you have, and don't be greedy or jealous of others. (1 Timothy 5:18)

Respect & Honor Spiritual Leaders

6. Respect and honor those who lead and teach you, such as your pastor or Sunday school teacher. (1 Timothy 5:19)

Be Honest & Truthful

7. Be honest and truthful in everything you say and do, and don't lie or cheat. (1 Timothy 5:20)

Stay Away From Harmful & Hurtful Things

8. Stay away from doing harmful or hurtful things to others, and always try to help and encourage them instead. (1 Timothy 5:21)

1 Timothy 5:16-21 NIV If any woman who is a believer has widows in her care, she should continue to help them and not let the church be burdened with them, so that the church can help those widows who are really in need. The elders who direct the affairs of the church well are worthy of double honor, especially those whose work is preaching and teaching. For Scripture says, "Do not muzzle an ox while it is treading out the grain," and "The worker deserves his wages."Do not entertain an accusation against an elder unless it is brought by two or three witnesses. But those elders who are sinning you are to reprove before everyone, so that the others may take warning. I charge you, in the sight of God and Christ Jesus and the elect angels, to keep these instructions without partiality, and to do nothing out of favoritism.

The Lord Knows Who Are His

2 Timothy 2:19 says "The Lord knows those who are his" to know who are his they keep his commandments and "confess the name of the Lord" and "must turn away from wickedness".

Keep God's Commandments

To keep God's commandments, we have to know what His commandments are, right? To Keep God's Commandments means to follow or to keep God's rules, his commandments and do them the way God wants us to do them. This is why we add them to this book and talk about them, so you will know what God's commandments are and how to do them the way God and Jesus wants us to do them.

Confess The Name Of The Lord

To Confess the name of the Lord is a special and important thing that we can do as believers in God. It means that we openly and proudly declare that we believe in Jesus and that He is our Savior and Lord.

But what does this really mean, to us as children?

Well, imagine you have a best friend whom you love and trust very much. You know that this friend is amazing, kind, and always there for you. Confessing the name of the Lord is a bit like telling everyone how awesome your best friend is and how much you love and trust them.

When we confess the name of the Lord, we are saying to everyone, "I believe in Jesus, and I trust Him with my life." We are telling others that we have a special relationship with Him, just like we have with our best friend. We are proud to be a part of His family, and we want others to know that too.

Confessing the name of the Lord also means that we are not afraid or embarrassed to talk about Jesus and what He has done for us. We may talk about how He loves us unconditionally, forgives our mistakes, and helps us when we're sad or scared. We may also talk about how He teaches us to be kind, patient, and loving towards others.

Sometimes, confessing the name of the Lord can be challenging, especially when others may not understand or believe the same things we do. But it's important to remember that we are not alone. Jesus is with us every step of the way, and we can always lean on Him for strength and courage.

So, confessing the name of the Lord is about expressing your love and trust in Jesus and sharing that love with others. It's like telling everyone how amazing your best friend is and how they have made your life better. Keep loving and trusting Jesus, and don't be afraid to share your faith with others. Remember, you are never alone because Jesus is always by your side!

Turn Away From Wickedness

Turning away from wickedness means choosing to do what is right and good instead of doing things that are wrong or hurtful. It means making decisions that make the world a better place and being kind to others.

Imagine if you were playing a game with your friends, and one of them started cheating or being mean to others. You might feel that it's not fair and it hurts your feelings. In that situation, turning away from wickedness would mean not joining in with your friend's bad behavior, but instead, standing up for what is right and fair. It means saying, "Cheating and being mean is not okay, and I won't be a part of it."

Sometimes, we may see people doing things that are not good, like lying or being unkind. We might be tempted to do the same things because we want to fit in or be like them. But turning away from wickedness means making the right choice, even if it's not the popular one. It means listening to our conscience, the little voice inside our head that tells us what is right and what is wrong.

2 Timothy 2:19 NIV "Nevertheless, God's solid foundation stands firm, sealed with this inscription: "The Lord knows those who are his," and, "Everyone who confesses the name of the Lord must turn away from wickedness."

Flee Bad Things & Pursue Godly Things

In 2 Timothy 2:22-25 tells us some commandments that tell us to run away or flee from bad things and pursue good or Godly things. Let's take a closer look at these commandments to understand them better.

Run Away From Bad Things

1. Run away from bad things: Just like when you see something scary or dangerous, you would run away from it, these commandments tell us to run away from things that are not good for us. It could be anything that makes us feel sad, angry, or does not make us kind and loving towards others.

Do What Is Right

2. Try to do what is right: This means that we should always try to make good choices and not do things that we know are wrong. We should be kind, honest, and helpful to others.

Love & Trust God With All Your Heart

3. Love and trust God with all your heart: This means that we should believe in God and love Him with all our heart. We can talk to Him, pray to Him, and trust that He is always there to help us.

Be Patient & Gentle

4. Be patient and gentle: It's important to be patient when things don't go our way or when someone is bothering us. We

should also be gentle with others, which means treating them kindly and not being rough or mean.

Don't Argue or Fight

5. Don't argue or fight with others: Sometimes, we may have disagreements with our friends or family, but these commandments tell us that it's important to try and solve problems peacefully. We should talk calmly and listen to each other instead of yelling or hitting.

Teach Others About God's Love

6. Teach others about God's love: We can share our faith and tell others about God's love by being kind, helpful, and showing them how much we care. We can also talk to them about God and how He loves us all.

2 Timothy 2:22-25 NIV Flee the evil desires of youth and pursue righteousness, faith, love and peace, along with those who call on the Lord out of a pure heart. Don't have anything to do with foolish and stupid arguments, because you know they produce quarrels. And the Lord's servant must not be quarrelsome but must be kind to everyone, able to teach, not resentful. Opponents must be gently instructed, in the hope that God will grant them repentance leading them to a knowledge of the truth,

Have Nothing To Do With Ungodly People

2 Timothy 3:2-5 is a list of commandments telling us to have nothing to do with people who do not have these qualities in these commandments. We are to stay away from people who have no form of godliness because they are not kind, not respectful to their parents, they are not thankful, they brag and are boastful, they are liars, they are not honest, and they are mean and hurtful.

Be Kind

This means being nice to others and treating them the way you would like to be treated. It's important to use kind words and not hurt anyone's feelings with mean words or actions.

Respect Your Parents

Your parents take care of you, love you, and want the best for you. So, it's important to listen to them, obey their rules, and show them love and respect.

Be Thankful

This means being grateful for all the good things in your life, like your family, friends, food, and toys. Remember to say "thank you" when someone does something nice for you.

Don't Brag or Boast

Don't brag or boast: It's not nice to show off or make others feel bad about themselves. Instead, we should be humble and happy for others when they do well.

Be Honest

Always tell the truth, even if it's hard. It's important to be honest with yourself and others, as it helps build trust and shows that you are a reliable person.

Don't Be Mean Or Hurtful

Avoid being mean to others, both with your words and actions. Instead, try to help, encourage, and support your friends and classmates.

2 Timothy 3:2-5 NIV "People will be lovers of themselves, lovers of money, boastful, proud, abusive, disobedient to their parents, ungrateful, unholy, without love, unforgiving, slanderous, without self-control, brutal, not lovers of the good, treacherous, rash, conceited, lovers of pleasure rather than lovers of God— having a form of godliness but denying its power. Have nothing to do with such people."

Demonstrate With Faith & Patience

The commandments in Hebrews 6:11-12 are about working hard, staying positive, being patient, trusting in good things, and learning from good people. If we remember these things and try to follow them, we can become better and happier people as we follow God.

Always Do Your Best

First, it says that we should "show diligence" in what we do. This means that we should try our best and work hard in everything we do, like schoolwork, chores, or even playing sports. It's important to put effort into things and not give up easily.

It's like when you have homework, and you put in a lot of effort to complete it nicely. That's what this commandment is telling us to do - to work hard and do good things.

Have Hope

Second, it says we should have "full assurance of hope." This means that we should always have a positive attitude and believe that good things will happen. Even when things are difficult or don't go as planned, we should keep hoping and not let go of our dreams.

The second commandment is about having hope. Hope means believing that good things will happen, even when things are difficult. It's like when you really want to go to a park, but it's raining outside. You can still hope that the rain will stop and you'll be able to go later. This commandment tells us to always have hope and believe that good things will come in the future.

Be Patient & Wait Calmly

Next, it talks about having "patience." This means that we should learn to wait calmly and not get frustrated when things take longer than we want. Being patient means understanding that some things just need time to happen, like growing a plant or learning a new skill.

The third commandment is about being patient. Patience means waiting calmly without getting upset or angry. It's like when you're waiting for your turn on a swing, and you have to wait for the person before you to finish. This commandment tells us to be patient and wait calmly, even when things don't happen right away.

Never Give Up

The verse also mentions "inherit the promises." This means that we should trust in the good things that God has promised for us. It's like when someone tells us they will give us a special gift or take us on a fun trip. We should believe that it will happen and be excited about it.

The fourth commandment is about not giving up. Sometimes, things can be really difficult, but this commandment tells us to keep going and not give up. It's like when you're learning to ride a bicycle, and you fall down a few times. You might feel like giving up, but this commandment tells us to keep trying and not give up, even when things are tough.

Trust In God

Lastly, it says that we should imitate those who have faith and patience. This means that we should look up to and learn from people who are kind, loving, and have strong beliefs. We can try to be like them by being helpful, caring, and believing in ourselves.

The fifth commandment is about trusting in God. Trust means believing and having faith in someone. This commandment tells us to trust in God, to believe in Him, and know that He will always be there for us. It's like when you have a really good friend, and you trust them to always be there for you when you need them.

Remember, when we started talking about these verses in in Hebrews 6:11-12, they are about working hard, staying positive, being patient, trusting in good things, and learning from good people. If we remember these things and try to follow them, we can become better and happier people for God.

Hebrews 6:11-12 NIV "We want each of you to show this same diligence to the very end, so that what you hope for may be fully realized. We do not want you to become lazy, but to imitate those who through faith and patience inherit what has been promised."

Draw Closer To God

The commandments from Hebrews 10:22-25 teach us how to be close to God, believe in our hopes, encourage others, and spend time with people who share our beliefs. They are important because they guide us to be good and loving individuals.

Let's take a closer look at these commandments in Hebrews 10:22-25 to understand them better so we know how to draw closer to God as a a believer in God.

Be Close To God

The first commandment says, "Let us draw near to God with a sincere heart." This means that we should try to be close to God and have a true and honest heart when we pray or talk to Him. It's like having a special friendship with God where we are always honest and open with God about everything in our life. God already knows everything about us anyway so why try to hide anything from Him. Right? We can tell Him anything because He will always love and care for us.

Believe &Trust In Our Hopes and Dreams

The second commandment says, "Let us hold unswervingly to the hope we profess." This means that we should always believe and trust in the good things that we say we believe in. We should never give up on our hopes and dreams.

Encourage & Help Other Be Kind and Do Good Things

The third commandment says, "Let us consider how we may spur one another on toward love and good deeds." This means that we should think about how we can encourage and help others to be kind and do good things. It's like being a good friend and supporting each other.

Spend Time With Others Who Believe In God

The fourth commandment says, "Let us not give up meeting together." This means that we should try to gather and spend time with other people who believe in God, like going to a church or a place of worship. It's like being part of a big family where we can learn from each other and grow together.

The commandments given in Hebrews 10:22-25 remind us how to be close to God, believe in our hopes, encourage others, and spend time with people who share our beliefs. I hope that helps you understand these commandments about how to draw closer to God!

Hebrews 10:22-25 NIV let us draw near to God with a sincere heart and with the full assurance that faith brings, having our hearts sprinkled to cleanse us from a guilty conscience and having our bodies washed with pure water. Let us hold unswervingly to the hope we profess, for he who promised is faithful. And let us consider how we may spur one another on toward love and good deeds, not giving up meeting together, as some are in the habit of doing, but encouraging one another —and all the more as you see the Day approaching.

Live In Peace With Everyone

In Hebrews 12:12-16 is a list of commandments telling us to live in peace with everyone. These commandments teaching us what to do when we feel sad or weak, to stay on the right path, to try to get along with everyone, to help others know about God, and to make sure no one is immoral.

This is a wide variety of commandments. Let's go a little deeper into each of these to help you understand each of them better, shall me?

When You Feel Sad or Weak

"Lift up your drooping hands and strengthen your weak knees."

This means that when you feel sad or weak, you should try to be strong and not give up. Just like when you have a boo-boo and it hurts, you try to be brave and not cry too much.

Stay On The Right Path

"Make straight paths for your feet, so that what is lame may not be put out of joint, but rather be healed."

This means that you should try to do the right things and stay on the right path. It's like when you have a toy car and you want it to go straight on the road without crashing into things. It's important to stay on the right track so that you don't get hurt.

Try To Get Along With Everyone

"Strive for peace with everyone, and for the holiness without which no one will see the Lord."

This means that you should try your best to get along with everyone and be kind. It's like when you're playing with your friends, you want to be friendly and not fight. And being holy means being good and doing what is right, so that you can be close to God.

Help Others Know About God's Love

"See to it that no one fails to obtain the grace of God; that no root of bitterness springs up and causes trouble, and by it many become defiled."

This means that we should help others to know about God's love and be kind to them. We shouldn't hold grudges or be mean because that can cause trouble and make others feel bad. It's like when someone accidentally steps on your favorite toy, instead of getting angry, you forgive them and continue to be friends.

Make Sure No One Is Immoral

"See to it that no one is immoral or unholy like Esau, who sold his birthright for a single meal."

This means that we should wait to do things that are meant for grown-ups, like getting married and having a family. We shouldn't do things that are wrong or make God sad. It's like when you have a special treat, you don't want to give it away for something not as good. You want to save it for the right time.

Hebrews 12:12-16 "Therefore, strengthen your feeble arms and weak knees. "Make level paths for your feet,"so that the lame may not be disabled, but rather healed. Make every effort to live in peace with everyone and to be holy; without holiness no one will see the Lord. See to it that no one falls short of the grace of God and that no bitter root grows up to cause trouble and defile many. See that no one is sexually immoral, or is godless like Esau, who for a single meal sold his inheritance rights as the oldest son."

Keep Loving One Another As Brothers & Sisters

In Hebrews 13:1-3, these commandments are basically about being loving, kind, and caring to everyone around us, whether they are our friends, family, strangers, or people who are having a tough time. It's important to treat others with love and respect because that's what makes the world a better place.

Love One Another

1. The first commandment is to love one another. This means we should be kind, caring, and show love to our family, friends, and even people we don't know very well. It's like being a good friend and treating others the way we want to be treated.

Be Kind To Strangers

2. The second commandment is to not forget to be kind to strangers. Strangers are people we don't know, like someone we meet for the first time. We should be friendly and welcoming to them, just like we would want others to be kind to us when we are new somewhere.

Remember Those Having A Tough Time

3. The third commandment is to remember those who are in prison or going through hard times. It's important to show empathy and compassion to people who are sad, lonely, or facing difficulties. We can help them feel better by sending them a kind message, praying for them, or doing something nice for them.

Hebrews 13:1-3 NIV "Keep on loving one another as brothers and sisters. Do not forget to show hospitality to strangers, for by so doing some people have shown hospitality to angels without knowing it. Continue to remember those in prison as if you were together with them in prison, and those who are mistreated as if you yourselves were suffering."

Don't Be Jealous or Envious Of What Others Have

Hebrews 13:5 is commandments about how we conduct ourselves with regard to jealousy and and being content in our lives. This verse is telling us not to be jealous of what others have, keep your lives free from the love of money, to be happy and grateful for the things we already possess, and that God will never leave you. It's like a gentle reminder to be content and appreciate the blessings in our lives.

Hebrews 13:5, God gives us some commandments, or rules, to follow. Let's break them down in a way that an elementary school child can understand:

Keep Yourself Free Of Love Of Money

This means we should not be too focused on wanting lots of money or things. Instead, we should be grateful for what we have and remember that people are more important than money.

Be Satisfied With What You Have

It's important to be happy and content with what we already have, rather than always wanting more and more. This helps us appreciate the things we have and not be too greedy.

God Will Never Leave You

This means that God is always with us, no matter what. We can trust Him and know that He will never abandon us. He loves us and will be with us through good times and bad times.

So, to summarize, this verse is telling us not to be jealous of what others have, to be happy and grateful for the things we already have, and that God will always be with us. It's like a gentle reminder to be content and appreciate the blessings in our lives.

Hebrews 13:5 Keep your lives free from the love of money and be content with what you have, because God has said, "Never will I leave you; never will I forsake you."

Respect The People Who Teach Us About God

The individual commandments in Hebrews 13:7 are about respecting the people who teach us about God. These commandments teach us to respect our leaders, appreciate our teachers, be strong in our choices, show love and kindness, be faithful in relationships, not be jealous, and be content with what we have.

Respect Our Leaders

The first commandment is to remember and respect our leaders or people who are in charge, like our teachers or parents. We should listen to them and learn from them because they can guide us in the right direction.

Appreciate Our Teachers

The second commandment is to remember and appreciate the people who have taught us about God and about being good. These people are like our spiritual leaders, such as pastors or religious teachers. We should be grateful for their teachings and follow their good examples.

Be Strong In Our Choices

The third commandment is about being strong and not easily influenced by bad things. It means we should not let others lead us into doing wrong or breaking the rules. We should always try to make good choices and do what is right.

Show Love & Kindness To Others

The fourth commandment is to show love and kindness to others. We should be friendly, help people when they need it, and be nice to everyone we meet. It's important to share and care for others, just like we would want them to do for us.

Be Faithful In Our Relationships

The fifth commandment is about being faithful and true to our marriage vows. This one might be a bit hard to understand at your age, but it means when we grow up and get married, we should always love and be loyal to our spouse.

Do Not Be Jealous

The sixth commandment is about not wanting or desiring things that belong to other people. It means we should be happy with what we have and not be jealous of others. We should appreciate the things we own and not try to take what belongs to someone else.

Be Content With What We Have

The seventh commandment is about being content with what we have. It means we should be happy and grateful for the things we own, our family, and our friends. We should not always want more and more, but instead be thankful for what we already have.

So, these are the individual commandments in Hebrews 13:7. They teach us to respect our leaders, appreciate our teachers, be strong in our choices, show love and kindness, be faithful in relationships, not be jealous, and be content with what we have. Following these commandments can help us be good and make the world a better place.

Hebrews 13:7 NIV "Remember your leaders, who spoke the word of God to you. Consider the outcome of their way of life and imitate their faith."

Don't Be Carried Away By Strange Teachings

The commandments in Hebrews 13:9 remind us to not be carried away by strange teachings. These commandments remind us to be careful about what we learn, not to worry too much about what we eat, not to rely only on rituals, and to always remember and follow the teachings of Jesus.

This is a vast array of commandments so lets look a little deeper into them to help understand them a little better.

Be Careful What We Believe

This means we should be careful about what we believe and listen to. We should only believe things that are true, good, and helpful to ourselves and other and not be fooled by strange or wrong ideas.

Have Kind & Loving Hearts

This means that we should try to have kind and loving hearts. We should be nice to others and help them when they need it. Grace means showing love and kindness to others, just like God shows us love and kindness.

The second commandment is about food. It says that it is good if our hearts are strengthened by grace and not by rules about what we can or cannot eat. This means that instead of worrying too much about what we eat, we should focus on being kind, loving, and showing grace to others.

Not By Eating Ceremonial Foods

This part might be a little tricky. It means that we don't need to follow certain rules about what we eat to be good people. What matters more is how we treat others and how we show love and kindness.

The third commandment tells us that it is good not to rely on rituals or ceremonies. It means that we should not think that doing specific actions or following certain rituals will make us better people. Instead, we should focus on having a good heart and treating others with kindness and respect.

Always Follow The Teachings of Jesus

The last commandment is about Jesus. It says that we should always remember and follow the teachings of Jesus, who is our leader and the one who showed us how to love and care for others.

So, the main message from this verse is that we should be careful about what we believe, have kind and loving hearts, and not worry too much about following certain rules about food. Instead, we should focus on being good to others and showing love and kindness, just like God does.

Hebrews 13:9 NIV "Do not be carried away by all kinds of strange teachings. It is good for our hearts to be strengthened by grace, not by eating ceremonial foods, which is of no benefit to those who do so."

Do Good & Share With Others

The commandments in Hebrews 13:15-17 teach us do good and share with others by remembering to thank God, to be kind to others, and obedient to the people who take care of us.

Always Remember To Thank God

1. The first commandment says, "Let us continually offer to God a sacrifice of praise." This means that we should always remember to thank God and say nice things about Him. It's like when you say "thank you" to your parents or friends when they do something nice for you.

Remember To Be Kind To Others

2. The second commandment says, "Do not forget to do good and to share with others." This means we should always try to be kind to others and share the good things we have with them. It's like when you share your toys with your friends or help someone who needs it.

Obey Teachers

3. The third commandment says, "Obey your leaders and submit to their authority." This means that we should listen to our parents, teachers, and other grown-ups who take care of us. They are like our leaders, and it's important to follow their instructions to stay safe and learn new things.

Hebrews 13:16-17 NIV "And do not forget to do good and to share with others, for with such sacrifices God is pleased. Have confidence in your leaders and submit to their authority, because they keep watch over you as those who must give an account. Do this so that their work will be a joy, not a burden, for that would be of no benefit to you."

Everything Good & Perfect Is From Above

The commandments in James 1:16-18 tell us everything good and perfect is from above. These commandments reminds us not to be fooled by false things, and to remember that everything good comes from God. It also tells us that God created everything and is always the same, and that He gave us life and guidance through the words of truth in the Bible.

Do Not Be Deceived

First, it says, "Do not be deceived." This means we should not believe something that is not true. We should be careful and make sure we understand things correctly.

Every Good & Perfect Gift Is From Above

Then it says, "Every good and perfect gift is from above." This means that all the good things we have in our lives come from God. The love of our family, the food we eat, and the beautiful nature around us are all gifts from God.

God Created Everything

Next, it says, "Coming down from the Father of the heavenly lights." This tells us that God is the one who created everything, including the stars and the sun. He is the Father of all the amazing things we see in the sky.

God Is Always The Same

After that, it says, "Who does not change like shifting shadows." This means that God is always the same. He doesn't change the way people sometimes do. He is constant and reliable, just like the sun that rises and sets every day.

God Gave Us LIfe

Finally, it says, "He chose to give us birth through the word of truth." This tells us that God gave us life and made us who we are. The "word of truth" refers to the teachings and messages in the Bible that guide us to live good and loving lives.

James 1:16-18 NIV "Don't be deceived, my dear brothers and sisters. Every good and perfect gift is from above, coming down from the Father of the heavenly lights, who does not change like shifting shadows. He chose to give us birth through the word of truth, that we might be a kind of firstfruits of all he created."

Quick To Listen, Slow To Speak & Anger

In James 1:19, there are three important commandments that are meant to help us become better people. These commandments are that we are to be quick to listen, slow to speak and slow to anger.

Let me explain them to you in a way will help you understand them better.

Be Quick To Listen

This means that we should always try to listen carefully when someone is talking to us. It's important to pay attention and not interrupt them. By doing this, we show respect to others and can understand their feelings and thoughts better.

Slow To Speak

This means that we should think carefully before we speak. Sometimes, we might feel like saying something mean or hurtful when we're angry or upset, but it's better to take a moment and calm down. By being slow to speak, we can choose our words wisely and avoid hurting others with our words.

Slow To Become Angry

This commandment tells us that it's important to control our anger. When we get angry, we might feel like yelling or hitting, but that's not the right way to handle it. Instead, we should take a deep breath and try to find a peaceful solution to the problem. Being slow to become angry helps us maintain good relationships with others.

James 1:19 NIV My dear brothers and sisters, take note of this: Everyone should be quick to listen, slow to speak and slow to become angry,

A CHILDREN'S GUIDE TO A GODLY WAY OF LIFE

Be Good & Follow God's Teachings

In James 1:21-22, the commandments are telling us to be good, listen to God's teachings, not just ignore them, and actually follow what God tells us to do. By doing these things, we can become better and make the world a happier place!

James 1:21-22 says, "Therefore, get rid of all moral filth and the evil that is so prevalent and humbly accept the word planted in you, which can save you. Do not merely listen to the word, and so deceive yourselves. Do what it says."

Let's explain these commandments in a simpler way:

Get Rid Of All Moral Filth & Evil

This means we should try to stay away from things that are bad or wrong. It's like cleaning up our thoughts and actions to make sure we are being kind and good to others.

Humbly Accept The Word Planted In You

This means we should be open and willing to listen to what God teaches us through the Bible. It's like being ready to learn and understand the good things God wants us to know.

Do Not Merely Listen To The Word

This means we shouldn't just hear what God says and then forget about it. We need to pay attention and take it seriously. It's like when someone gives us important instructions, we should remember and follow them.

Do What It Says

This is the most important commandment from James 1:21-22! It means we should actually do what God tells us in the Bible. It's like when our parents give us rules, we should follow them and do what they say.

So, to summarize, the commandments from James 1:21-22 are telling us to be good, listen to God's teachings, not just ignore them, and actually follow what God tells us to do. By doing these things, we can become better and make the world a happier place!

James 1:21-22 NIV "Therefore, get rid of all moral filth and the evil that is so prevalent and humbly accept the word planted in you, which can save you. Do not merely listen to the word, and so decide yourselves. Do what it says."

Treat Everyone Fairly

James 2:1-4, God gives us important commandments commandments from God that remind us to treat everyone equally, not judge people by their appearance or social status, and to be kind and loving to everyone we meet.

Let's break them down and explain them in a way that is easier to understand.

Don't Show Favoritism

"My brothers and sisters, believers in our glorious Lord Jesus Christ must not show favoritism."

This means that we should treat everyone equally and not have favorites. It's like when you have a group of friends, you shouldn't only play with one friend and ignore the others. Instead, we should be kind and friendly to everyone, no matter where they come from or what they look like.

This commandment is to not show favoritism. This means that we should treat everyone equally, no matter how they look or where they come from. We should not think that some people are better than others or treat someone special just because they have nice things or look different.

Don't Judge By How People Look Or What They Have

"Suppose a man comes into your meeting wearing a gold ring and fine clothes, and a poor man in filthy old clothes also comes in."

Here, God is saying that we shouldn't judge people by how they look or what they have. It's like when someone comes to our classroom wearing fancy clothes and someone else comes wearing old, dirty clothes. We shouldn't treat the person with fancy clothes better just because they have nice things. Instead, we should be kind to both of them and treat them equally.

This commandment is about treating people who are rich or have nice things differently than people who may not have as many things. James says that we should not give extra attention or treat them better just because of their belongings. We should be fair and kind to everyone, no matter if they have many things or not.

Don't Judge People By Their Appearance

"If you show special attention to the man wearing fine clothes and say, 'Here's a good seat for you,' but say to the poor man, 'You stand there' or 'Sit on the floor by my feet,'"

God is telling us not to treat people differently based on their appearance or social status. It's like if we invite someone important to our class and give them the best seat, but tell someone who doesn't seem important to stand in the back or sit on the floor. This is not fair. We should treat everyone with respect and make sure everyone feels welcome and included.

This commandment is to not judge people by their appearance or make assumptions about them based on how they look or what they wear. James tells us that we should not think that someone is more important just because they dress nicely or that someone is less important because they may have old or torn clothes. We should remember that what matters most is how kind and caring a person is on the inside, not what they wear.

Don't Discriminate

"Have you not discriminated among yourselves and become judges with evil thoughts?"

God is saying that when we treat people unfairly or judge them based on how they look or what they have, it's not good. It's like if we start thinking bad things about others just because they are different from us. Instead, we should be kind, loving, and accepting of everyone, just like Jesus taught us.

This last commandment is to not make distinctions or separate people into groups based on how much money they have or where they come from. James tells us that we should not treat someone better just because they are rich or look important. We should treat everyone with kindness and respect, no matter their background or how much money they have.

The commandments in James 2:1-4 teach us to treat everyone fairly, not to show favoritism, not to judge people by their appearance, and not to make distinctions based on money or background. It's all about being kind and treating others the way we would like to be treated.

James 2:1-4 NIV "My brothers and sisters, believers in our glorious Lord Jesus Christ must not show favoritism. Suppose a man comes into your meeting wearing a gold ring and fine clothes, and a poor man in filthy old clothes also comes in. If you show special attention to the man wearing fine clothes and say, "Here's a good seat for you," but say to the poor man, "You stand there" or "Sit on the floor by my feet," have you not discriminated among yourselves and become judges with evil thoughts?"

Love Your Neighbors As Yourself

The commandments in James 2:8-11 remind us Love Your Neighbor As Yourself. We obey these commandments by being kind, fair, obedient, accepting, and gentle with others. These commandments help us understand how to treat people with love and respect, just like we would want to be treated.

Treat Others The Way You Want To Be Treated

The first commandment talks about loving your neighbor as yourself. It means that we should treat others the way we want to be treated. We should be kind, helpful, and caring towards everyone, just like we would want them to treat us.

Don't Show Favoritism

The second commandment talks about showing favoritism. It means that we shouldn't treat some people better than others just because they are rich or have nice things. We should treat everyone equally, whether they are rich or poor, young or old, or from a different background.

Obey The Rules and Laws

The third commandment talks about breaking the law. It means that we should try our best to obey the rules and laws that are in place to keep us safe and happy. We should respect authority and do what is right.

Don't Judge Others

The fourth commandment talks about not judging others. It means that we should not make fun of or look down on someone just because they are different from us or have made mistakes. We should be understanding and forgiving towards others. We should always speak kindly and avoid saying mean or hurtful things. It's important to use our words to build others up and not tear them down.

Speak With Kindness & Encouragement

The fifth commandment talks about speaking with kindness. It means that we should use our words to encourage and help others, instead of using them to hurt or bring them down. We should think before we speak and choose our words wisely.

James 2:8-11 NIV "If you really keep the royal law found in Scripture, "Love your neighbor as yourself," you are doing right. But if you show favoritism, you sin and are convicted by the law as lawbreakers. For whoever keeps the whole law and yet stumbles at just one point is guilty of breaking all of it. "

Submit Yourself To God

The commandments in James 4:7-11 are about submitting yourself to God. The commandments remind us to listen to God, be strong against bad things, be close to God, be good to others, have kind thoughts, be humble, and use our words for kindness. Following these commandments helps us become better people and make the world a happier place

Let's break the commandments down in a way that is easier for us to understand.

Obey God

This means that we should listen to God and do what He tells us. Just like how you listen to your parents or teachers, we should listen to God because He loves us and knows what is best for us.

Resist The Devil

The devil is like a sneaky bad guy who tries to make us do things that are wrong or not nice. We should be strong and say "no" to the devil when he tries to tempt us. It's like saying "I won't do what you want me to do because it's not right."

Draw Near To God

This means that we should try to be close to God and have a good relationship with Him. We can do this by talking to Him through prayer, reading the Bible, and going to church. When we are close to God, we feel happy and safe.

Cleanse Your Hands

This means that we should try to do things that are good and helpful to others. We should be kind, share our toys, and help our friends and family. Just like when we wash our hands to keep them clean, we should also keep our actions clean by being good to others.

Purify Your Hearts

Our hearts are where our feelings and thoughts are. We should try to have good thoughts and feelings towards others. For example, we should forgive people if they make mistakes and not hold grudges. It's like having a heart that is full of love and kindness.

Be Humble

Being humble means not thinking that we are better than others. We should treat everyone with kindness and respect, no matter who they are. It's like being friendly to everyone and not bragging about ourselves.

Don't Speak Evil Against One Another

This means that we should not say mean or hurtful things about other people. We should use our words to encourage and uplift others. It's like using our words to make people feel happy and loved.

In summary, the commandments from James remind us to listen to God, be strong against bad things, be close to God, be good to others, have kind thoughts, be humble, and use our words for kindness. Following these commandments helps us become better people and make the world a happier place

James 4:7-11 NIV "Submit yourselves, then, to God. Resist the devil, and he will flee from you. Come near to God and he will come near to you. Wash your hands, you sinners, and purify your hearts, you double-minded. Grieve, mourn and wail. Change your laughter to mourning and your joy to gloom. Humble yourselves before the Lord, and he will lift you up. Brothers and sisters, do not slander one another. Anyone who speaks against a brother or sister[d] or judges them speaks against the law and judges it. When you judge the law, you are not keeping it, but sitting in judgment on it."

Be Humble And Respectful Towards God

In James 4:13-15 the commandments are about being humble and respectful toward God. The commandments are telling us not to boast about our future plans, to remember that we can't predict what will happen, and to always acknowledge that God is in control of our lives. It's like a reminder to be humble and respectful towards God and others.

Let's look a little deeper into each commandment to understand it better.

Do Not Boast About Your Future Plans

The first commandment says, "Come now, you who say, 'Today or tomorrow we will go to such and such a city, spend a year there, buy and sell, and make a profit.'"

This means that we shouldn't boast or brag about our plans for the future. We shouldn't say things like, "Oh, I'm going to do this and that, and I'm going to make so much money." It's not nice to show off and act like we know what will happen in the future.

We Can't Predict What Will Happen In The Future

The second commandment says, "Whereas you do not know what will happen tomorrow. For what is your life? It is even a vapor that appears for a little time and then vanishes away."

This means that we can't predict or know what will happen in the future. Our life is like a tiny cloud that appears for a short time and then disappears. So, it's not a good idea to think we have full control over everything because we really don't.

Always Acknowledge God Is In Control Of Everything

The third commandment says, "Instead, you ought to say, 'If the Lord wills, we shall live and do this or that.'"

This means that when we make plans for the future, we should always remember that it's up to God if those plans will happen. We should say things like, "If God allows it, I will do this or that." It's important to show humility and acknowledge that God is in control of everything.

James 4:13-15 NIV "Now listen, you who say, "Today or tomorrow we will go to this or that city, spend a year there, carry on business and make money." Why, you do not even know what will happen tomorrow. What is your life? You are a mist that appears for a little while and then vanishes. Instead, you ought to say, "If it is the Lord's will, we will live and do this or that."

Be Patient Until The Lord's Coming

In James 5:7-12 the commandments are about being patient until the Lord's coming. The commandments are about being patient, not complaining, remembering the prophets, being patient, when you will do something, you do it, and not swearing.

Let's look a little deeper into each commandment so we understand it better, shall we?

Be Patient

Be patient, just like a farmer.

You know how a farmer plants seeds and waits for them to grow into beautiful plants? Well, we should also learn to be patient and wait for good things to happen in our lives. Sometimes, we might want something right away, but it's important to remember that good things take time.

Don't Complain

Don't complain about each other.

It's not nice to say mean things about other people. We should always try to be kind and understanding. If someone does something that upsets us, it's better to talk it out and find a solution instead of complaining or saying hurtful things.

Listen To The Teachings of The Prophets

Remember the prophets.

Prophets are special people who teach us about God's love and guidance. We should listen to their wise words and learn from them. They can teach us how to be good and make good choices in our lives.

Be Strong & Patient

Be patient like Job.

Job was a person in the Bible who had a lot of challenges and tough times, but he stayed strong and patient. We should try to be like him and not give up when things get difficult. It's important to remember that tough times will pass, and good things will come.

When You Say You Will Do Something, Do It

Let your "yes" mean yes and your "no" mean no.

This means that when we say we will do something, we should keep our promise. It's important to be honest and truthful in our words and actions. When we make a promise, we should try our best to keep it.

Do Not Swear

Don't swear.

This doesn't mean not to use bad words, but rather not to make promises or say things we don't really mean. We should always think before we speak and be careful with our words. It's better to be honest and true in what we say.

Using bad words makes us seems less intelligent that we are so using bad words only hurts us in the long run. So even though we don't take this to mean we not using bad words any more, it's still not good to use bad words.

Using bad words is disrespectful to most people still. One of our commandments is to be respectful to those around us, so for that commandment, we still wouldn't use bad words, would we?

James 5:7-12 NIV "Be patient, then, brothers and sisters, until the Lord's coming. See how the farmer waits for the land to yield its valuable crop, patiently waiting for the autumn and spring rains. You too, be patient and stand firm, because the Lord's coming is near. Don't grumble against one another, brothers and sisters, or you will be judged. The Judge is standing at the door! Brothers and sisters, as an example of patience in the face of suffering, take the prophets who spoke in the name of the Lord. As you know, we count as blessed those who have persevered. You have heard of Job's perseverance and have seen what the Lord finally brought about. The Lord is full of compassion and mercy. Above all, my brothers and sisters, do not swear—not by heaven or by earth or by anything else. All you need to say is a simple "Yes" or "No." Otherwise you will be condemned."

Prayer Of A Righteous Person

In James 5:16, it says, "Therefore confess your sins to each other and pray for each other so that you may be healed. The prayer of a righteous person is powerful and effective."

In summary, James 5:16 the commandments teach us to be honest, kind, forgiving, and to pray for one another because the prayer of a righteous person is powerful and effective.

Now, let's break it down into simpler words:

Be Honest

This means always telling the truth and not telling lies. God wants us to be truthful and trustworthy. When you do something wrong or make a mistake, it's important to admit it to someone you trust, like a friend, family member, or even a grown-up. It's about being honest and not keeping secrets.

Be Kind

Being kind means showing love and respect to everyone, including your family, friends, and even people you don't know. It's important to treat others the way you want to be treated.

Forgive Others

Forgiving means letting go of anger or grudges and choosing to be kind even when someone hurts your feelings. It's like giving them a second chance.

Forgiving allows us to Heal. Healing means to feel better. When we confess our mistakes and pray for others, it can help us feel better inside. It's like a way to find peace and forgiveness.

Pray for Each Other

Praying means talking to God. It's important to pray not just for ourselves but also for other people. When we pray for others, it shows that we care about them and want good things for them.

The commandments in James 5:16 tell us God wants us to be honest, kind, forgiving, and to pray for one another. These commandments help us to be good and loving people.

James 5:16 NIV "Therefore confess your sins to each other and pray for each other so that you may be healed. The prayer of a righteous person is powerful and effective."

Be Holy

In simple words, the commandments in 1 Peter 1:13-17 tell us to "Be Holy" and think before we act, be in control of ourselves, trust in Jesus, be good and kind, and not let our old bad habits control us.

Think Before We Act

Be ready to think.

This means that we should always be prepared to use our thinking skills and make good choices. We should think before we act and consider what is right and wrong.

Be In Control Of Ourselves

Be self-controlled.

Self-control means being in charge of our own actions and not letting our feelings or desires control us. It's like being the boss of our own behavior and making sure we do the right thing.

Trust In Jesus

Set your hope fully on the grace of Jesus.

This means that we should believe and trust in Jesus and His love for us. We should have hope and faith in Him and know that He is always with us and will take care of us.

Be Good and Kind

Be holy.

Being holy means being like Jesus and trying our best to do what is good and right. We should be kind, loving, and helpful to others, just like Jesus taught us.

Don't Let Bad Habit Control Us

Don't be shaped by your desires from before you knew God.

This means that we should not let our old bad habits or wrong desires control us. Instead, we should try to make good choices and follow God's teachings.

1 Peter 1:13-17 NIV "Therefore, with minds that are alert and fully sober, set your hope on the grace to be brought to you when Jesus Christ is revealed at his coming. As obedient children, do not conform to the evil desires you had when you lived in ignorance. But just as he who called you is holy, so be holy in all you do; for it is written: "Be holy, because I am holy." Since you call on a Father who judges each person's work impartially, live out your time as foreigners here in reverent fear."

Living In Harmony With One Another

1 Peter 3:8-12 provides commandments for living in harmony with one another. These commandments tell us to be like minded, be sympathetic, to love one another, be compassionate, be humble, to not repay evil with evil or insult with insult, to repay evil with a blessing, to keep your tongue from evil and your lips from deceitful speech, to turn from evil and do good, to turn from evil, to seek peach and pursue it, and finally that God is always watching us.

1 Peter 3:8-12 says, "Finally, all of you, be like-minded, be sympathetic, love one another, be compassionate and humble. Do not repay evil with evil or insult with insult. On the contrary, repay evil with blessing, because to this you were called so that you may inherit a blessing. For, 'Whoever would love life and see good days must keep their tongue from evil and their lips from deceitful speech. They must turn from evil and do good; they must seek peace and pursue it. For the eyes of the Lord are on the righteous and his ears are attentive to their prayer, but the face of the Lord is against those who do evil.'"

There are a lot of commandments in 1 Peter 3:8-12, so let's explain these commandments one by one:

Be Like Minded

This means that we should try to think and agree on things together, like having similar thoughts or opinions. We should try to understand and care about what other people are feeling. We should treat others with love, kindness, and respect. We should also be humble, which means not thinking we are better than anyone else.

Be Sympathetic

This means that we should show understanding and kindness to others when they are going through a difficult time or feeling sad. even if someone is mean to us, we shouldn't be mean back. Instead, we should be kind and forgive them. We should respond with good words and actions, even if others are not nice to us.

Love One Another

We should care for and show love to everyone around us, like our family, friends, and even people we might not know very well.

Be Compassionate

This means we should have a heart that cares about others and wants to help them when they are in need.

Be Humble

We should not brag or think we are better than others. Instead, we should be modest and treat everyone with respect.

Do Not Repay Evil With Evil Or Insult With Insult

If someone treats us badly or says mean things, we should not try to hurt them back. Instead, we should respond with kindness and forgiveness. Even if someone is mean to us, we shouldn't be mean back. Instead, we should be kind and forgive them. We should respond with good words and actions, even if others are not nice to us.

Repay Evil With Blessing

Instead of being mean to someone who is mean to us, we should do something nice for them. This way, we can show them the right way to behave and hopefully make them feel better.

Don't Say Mean Or Hurtful Things

This means we should not say mean or hurtful things to others, and we should always tell the truth. We should be careful with our words. We should not say mean or hurtful things to others. Instead, we should speak truthfully and kindly.

Turn From Evil & Do Good

We should stay away from doing bad things and focus on doing good things that help others and make the world a better place.

Seek Peace & Pursue It

We should always try to make peace and keep the peace between us. We should do good things and try to bring peace to the world. We should always try to make things better and not cause harm.

God Is Always Watching Us

The last commandment in 1 Peter 3:8-12 says, "For the eyes of the Lord are on the righteous and his ears are attentive to their prayer, but the face of the Lord is against those who do evil." This means that God is always watching us. When we do good things and follow these commandments, God is happy with us. But if we do bad things, God is not pleased.

1 Peter 3:8-12 NIV "Finally, all of you, be like-minded, be sympathetic, love one another, be compassionate and humble. Do not repay evil with evil or insult with insult. On the contrary, repay evil with blessing, because to this you were called so that you may inherit a blessing. For "Whoever would love life
  and see good days
must keep their tongue from evil
  and their lips from deceitful speech. They must turn from evil and do good;
  they must seek peace and pursue it. For the eyes of the Lord are on the righteous
  and his ears are attentive to their prayer,
but the face of the Lord is against those who do evil."

Explain Why You Believe In God

The commandments in Peter 3:15-17 are telling us to be ready to explain why we believe in God, to be kind and polite to others, to always do the right thing, and to show others how good we are.

Love God

God wants us to love Him with all our hearts. He is our creator and loves us very much. We can show our love by talking to Him, praying, and thanking Him for all the good things in our lives.

Be Ready To Explain Why You Believe In God

God wants us to be ready to explain to others why we believe in Him and why we have hope in our hearts. This means that if someone asks us about our faith or wants to know more about God, we should be able to tell them in a kind and gentle way.

Be Kind & Respectful

God wants us to be kind and respectful to everyone we meet. This means treating others the way we want to be treated. We should use kind words, share, help others, and be a good friend. We should treat them nicely and not be mean or rude.

Do Good & Avoid Evil

God wants us to do good things and avoid doing things that are not right. We should always try to make good choices and be honest, even when no one is watching. We should also try to help others and be a good example for them.

This part of the verse says, "Keeping a clear conscience." A clear conscience means that we should try to always do the right thing and not feel guilty about it. We should listen to our hearts and follow what we know is right and good.

Trust In God

God wants us to trust Him and have faith in Him. This means believing that He is always with us, guiding and protecting us. We can trust that He loves us and wants the best for us, even when things are difficult.

Always Show Others How Good We Are

Lastly, this part of the verse says, "so that those who speak maliciously against your good behavior in Christ may be ashamed of their slander." This part of the verse means that when we act in a good and kind way, even if others say mean things about us, they will realize that they were wrong. Our good behavior can make them feel sorry for saying bad things about us.

1 Peter 3:15-17 NIV "But in your hearts revere Christ as Lord. Always be prepared to give an answer to everyone who asks you to give the reason for the hope that you have. But do this with gentleness and respect, keeping a clear conscience, so that those who speak maliciously against your good behavior in Christ may be ashamed of their slander. For it is better, if it is God's will, to suffer for doing good than for doing evil."

Living For The Will Of God

In 1 Peter 4:1-15 shares with us commandments about Living For The Will of God. These commands teach us things like: Be ready to suffer, Don't give in to sin, Love and serve others, use your gifts to help, be hospitable, speak good words, and use everything for God's glory.

But what do all of these mean? Let's dig in a little deeper and find out, shall we?

Be Ready To Suffer

Be ready to suffer: Peter tells us that sometimes in life, we might face difficult or challenging situations. But he encourages us to be strong and keep going, even when things are tough.

Don't Give In To Sin

Don't give in to sin: Peter asks us to remember not to do things that are wrong or hurtful to others. Instead, he wants us to always try to do what is right and make good choices.

Love & Serve Others

Love and serve others: Peter tells us to love and care for one another. This means being kind, helpful, and treating others the way we want to be treated. We should do nice things for others and try to make them happy.

Use Your Gifts To Help

Use your gifts to help: Peter also tells us that each of us has special talents or abilities. He wants us to use these gifts to help others and make the world a better place. So, if you are good at drawing, you can make beautiful pictures to brighten someone's day. If you are good at singing, you can use your voice to bring joy to others.

Be Hospitable

Be hospitable: Peter says to welcome others into our homes and lives. This means being friendly and making people feel welcome and comfortable when they visit us. We should share with them and show them kindness.

Speak Good Words

Speak good words: Peter asks us to use our words wisely. We should speak kindly and not say mean things or hurt others' feelings. Our words should be helpful and make others feel good about themselves.

Use Everything For God's Glory

Use everything for God's glory: Peter reminds us that everything we have is a gift from God. Whether it's our toys, our abilities, or our time, we should use them in a way that pleases God and brings honor to Him.

1 Peter 4:1-15 NIV "Therefore, since Christ suffered in his body, arm yourselves also with the same attitude, because whoever suffers in the body is done with sin. As a result, they do not live the rest of their earthly lives for evil human desires, but rather for the will of God. For you have spent enough time in the past doing what pagans choose to do—living in debauchery, lust, drunkenness, orgies, carousing and detestable idolatry. They are surprised that you do not join them in their reckless, wild living, and they heap abuse on you. But they will have to give account to him who is ready to judge the living and the dead. For this is the reason the gospel was preached even to those who are now dead, so that they might be judged according to human standards in regard to the body, but live according to God in regard to the spirit. The end of all things is near. Therefore be alert and of sober mind so that you may pray. Above all, love each other deeply, because love covers over a multitude of sins. Offer hospitality to one another without grumbling. Each of you should use whatever gift you have received to serve others, as faithful stewards of God's grace in its various forms. If anyone speaks, they should do so as one who speaks the very words of God. If anyone serves, they should do so with the strength God provides, so that in all things God may be praised through Jesus Christ. To him be the glory and the power for ever and ever. Amen. Dear friends, do not be surprised at the fiery ordeal that has come on you to test you, as though something strange were happening to you. But rejoice inasmuch as you participate in the sufferings of Christ, so that you may be overjoyed when his glory is revealed. If you are insulted because of the name of Christ, you are blessed, for the Spirit of glory and of God rests on you. If you suffer, it should not be as a murderer or thief or any other kind of criminal, or even as a meddler."

Grown-Ups Have Wisdom To Share

In 1 Peter 5:5-9, the commandments from God tell us grown-ups have lots of wisdom to share with you and they remind us to be humble, not worry too much, be alert, and remember that God is always with us. They help us to live a good and happy life, treating others kindly and trusting in God's love.

1 Peter 5:4-9 tells us, "Listen to the grown-ups and be respectful to them. They have lots of wisdom to share with you. When you're humble, it means you don't think you're better than others. Instead, you think about how you can help and be kind to everyone around you. Remember, God loves you and wants to take care of you, so give all your worries to Him. Be strong and don't let scary things make you afraid. Trust in God, and He will help you stay safe."

Let's dig a little deeper into 1 Peter 5:4-9 to understand these commandments better.

Be Humble

The first commandment is to be humble.

Humility means not thinking you are better or more important than others. God wants us to treat everyone with kindness and respect, just like how we want to be treated.

"Become clothed with humility towards one another, because God opposes the proud but gives grace to the humble." - 1 Peter 5:5

Be Careful & Don't Worry

The second commandment is to be careful and not worry too much.

Sometimes, we might have worries or fears, but we can give all those worries to God. He loves us and cares for us, so we don't need to be afraid.

"Casting all your anxiety on him, because he cares about you." - 1 Peter 5:7

Be Alert & Watch For Bad Things

The third commandment is to be alert and watch out for bad things.

There might be times when we feel sad or angry, but we shouldn't let those feelings control us. Instead, we should be strong and have self-control.

"Be sober-minded and alert. Your adversary the devil prowls around like a roaring lion, seeking someone to devour." - 1 Peter 5:8

You Are Not Alone, God Is Always With You

The fourth commandment is to always remember that we are not alone. God is always with us, even when we face difficult times. We can trust Him and know that He will take care of us.

"Resist him, firm in your faith, knowing that the same kinds of suffering are being experienced by your brotherhood throughout the world." - 1 Peter 5:9

So, remember these commandments from God remind us to be humble, not worry too much, be alert, and remember that God is always with us. They help us to live a good and happy life, treating others kindly and trusting in God's love.

1 Peter 5:5-9 NIV "In the same way, you who are younger, submit yourselves to your elders. All of you, clothe yourselves with humility toward one another, because, 'God opposes the proud but shows favor to the humble.' Humble yourselves, therefore, under God's mighty hand, that he may lift you up in due time. Cast all your anxiety on him because he cares for you. Be alert and of sober mind. Your enemy the devil prowls around like a roaring lion looking for someone to devour. Resist him, standing firm in the faith, because you know that the family of believers throughout the world is undergoing the same kind of sufferings."

Be Spotless, Blameless & At Peace With God

2 Peter 3:14 says, 'So then, dear friends, since you are looking forward to this, make every effort to be found spotless, blameless and at peace with him.' This means that we should try our best to live good lives, without doing anything wrong, and to be peaceful with God.

Although 2 Peter 3:14 doesn't list specific commandments from God, but it does tell us how we should live our lives.

Let me explain it to you in a way that is easy to understand.

The Bible teaches us that God loves us very much and wants us to live in a special way that makes Him happy. So where 2 Peter 3:14, it says, "Make every effort to be found spotless, blameless and at peace with him.", we need to be found spotless, blameless, and at peace with Him, who is God.

Spotless

This means we should try our best to keep our hearts and minds clean by being kind and loving to others. We should avoid doing things that hurt others or ourselves.

Blameless

This means we should try to do what is right and follow God's teachings. We should be honest, respectful, and obey our parents and teachers. We should treat everyone with kindness and fairness.

At Peace With Him

This means we should have a good relationship with God. We can talk to Him through prayer and listen to His words in the Bible. We should trust Him and believe in His love for us.

So, these verses remind us to live a good life by being kind, doing what is right, and having a close relationship with God. This will make God happy and bring peace to our hearts.

2 Peter 3:14 NIV " 'So then, dear friends, since you are looking forward to this, make every effort to be found spotless, blameless and at peace with him.' This means that we should try our best to live good lives, without doing anything wrong, and to be peaceful with God."

Grow in Grace & Knowledge

2 Peter 3:18. It says, "But grow in the grace and knowledge of our Lord and Savior Jesus Christ. To him be glory both now and forever! Amen."

In this verse, 2 Peter 3:18, Peter is telling us something important. He is giving us commandments from God that God wants us to grow in two things: grace and knowledge.

Let's explore these commandments a little deeper to learn about Grace and Knowledge.

Grow In God's Grace

First, let's talk about grace. Grace means God's love and kindness towards us, even when we make mistakes. It's like when you do something wrong, but your parents still love you and forgive you. God's grace is even bigger and better than that! Peter wants us to grow in experiencing and understanding God's grace more and more.

Grow In Knowledge of Jesus

Second, knowledge means learning and understanding things. Peter wants us to grow in knowing more about our Lord and Savior Jesus Christ. Just like you learn new things every day, like math or science, Peter wants us to learn more about Jesus and how awesome He is.

So, the commandment here is to keep growing in God's grace and knowledge of Jesus. It's like a reminder for us to keep learning about God and how much He loves us, and to keep growing in being kind and loving to others.

Remember, God loves you so much and wants you to keep growing in His grace and knowledge. Let's give Him glory by doing that, now and forever! Amen!

2 Peter 3:18 NIV "But grow in the grace and knowledge of our Lord and Savior Jesus Christ. To him be glory both now and forever! Amen."

Don't Love Anything More Than You Love God

In 1 John 2:15 we are given a commandment to "not love the world or anything in the world because love for the Father is not in them". But what does this mean?

In simple words, it means that we should not love the things of this world too much. What are the things of this world? Well, it means we should not love things like toys, candy, or video games more than we love God.

Now, this doesn't mean that we can't enjoy these things. It's okay to have fun and play with toys or eat candy, but we should not let them become the most important things in our lives. Instead, we should love God the most because He is our Heavenly Father.

So, it's like saying that we need to remember that God is the most important and should always come first in our hearts. We can still have fun with toys and enjoy other things, but God should be the most important love in our lives.

1 John 2:15 NIV "Do not love the world or anything in the world. If anyone loves the world, love for the Father is not in them."

Reminder To Keep Following Jesus

The Bible verse is 1 John 2:28, and it says: "And now, dear children, continue in him, so that when he appears we may be confident and unashamed before him at his coming."

Overall, this verse is a reminder to keep following Jesus, but what exactly does this mean to us? Let's take a closer look at this verse.

Stay Close To Jesus

This verse in 1 John 2:28 is a reminder for us to stay close to Jesus. It's like having a best friend who we want to always be with. So, John, who wrote this verse, says that we should keep following Jesus and staying connected to him.

Keep Believing In Jesus

When it says "continue in him," it means that we should keep believing in Jesus and doing the things that he taught us. We can do this by praying, reading the Bible, and trying to be kind to others, just like Jesus was.

Be Proud Of Yourself For Believing In Jesus

The verse also talks about being confident and unashamed when Jesus comes back. It's like when we do something good and we feel proud of ourselves because we know we did the right thing. We want to be like that when Jesus returns, so we won't feel ashamed but instead happy and confident because we have been doing what he wants us to do.

Remember to keep following Jesus! It's like having the coolest person ever as your best friend, And Jesus will always be with you, guiding you to make good choices.

1 John 2:28 NIV "And now, dear children, continue in him, so that when he appears we may be confident and unashamed before him at his coming."

A CHILDREN'S GUIDE TO A GODLY WAY OF LIFE

How To Know Who Are God's Children

The Bible verse in 1 John 3:10-23 starts off telling us how to know who children of God are and who the children of the devil are. It tells us plainly that "anyone who does not do what is right is not God's child, nor anyone who does not love their brother or sister".

But, what does all of this mean to us as a "children" mean? Let's take a much deeper look at this to find out, shall we?

Love Each Other

Love Each Other

The Bible tells us that we should love our brothers and sisters. That means we should be kind, helpful, and treat others the way we want to be treated. These verses and all through the Bible it tells us to "Love Each Other". It is the reason God sent His son Jesus back to earth for us, Love. God wanted us to know what real love was. To be one of God's children, we have to love each other.

Don't Be Like Bad People

Don't Be Like the Bad People

We should not act like the bad people who do bad things. We should be good and do what is right.

Help Those In Need

Help Those in Need

If we see someone who needs help, we should try our best to help them. It could be as simple as sharing our toys or comforting someone who is sad.

Believe In Jesus

Believe in Jesus

We need to believe in Jesus and trust Him. He loves us and wants us to follow Him.

Obey God's Commandments

Obey God's Commands

God wants us to follow His rules. God's rules are His commandments. We should listen to our parents, be honest, and not say mean things to others.

Show Love For Others With Our Actions

Love Others with Actions

It's not enough to say we love others, we need to show it through our actions. We can do this by sharing, being kind, and forgiving others when they make mistakes.

Trust in Jesus

Believe in Jesus' Name

To believe in Jesus' name, we must trust in Jesus and have faith in Him. He is the one who can save us and make us better people.

A CHILDREN'S GUIDE TO A GODLY WAY OF LIFE

Love One Another The Way God Loves Us

Love One Another

We should love everyone around us, just like how God loves us. We can show love by being patient, understanding, and helping others.

These commandments are meant to help us both become better children of God and to help us know who are children of God.

Also, if someone says they believe in God but they aren't doing these things, then they really aren't children of God or they haven't quite gotten to the point in their lives where they are children of God. We know we may not be able to trust the things they say as being completely true yet and we can help them understand and believe in God because we are children of God and know these things about being children of God.

1 John 3:10-23 NIV "This is how we know who the children of God are and who the children of the devil are: Anyone who does not do what is right is not God's child, nor is anyone who does not love their brother and sister. For this is the message you heard from the beginning: We should love one another. Do not be like Cain, who belonged to the evil one and murdered his brother. And why did he murder him? Because his own actions were evil and his brother's were righteous. Do not be surprised, my brothers and sisters, if the world hates you. We know that we have passed from death to life, because we love each other. Anyone who does not love remains in death.

Anyone who hates a brother or sister is a murderer, and you know that no murderer has eternal life residing in him. This is how we know what love is: Jesus Christ laid down his life for us. And we ought to lay down our lives for our brothers and sisters. If anyone has material possessions and sees a brother or sister in need but has no pity on them, how can the love of God be in that person? Dear children, let us not love with words or speech but with actions and in truth. This is how we know that we belong to the truth and how we set our hearts at rest in his presence: If our hearts condemn us, we know that God is greater than our hearts, and he knows everything. Dear friends, if our hearts do not condemn us, we have confidence before God and receive from him anything we ask, because we keep his commands and do what pleases him. And this is his command: to believe in the name of his Son, Jesus Christ, and to love one another as he commanded us."

Test What You Hear To Know It's From God

In 1 John 4:1, John is writing a letter to children like you, and he wants to give you an important commandment. He says that you should be careful about what you believe. Not everything you hear is true or comes from God, so it's essential to test it.

Testing means that you should ask yourself some questions:

Is what you heard good and kind?

Does it match with the things God teaches us in the Bible?

Does it make you feel happy and peaceful inside?

If the answer is "yes" to these questions, then it's likely from God.

But if the answer is "no" or you feel confused, it might not be from God.

1 John 4:1 NIV "Dear children, do not believe everything you hear. Instead, test what you hear to see if it is from God or not."

How We Should Love Others

1 John 4:7-8 is all about how we should love others, just like how God loves us. So, let's break it down in a way that you can understand, okay?

Love Comes From God

Love Comes from God

God is all about love! He is the biggest, most amazing source of love in the whole wide world. When we love others, it's like we're sharing a piece of God's love with them.

Spread Love Everywhere To Everyone

Everyone Should Love

God wants everyone to love each other. That means we should treat everyone with kindness, respect, and care. We should be like little love superheroes, spreading love everywhere we go!

Knowing God Is Knowing Love

Knowing God = Knowing Love

When we know God, we also know what love is all about. It's like learning how to be a loving person by looking at God as the perfect example. God is love, and that's pretty awesome!

If You Don't Love, You Don't Know God

If You Don't Love, You Don't Know God

If someone doesn't love others, it means they don't really know God. God wants us to be loving, and if we're not, then we're missing out on something really special.

It pretty easy to understand when it's explained this way, isn't it?

The most important thing is to remember to love others. That's what God wants most from all of us. So, let's go out there and spread love like confetti! Sprinkle a little of it around everywhere you go!

1 John4:7-8 NIV "Beloved, let us love one another, for love is from God, and whoever loves has been born of God and knows God. Anyone who does not love does not know God, because God is love."

Loving Others & Loving God

Everything in the Bible book of John is about love, as we are seeing, right? In the verses in 1 John 4:11-12, we have commandments about loving others and loving God.

Let's dive into these two commandments in this verse.

Love One Another As God Loves Us

Love Each Other

The first commandment in 1 John 4:11-12 is to love each other. This means being kind, caring, and nice to everyone around you. Just like how God loves us, we should show love to our family, friends, and even people we don't know very well. Love makes the world a better place! Love is so super important!

Love Comes From God

Love Comes from God

The second commandment says that love comes from God.

God is the source of all love and He showed us His love by sending Jesus to save us. So, when we love others, we are actually sharing God's love with them! Isn't that amazing?

No One Has Seen God

No One Has Seen God

The third commandment tells us that no one has seen God. We can't see Him with our eyes, but we can feel His love in our hearts. So, even though we can't see Him, we can still love Him by loving others. When we love, we show that we believe in God and His love for us.

Love One Another

Love One Another

The fourth commandment in 1 John4:11-12 reminds us to love one another. When we love others, God's love lives in us. And when His love lives in us, it shines through us and makes us happy. So, let's be loving to everyone we meet and spread God's love all around!

God Lives In Our Heart

God Lives In Us

Where it says "God lives in us.", it means that when we love others, God's love shines through us. So, when you do nice things for people, it's like showing them God's love and making them feel happy.

Remember, these commandments teach us how to love just like God loves us. They are like a special guide to help us be kind, caring, and show love to others. By following these commandments, we can make the world a better place and make God proud.

So, let's always remember to love each other and share God's love with eve

Isn't that cool? God wants us to love others just like He loves us. So, always try your best to be loving and show kindness to everyone you meet. This way, you'll be following the commandments from 1 John 4:11-12.

Remember, love is a superpower that we can all have, and it makes the world a better place. So, go out there and spread some love!

1 John 4:11-12 NIV "Dear friends, since God so loved us, we also ought to love one another. No one has ever seen God; but if we love one another, God lives in us and his love is made complete in us."

Believe & Say Jesus Is God's Son

In the Bible verse 1 John 4:15-16 God gives us more commandments about loving God, believing in Jesus, loving others, and God living in us once we acknowledge or really believe the Jesus is God's son.

Overall, this verse is saying that if we believe and say that Jesus is God's Son, then God lives inside us and we live in God too. It means that when we believe in Jesus, we become connected to God and He loves us very much. We can trust and depend on God's love for us because it is always there.

Let's take a little deeper look into what God is talking about with these verses and commandments. Ready?

Love God

Love God:

You know how we love our family and friends? Well, we should also love God because He loves us so much. He is like our heavenly Father who always takes care of us.

Believe Jesus Is God's Son

Believe in Jesus:

Jesus is God's special Son who came to earth to show us how much God loves us. We need to believe in Him and trust Him, just like we trust our parents or teachers.

Love Others As God Loves Us

Love Others:

Just like we love our family and friends, we should also love everyone around us. God wants us to be kind, helpful, and treat others the way we want to be treated.

God Lives In Your Heart

God Lives in Us:

When we believe in Jesus and love others, God lives inside our hearts. He helps us be good and makes us feel warm and happy inside.

Where it says "God lives in us", remember we talked about before imagining you have a very special friend who loves you very much. This friend is always with you, even when you can't see them. They live right inside your hear?

In the same way, the Bible tells us that God, who is like the best friend we could ever have, lives inside us too. He loves us so much that He wants to be close to us all the time.

When we are kind to others, share our toys, or help someone in need, it's like we are showing God's love to the world. It's like we are letting God's light shine through us, just like a flashlight shines in the dark.

God is love, and when we let His love shine through us, it makes us feel happy and brings joy to others. So, when we hear that "God lives in us," it means that His love is always with us, guiding us to do good things and be kind to others.

Remember, this verse 1 John 4:15-16. It reminds us to love God, believe in Jesus, love others, and know that God lives in us when we do these things.

1 John 4:15-15 NIV "If anyone acknowledges that Jesus is the Son of God, God lives in them and they in God. And so we know and rely on the love God has for us. God is love. Whoever lives in love lives in God, and God in them."

Love Everyone As Much As We Love Our Family

In 1 John 4:21, God gives us this seemingly same command again as a commandment, that "Anyone who loves God must also love their brothers and sisters".

What does this really mean to us and why is it important to us?

This verse tells us that God has given us a special commandment. The commandment is that if we love God, it is important for us to also love our brothers and sisters.

When we say "brothers and sisters," it doesn't just mean our siblings, but it means everyone around us. We should treat everyone with kindness, respect, and love, just like we would treat our own family members. God has taken it a step further this time, hasn't He?

God is now saying we have to love others as much as we love our own families, isn't He? That's a lot of love we have to show to people we don't know or people who may not even like us, isn't it?

Remember, it's important to love and care for others as much as we do our family because that's what God wants us to do.

1 John 4:21 NIV "And he has given us this command: Anyone who loves God must also love their brother and sister."

Nothing Has Importance Over God

In the Bible, 1 John 5:21 it says, "Dear children, keep yourselves from idols." This means that we should be careful not to worship or give too much importance to things that are not God. Idols can be objects or activities that distract us from loving and obeying God.

God wants us to love Him above all else and put Him first in our lives. He doesn't want us to worship anything or anyone other than Him. Some examples of idols could be toys, video games, or even wanting to be popular or look a certain way. These things are not bad in themselves, but when we start to care about them more than God, it becomes a problem.

So, the commandment in 1 John 5:21 is a reminder for us to always remember that God is the most important and to not let anything else take His place in our hearts. We should love, trust, and follow Him with all our hearts.

Remember, God loves us very much and wants what is best for us. So, let's keep ourselves from idols and focus on loving and obeying God above everything else!

1 John 5:21 NIV "Little children, keep yourselves from idols."

Doing What Is Good

3 John 1:11, and it says, "Dear friend, do not imitate what is evil but what is good. Anyone who does what is good is from God. Anyone who does what is evil has not seen God."

Do Not Copy Bad Things

Let's talk about this Bible verse. It says that we should not copy or do bad things, but instead, we should do good things. When we do good things, it means we are following God and showing that we know Him. But if we do bad things, it means we haven't really known God yet.

Copy Good Things

This verse also tells us to "imitate … what is good. Anyone who does what is good is from God." When we do the things that Jesus taught us to do, the way Jesus taught us to do things while He was here on earth and we follow God's commandments, we are imitating what is good, aren't we? Copying or imitating what is good is showing God that we understand what He wants us to do, isn't it? God likes it when we do the right thing and live in a Godly Way for Him.

Following God's commandments is living our lives in a Godly Way, the way He wants us to live, isn't it? So when we do what the commandments tell us to do we are living a Godly Way of Life and when we copy or do the things Jesus did with the way He handled things like Anger or Forgiving people or dealing with other things He had to do when He was here on the earth, we are living our lives in a Godly Way, and God is very happy we copy or imitate what is good.

3 John 1:11 NIV "Dear friend, do not imitate what is evil but what is good. Anyone who does what is good is from God. Anyone who does what is evil has not seen God."

Building You Faith

Jude 1:20-23 gives us four commandments to help us build our faith. These commandments are about continuing to building your faith, showing God's love, staying away from bad things, and helping others who are struggling.

Keep Building Your Faith

Keep Building your Faith up:

Just like when we play with blocks or Legos, we can build things up, like a tower or a house. The first commandment is to build ourselves up. This means we should try to become better and stronger in our faith and love for God. Now, what does that mean really? Well, it's like building a strong and sturdy house. Just like you need a solid foundation for a house, you also need a strong foundation for your faith.

Imagine your faith is like a house. You want it to be strong and unshakable, right? So, how do you build it up? You do that by learning more about God, His teachings, and His love for us. You can do this by reading the Bible, going to Sunday school, or talking to your parents and teachers about God.

Pray In The Holy Spirit

Pray in the Holy Spirit:

Prayer is like talking to God. The second commandment is to "pray in the Holy Spirit". It means we should talk to God with a pure heart and ask for His help and guidance. The Holy Spirit can help us pray in the right way.

Prayer is like talking to God. It's important because it helps us connect with Him and grow closer to Him. When you pray, you can thank God for all the good things in your life, ask for help when you're feeling sad or scared, and even just have a conversation with Him like you would with a friend.

Keep Yourselves In God's Love

Keep yourselves in God's love:

God loves us so much, and He wants us to love Him too. The third commandment is to always stay in God's love. We can do this by obeying His commandments and showing kindness and love to others.

Where the verse says, "keep yourselves in God's love." This means that we should always remember that God loves us so much. He cares for us and wants what's best for us. So, we should try to live in a way that pleases Him. We can do this by being kind to others, helping those in need, and following His commandments.

Show Mercy To Others

Show mercy to others:

Mercy means being kind and forgiving to people, even when they make mistakes or do something wrong. The fourth commandment is to show mercy to others, just like God shows mercy to us. We should forgive and help others when they need it.

Help Others In Need

Save others from danger:

Imagine if your friend was about to touch something hot and you warned them to stop. The fifth commandment is to help save others from danger. We need to care about others and try to keep them safe, both physically and spiritually.

So, these are the commandments from Jude 1:20-23. They remind us to build ourselves up, pray in the Holy Spirit, stay in God's love, show mercy to others, and help save others from danger.

Following God's commandments can help us become better and happier people.

Jude 1:20-23 NIV "But you, dear friends, by building yourselves up in your most holy faith and praying in the Holy Spirit, keep yourselves in God's love as you wait for the mercy of our Lord Jesus Christ to bring you to eternal life. Be merciful to those who doubt; save others by snatching them from the fire; to others show mercy, mixed with fear—hating even the clothing stained by corrupted flesh."

Be Ready For Jesus To Come Back To Earth

In Revelation 3:11 Jesus tells us some commandments for when He is coming back to earth one day. Jesus wants us to be ready for Hm to come back, He wants us to live in a way that pleases Him, He wants us to hold on to our Faith, His teachings and not let go of our belief in God and the love He has for us, and also to stay faithful to Him and keep following His commandments so we can get into Heaven.

This is a lot of commandments so let's break these commandments down to make them easier to understand.

Jesus Is Coming Soon

"I am coming soon":

This means that Jesus is telling us that He will come back to Earth one day. He wants us to be ready and live in a way that pleases Him.

Hold On To Your Beliefs

"Hold on to what you have":

Jesus wants us to hold on tightly to the good things we have, like our faith in Him and His teachings. It means we should not let go of our belief in God and the love He has for us.

Stay Faithful to God

"So that no one will take your crown":

The word "crown" represents the reward we will receive from God if we stay faithful to Him. Jesus wants us to keep doing good things and following His commandments so that nobody can take away the special reward we will get in Heaven.

So, to summarize, Jesus is telling us to stay faithful, hold on to our beliefs, and keep doing good things until He comes back. This way, we can receive a special reward from God that nobody can take away.

Revelation 3:11 NIV "I am coming soon. Hold on to what you have, so that no one will take your crown."

Be Eager To Do Right

In Revelation 3:18-19, Jesus is commanding us to value things that are important to Him over things that are important to the world such as gold and being rich. It isn't always easy to read between the lines to follow Jesus's line of thinking when He says it in ways like this "I advise you to buy gold from me, pure and shining, so that you become rich. Also buy white clothes from me…".

Let's break these down and make them easier to understand.

Value Things That Are Important To Jesus

Buy gold from God.

This means to value things that are important to Him, like being kind, honest, and loving. These values will make you rich in a different way - rich in goodness and happiness.

Buy White Clothes From God & Wear Them

Buy white clothes from God and wear them.

This means to choose to do good things and make good choices, so you can cover up any mistakes or things you might feel ashamed of. It's like wearing a beautiful, clean outfit that shows you're trying to be your best.

Ask God For Wisdom & Understanding

Buy medicine to put on your eyes, so you can see clearly.

This means to ask God for wisdom and understanding, so you can make good choices and see things the way He wants you to see them. It's like putting on special glasses that help you see things clearly.

God Corrects & Punishes Us Because He Loves Us

Remember, God loves you very much. Sometimes, when you do something wrong, He might correct you or show you the right way to do things. It's because He cares about you and wants you to grow into a good and kind person. So, always be eager to do what is right and change your heart to be better.

Revelation 3:18-19 NIV 'I advise you to buy gold from me, pure and shining, so that you will become rich. Also, buy white clothes from me and wear them, so you can cover your shameful nakedness. And buy medicine to put on your eyes, so you will be able to see. I correct and punish those I love. So be eager to do right and change your hearts.'

Thirsty for God's Love

The Bible verse Revelation 22:17 is telling us that when we are thirsty for God's love and forgiveness, we should go to Him. And once we have received His love, we should share it with others and invite them to experience it too. God wants everyone to know His love and have a chance to receive it.

Go To God When We Need His Love & Forgiveness

1. The first commandment is about being thirsty. It says that if we are thirsty for God's love and forgiveness, we should come to Him. Just like when we are really thirsty for a drink, we go to get some water, we should go to God when we need His love and forgiveness.

Share God's Love & Forgiveness

2. The second commandment is about inviting others. It says that if we have found God's love and forgiveness, we should tell others about it. It's like when we find a really cool toy or discover a yummy treat, we want to share it with our friends and family. God wants us to do the same and share His love with others.

Come Receive God's Love & Forgiveness

3. The third commandment is about receiving God's gift. It says that if anyone wants to have God's love and forgiveness, they can come and receive it. It's like when someone gives us a present, we can choose to accept it with joy. God's love and forgiveness are the best gifts we can ever receive!

Revelation 22:17 NIV "The Spirit and the bride say, 'Come!' And let the one who hears say, 'Come!' Let the one who is thirsty come; and let the one who wishes take the free gift of the water of life."

Death

Jesus taught us that death is not the end, but a new beginning. He told us that when we die, our souls will live on forever with Him in heaven.

What did Jesus teach us about death? Jesus taught us that death is not the end, but a new beginning. He told us that when we die, our souls will live on forever with Him in heaven. Even though death may feel sad and scary, Jesus gives us hope and comfort by promising eternal life.

Death Isn't The End, But A New Beginning

1. John 11:25-26 - Jesus said, "I am the resurrection and the life. The one who believes in me will live, even though they die; and whoever lives by believing in me will never die."

This means that even though our bodies may stop working and we pass away, our spirits will continue to live with Jesus forever. Jesus is the source of life, and trusting in Him brings us everlasting life.

John 11:25-26 NIV Jesus said to her, "I am the resurrection and the life. The one who believes in me will live, even though they die; and whoever lives by believing in me will never die. Do you believe this?"

Our Souls Live forever In Heaven If We Believe In Jesus

2. John 14:2-3 - Jesus said, "My Father's house has many rooms; if that were not so, would I have told you that I am going there to prepare a place for you? And if I go and prepare a place for you, I will come back and take you to be with me, that you also may be where I am."

Jesus assures us that He is preparing a special place for us in heaven. When we die, He will come to take us there so we can be with Him forever. This shows His love and care for us, even after death.

John 14:2-3 NIV My Father's house has many rooms; if that were not so, would I have told you that I am going there to prepare a place for you? And if I go and prepare a place for you, I will come back and take you to be with me that you also may be where I am.

Jesus Comforts Us When We Are Sad

3. Matthew 5:4 - Jesus said, "Blessed are those who mourn, for they will be comforted."

When someone we love dies, it's natural to feel sad and miss them. But Jesus promises to comfort us during those difficult times. He understands our grief and is always there to bring us peace and solace.

Matthew 5:4 NIV Blessed are those who mourn, for they will be comforted.

Remember, even though death can be hard to understand, Jesus wants us to trust Him and have faith that He has a wonderful plan for us even after we pass away. We can find hope and comfort in His teachings, knowing that He loves us and will be with us forever.

How Jesus Dealt With Death

The Bible gives us an example of how Jesus dealt with death in how He deals with learning of John the Baptist's death. Jesus and John The Baptist were cousins and they were very close friends as well.

We know they were cousins because Luke 1:36 tells us that Elizabeth, John's mother, is a cousin of Mary's, Jesus's Mother.

Luke 1:36 KJV And, behold, thy cousin Elisabeth, she hath also conceived a son in her old age: and this is the sixth month with her, who was called barren.

We also know John was the one who baptized Jesus in the Jordan. John and those in the vicinity witnessed the heavens open and the Holy Spirit descend like a dove. They heard the declaration of God's beloved son. Jesus and John were close.

I really love reading this passage because I can see it in my mind so well. I can just imagine how everyone present that day must have felt watching and hearing it must have felt and the impression it left with them for the rest of their lives.

Matthew 3:13-17 NIV, Then Jesus came from Galilee to the Jordan to be baptized by John. But John tried to deter him, saying, "I need to be baptized by you, and do you come to me?" Jesus replied, "Let it be so now; it is proper for us to do this to fulfill all righteousness." Then John consented. As soon as Jesus was baptized, he went up out of the water. At that moment heaven was opened, and he saw the Spirit of God descending like a dove and alighting on him. And a voice from heaven said, "This is my Son, whom I love; with him I am well pleased."

The first thing Jesus does when He hears the news of John's death in Mark 6:30-32, is to go through the first stage of grief, isolation. As Jesus often does when He isolates Himself, He is taking time to pray, not isolate himself out of despair or hopelessness. This is the first thing we can learn from Jesus. Jesus takes time in the mornings, and evenings to isolate Himself for prayer everyday so in His time of grief, He does the same thing when He learned of the death of a family member, He isolated Himself for a time of prayer, a time with God.

Mark 6:30-32 The apostles returned to Jesus and told him all that they had done and taught. And he said to them, "Come away by yourselves to a desolate place and rest a while." For many were coming and going, and they had no leisure even to eat. And they went away in the boat to a desolate place by themselves.

The next thing Jesus did, was spend time in healing and service to others. In Mark 6:34, it tells us "they were like sheep without a shepherd. And he began to teach them many things." Jesus got right back to doing what He was sent here to do, "he began to teach them many things?

Mark 6:34 KJV, And Jesus, when he came out, saw much people, and was moved with compassion toward them, because they were as sheep not having a shepherd: and he began to teach them many things.

Matthew 14:13-21 tells us there were well over 5,000 men plus women and children who were not counted in the 5,000 waiting for Jesus when He returned from His prayer time. All of these men, women and children needing His teaching, healing and apparently food. Jesus did what He was sent here to do. He taught them. He healed them. Then He took five loaves of bread and the two fish and with His ability to perform miracles, He fed the entire crowd with food left over. Jesus continued with His life and did what He did best, what He had been sent here to do. He did not let His grief lock Him into despair, He used it to inspire Him to humbly help others.

Jesuses incredible example of how to handle loss and grief by serving our fellow humans when we lose one. He prayed and then expressed his grief of the loss of his family through serving those who had become his family which is expressed in His "love each other as I have loved you", John 13:34. Jesus did not stay there with the crowd for days and days on end. He isolated and prayed; He came back and taught, healed and fed those waiting for Him; then He went back to His normal life.

Matthew 14:13-21KJV, Now when Jesus heard this, he withdrew from there in a boat to a desolate place by himself. But when the crowds heard it, they followed him on foot from the towns.

When he went ashore he saw a great crowd, and he had compassion on them and healed their sick. Now when it was evening, the disciples came to him and said, "This is a desolate place, and the day is now over; send the crowds away to go into the villages and buy food for themselves." But Jesus said, "They need not go away; you give them something to eat." They said to him, "We have only five loaves here and two fish." And he said, "Bring them here to me." Then he ordered the crowds to sit down on the grass, and taking the five loaves and the two fish, he looked up to heaven and said a blessing. Then he broke the loaves and gave them to the disciples, and the disciples gave them to the crowds. And they all ate and were satisfied. And they took up twelve baskets full of the broken pieces left over. And those who ate were about five thousand men, besides women and children.

John 13:34 KJV, A new commandment I give unto you, That ye love one another; as I have loved you, that ye also love one another.

It's easy to hide away, be angry, or even be depressed when we encounter the grief that accompanies death. We have all been there. Jesus showed us a new and more exceptional way to deal with our grief.

What did Jesus teach us about how He dealt with death?

1. Take time to isolate yourself and pray, take some time with God. Commune with our Creator. But don't lock yourself in despair or depression.

2. Serve our fellow humans when we lose one. Find somewhere where whatever you do best can serve the needs of others and go do it.

3. Get on with your life. Love goes on and on. Just like the circle of life.

A CHILDREN'S GUIDE TO A GODLY WAY OF LIFE

Eating & Drinking

Jesus taught us that what we eat and drink is important, not just for our bodies, but also for our hearts and minds. He wanted us to understand that we should be careful about what we put into our bodies because it can affect our thoughts and actions.

Our Words & Actions Can Make Us Unclean

In the Bible, Jesus tells us that it's not just the physical food that matters, but also the things we say and do. In Matthew 15:11, Jesus said, "It is not what goes into your mouth that makes you unclean, but what comes out of it". This means that it's not just about the food we eat, but also about the words we speak and the actions we take.

Matthew 15:11 "What goes into someone's mouth does not defile them, but what comes out of their mouth, that is what defiles them."

Be Thankful For Our Food & Share With Others

Jesus also taught us about being grateful for the food we have. He showed us this when he fed a large group of people with just a few loaves of bread and fish in Matthew 14:13-21. After everyone had eaten, there were even leftovers! This reminds us to be thankful for the food we have and to share with others who may not have enough.

Matthew 14:13-21 "When Jesus heard what had happened, he withdrew by boat privately to a solitary place. Hearing of this, the crowds followed him on foot from the towns. When Jesus landed and saw a large crowd, he had compassion on them and healed their sick. As evening approached, the disciples came to him and said, "This is a remote place, and it's already getting late. Send the crowds away, so they can go to the villages and buy themselves some food." Jesus replied, "They do not need to go away. You give them something to eat." "We have here only five loaves of bread and two fish," they answered. "Bring them here to me," he said. And he directed the people to sit down on the grass. Taking the five loaves and the two fish and looking up to heaven, he gave thanks and broke the loaves. Then he gave them to the disciples, and the disciples gave them to the people. They all ate and were satisfied, and the disciples picked up twelve basketfuls of broken pieces that were left over. The number of those who ate was about five thousand men, besides women and children."

Love and Care For Our Bodies

Another important thing Jesus taught us is to love and care for our bodies. In 1 Corinthians 6:19, Jesus said, "Your body is a temple of the Holy Spirit" . This means that our bodies are special and should be treated with respect. We should try to eat healthy foods and take care of ourselves so that we can be strong and able to do good things.

1 Corinthians 6:19 NIV Do you not know that your bodies are temples of the Holy Spirit, who is in you, whom you have received from God? You are not your own;

Overall, Jesus wanted us to understand that what we eat and drink is important, but it's not just about the physical things. It's also about what we say, how we treat our bodies, and being grateful for the food we have. By following Jesus' teachings, we can learn to make good choices and take care of ourselves in a way that pleases God.

Physical Food vs Spiritual Sustenance

Jesus gave us an example of physical food versus spiritual sustenance in John 6:53-57. In these verses, Jesus tells us "unless you eat the flesh of the Son of Man and drink his blood, you have no life in you. Whoever feeds on my flesh and drinks my blood has eternal life". Jesus is contrasting between *physical* food and *spiritual* food which sets the stage for Jesus' statement that we must eat His flesh and drink His blood. Jesus goes on to explain that it is not physical bread that the world needs, but spiritual bread in John 6:35, John 6:48 and John 6:51.

John 6:35 And Jesus said unto them, I am the bread of life: he that cometh to me shall never hunger; and he that believeth on me shall never thirst.

John 6:48 KJV, "I am that bread of life."

John 6:51 KJV, "I am the living bread which came down from heaven: if any man eat of this bread, he shall live for ever: and the bread that I will give is my flesh, which I will give for the life of the world."

To further help them understand, uses the manna that had been eaten in the time of Moses to contrast to Himself in John 6:49-50 He says, "Your ancestors ate the manna in the wilderness, yet they died. But here is the bread that comes down from heaven, which anyone may eat and not die." Jesus is explaining that like manna, Jesus came down from heaven and, like manna, Jesus gives life; however unlike manna, the life Jesus gives lasts for eternity.

John 6:49-50 KJV, Your fathers did eat manna in the wilderness, and are dead. This is the bread which cometh down from heaven, that a man may eat thereof, and not die.

John 6:53-57 ESV, "So Jesus said to them, "Truly, truly, I say to you, unless you eat the flesh of the Son of Man and drink his blood, you have no life in you. Whoever feeds on my flesh and drinks my blood has eternal life, and I will raise him up on the last day. For my flesh is true food, and my blood is true drink. Whoever feeds on my flesh and drinks my blood abides in me, and I in him. As the living Father sent me, and I live because of the Father, so whoever feeds on me, he also will live because of me."

John 6:35 "*And Jesus said unto them, I am the bread of life: he that cometh to me shall never hunger; and he that believeth on me shall never thirst.*"

John 6:48 KJV, "*I am that bread of life.*"

John 6:51 KJV, "*I am the living bread which came down from heaven: if any man eat of this bread, he shall live for ever: and the bread that I will give is my flesh, which I will give for the life of the world.*"

John 6:49-50 KJV, "*Your fathers did eat manna in the wilderness, and are dead. This is the bread which cometh down from heaven, that a man may eat thereof, and not die.*"

Hebrews 3:3 "*For Jesus has been counted worthy of more glory than Moses—as much more glory as the builder of a house has more honor than the house itself.*"

Enemies

Jesus taught us many important lessons, including how to treat our enemies. Even though it can be hard, Jesus wants us to show love and kindness to everyone, even those who might not be very nice to us. He taught us that instead of seeking revenge or being mean back to our enemies, we should do good things for them.

The Bible tells us an "enemy" is someone who does not like us and wants to harm us.

"Love" is from the word *agape* and it means to seek someone else's welfare or their good over our own good, even if to do so requires a sacrifice.

"Good" means to act for the advantage of another person. It doesn't seem to makes sense for us to work toward the best for someone, an enemy, who actively wants to cause hardship, to us. However, this commandment is to seek the other person's good, not to enable enable, endorse, or cooperate in their abuse or evil. In other words, we are to help them do better, to become good.

Here are some Bible verses that talk about what Jesus taught us about enemies:

Love Your Enemies & Pray For Them

Matthew 5:44 says, "But I say to you, love your enemies and pray for those who persecute you."

This verse tells us that Jesus wants us to love our enemies and even pray for them. It can be tough, but when we show love and pray for our enemies, we are following Jesus' teachings.

Matthew 5:44 NIV "But I say to you, love your enemies and pray for those who persecute you."

Love Your Enemies & Do Good To Them

Luke 6:27 says, "But to you who are listening I say: Love your enemies, do good to those who hate you."

Here, Jesus tells us to love our enemies and do good things for them, even if they hate us. It might seem strange, but when we show kindness and love to our enemies, we are showing them God's love too.

Luke 6:27-31 ESV "But I say to you who hear, Love your enemies, do good to those who hate you,

Feed & Give Your Enemies Drink

Romans 12:20 says, "On the contrary: 'If your enemy is hungry, feed him; if he is thirsty, give him something to drink. In doing this, you will heap burning coals on his head.'"

This verse teaches us that when our enemies are in need, we should help them. By doing this, we are showing them God's love and it can even change their hearts.

Romans 23:30 "On the contrary: 'If your enemy is hungry, feed him; if he is thirsty, give him something to drink. In doing this, you will heap burning coals on his head.'"

Remember, Jesus wants us to love everyone, even our enemies. It can be challenging, but when we follow Jesus' teachings and show love and kindness to our enemies, we become more like Him.

Faith / Believe

Faith, according to the Bible, is believing in something even if we can't see it with our eyes. It's like when you believe that the sun will rise every morning, even if you can't see it before you go to bed. Faith is trusting in something or someone without needing proof.

Faith Is Trusting Without Needing Proof

Faith and believing are important concepts in the Bible. They mean trusting in something or someone even though you cannot see or touch them. In the Bible, it means having trust in God and His promises.

Faith Is Believing Even If We Can't See It

One Bible verse that talks about faith is Hebrews 11:1. It says, "Now faith is confidence in what we hope for and assurance about what we do not see." This means that faith is being sure about something we hope for, even if we can't see it right now.

Let's break this verse down so that we can understand faith and believing a little better.

We talked about "Faith" means believing in something even if we can't see it. It's like when you believe in things that you can't touch or see, like love, dreams, or the wind. Faith is having confidence or trust in something or someone, just like when you trust your parents to take care of you or your friends to be there for you.

The verse also talks about "hope." Hope is when we have a strong desire or wish for something good to happen in the future.

It's like when you hope to get a new toy for your birthday or hope for a sunny day to go to the park.

The verse says that faith is being confident in what we hope for. So, it means that when we have faith, we believe in the things we hope for, even if we can't see or touch them yet. It's like having a strong belief that good things will happen, even if we can't see them happening right now.

Lastly, the verse talks about "assurance." Assurance means being sure or certain about something. So, faith is also about being sure of things we can't see. It's like when you trust that the sun will rise tomorrow, even though you can't see it happening right now. You are confident that it will happen.

In summary, Hebrews 11:1 tells us that faith is having confidence in the things we hope for and being sure of things we can't see. It teaches us to believe in good things and trust that they will happen, even if we can't see them right now.

Hebrews 11:1 NIV Now faith is confidence in what we hope for and assurance about what we do not see.

Blessed Are Those Who Haven't Seen Yet Believed

Another verse is John 20:29. Here, Jesus says to Thomas, "Because you have seen me, you have believed; blessed are those who have not seen and yet have believed." This verse tells us that it's a special thing to believe in God even though we cannot see Him.

John 20:29 NIV Then Jesus told him, "Because you have seen me, you have believed; blessed are those who have not seen and yet have believed."

Everything Is Possible When You Believe

In the book of Mark, there is a story about a man whose son was very sick. He asked Jesus to heal his son, and Jesus told him, in Mark 9:23, "Everything is possible for one who believes". This verse teaches us that if we truly believe in God, amazing things can happen.

So, in summary, faith and believing mean having trust in God and His promises, even when we can't see or touch Him. It's about being sure of something we hope for and knowing that God can do great things if we believe in Him.

Faith, according to the Bible, is believing in something even if we can't see it with our eyes. It's like when you believe that the sun will rise every morning, even if you can't see it before you go to bed. Faith is trusting in something or someone without needing proof.

For example, you have faith in your parents because you know they love and take care of you, even if you don't see them every minute of the day. You have faith that your favorite chair will hold you up when you sit on it, even though you can't see the inside.

In the Bible, having faith in God means believing and trusting in Him, even if we can't see Him physically. We trust in His love, goodness, and promises. It's like having a best friend who is always there for you, even if you can't see them right next to you.

Having faith doesn't mean we never have doubts or questions. It's normal to wonder and ask, but faith helps us hold on to hope and believe in things that are important to us. It's like a strong foundation that keeps us steady even when things are difficult or uncertain.

Just like how we have faith in many things in our everyday life, having faith in God means putting our trust in Him and his plan for us. It's a special kind of belief that gives us hope, strength, and peace, even when we can't see all the answers.

A CHILDREN'S GUIDE TO A GODLY WAY OF LIFE

Family

*Jesus taught us **Family** extends beyond our biological relatives to include all follow God's teachings and who love and care for us and whom we love and care for to our friends, neighbors, and even strangers.*

Jesus taught us that family is not just about our biological relatives, but it includes all those who love and care for us, and whom we love and care for. He showed us that our family extends beyond our parents, siblings, and cousins to include our friends, neighbors, and even strangers.

Family Extends Beyond Our Biological Relatives

In the Bible, Jesus spoke about the importance of loving and caring for one another. In one instance, Jesus was told that his mother and brothers were waiting for him. He replied, "Who is my mother, and who are my brothers?" Then he pointed to his disciples and said, in Matthew 12:48-50, "Here are my mother and my brothers. For whoever does the will of my Father in heaven is my brother and sister and mother."

Matthew 12:48-50 NIV He replied to him, "Who is my mother, and who are my brothers?" Pointing to his disciples, he said, "Here are my mother and my brothers. For whoever does the will of my Father in heaven is my brother and sister and mother."

This means that Jesus considered all those who follow God's teachings as his family. He wanted us to understand that our connection with others is not limited by blood relations but by the love and support we offer each other.

In Luke 10:25-37, Jesus also taught us to show kindness and compassion to everyone, just like a family would. In the story of the Good Samaritan, Jesus taught that we should help others in need, no matter who they are. He explained that our neighbors are not just the people who live near us but anyone who needs our help.

Jesus taught us that family is not only about blood ties but about love, kindness, and caring for one another. We should treat everyone we meet with love and respect, just as we would treat our own family.

Luke 10:25-37 NIV On one occasion an expert in the law stood up to test Jesus. "Teacher," he asked, "what must I do to inherit eternal life?" "What is written in the Law?" he replied. "How do you read it?" He answered, "'Love the Lord your God with all your heart and with all your soul and with all your strength and with all your mind'[a]; and, 'Love your neighbor as yourself.' " "You have answered correctly," Jesus replied. "Do this and you will live." But he wanted to justify himself, so he asked Jesus, "And who is my neighbor?" In reply Jesus said: "A man was going down from Jerusalem to Jericho, when he was attacked by robbers. They stripped him of his clothes, beat him and went away, leaving him half dead. A priest happened to be going down the same road, and when he saw the man, he passed by on the other side. So too, a

Levite, when he came to the place and saw him, passed by on the other side. But a Samaritan, as he traveled, came where the man was; and when he saw him, he took pity on him. He went to him and bandaged his wounds, pouring on oil and wine. Then he put the man on his own donkey, brought him to an inn and took care of him. The next day he took out two denarii[c] and gave them to the innkeeper. 'Look after him,' he said, 'and when I return, I will reimburse you for any extra expense you may have.' "Which of these three do you think was a neighbor to the man who fell into the hands of robbers?" The expert in the law replied, "The one who had mercy on him." Jesus told him, "Go and do likewise."

Fear

Fear is a natural human emotion, a feeling we have when we are scared or worried about something. Fear is a natural emotion that helps us stay safe and protected.

Fear is a feeling we have when we are scared or worried about something. It's like when you see a big, scary spider or when you're afraid of the dark. Fear is a natural emotion that helps us stay safe and protected. Sometimes, fear can make our hearts beat faster, our bodies feel shaky, or even make us want to run away.

In the Bible, there are many verses that talk about fear and how we can find comfort and strength in God when we are afraid. Here are a few Bible verses to help us find comfort and strength in God:

God Will Strengthen You & Help You

"Fear not, for I am with you; be not dismayed, for I am your God; I will strengthen you, I will help you, I will uphold you with my righteous right hand." - Isaiah 41:10

This verse reminds us that God is always with us, even when we're scared. He promises to give us strength and help us through difficult times.

Isaiah 41:10 NIV 10 So do not fear, for I am with you; do not be dismayed, for I am your God. I will strengthen you and help you; I will uphold you with my righteous right hand.

A CHILDREN'S GUIDE TO A GODLY WAY OF LIFE

Put Your Trust In God

"When I am afraid, I put my trust in you." Psalm 56:3

This verse tells us that when we feel scared, we can trust in God. We can talk to Him and ask Him for comfort and peace.

Psalm 56:3 NIV "When I am afraid, I put my trust in you."

God Gave You A Spirit Of Power, Love & Self Control

3. "For God gave us a spirit not of fear but of power and love and self-control." - 2 Timothy 1:7

This verse reminds us that God has given us His spirit, which helps us to be brave and have self-control. We can rely on God's power and love to overcome our fears.

2 Timothy 1:7 NIV "For God gave us a spirit not of fear but of power and love and self-control."

Remember, it's okay to feel afraid sometimes. But we can always turn to God and His Word for comfort and strength.

Jesus taught us many things about fear. He wanted us to understand that we don't have to be afraid because He is always with us and He loves us very much.

You Are Very Special & Important To God

In Matthew 10:31, it says, "So don't be afraid; you are worth more than many sparrows." This means that you are very special and important. Just like how God takes care of the little sparrows, He also takes care of you because you are valuable to Him. So, you don't need to be scared or worried because God loves and protects you. Remember, you are precious and always in God's loving hands!

Matthew 10:31 NIV "So don't be afraid; you are worth more than many sparrows."

Be Strong & Courageous, God Is With You

Another verse that can help us control our fear is found in the book of Joshua 1:19, which says, "Have I not commanded you? Be strong and courageous. Do not be afraid; do not be discouraged, for the Lord your God will be with you wherever you go." This verse reminds us that God is always with us, no matter where we are or what we are facing. We can be brave and not be afraid because God is by our side. This verse teaches us about fear and how Jesus wants us to handle it.

Imagine you're about to start a new adventure, like going to a new school or trying something you've never done before. Sometimes, we might feel scared or worried. But Jesus tells us that we don't need to be afraid. We can "Be strong and courageous" and be brave and confident because God is always there with us, no matter where we go.

Jesus knows that fear can make us feel discouraged, which means feeling sad or down. But He wants us to remember that He is always by our side, giving us strength and helping us through any situation. We can trust in Him and have faith that He will take care of us.

Joshua 1:19 NIV "Have I not commanded you? Be strong and courageous. Do not be afraid; do not be discouraged, for the Lord your God will be with you wherever you go."

Put Your Trust In God

Another verse that can help us understand Controlling our fear is Psalm 56:3, which says, "When I am afraid, I put my trust in you." This means that when we feel scared, we can turn to Jesus and trust Him to take away our fears. He is like a loving friend who is always there to listen and comfort us.

Psalm 56:3 NIV "When I am afraid, I put my trust in you."

Pray To God About Everything

So, no matter what we face, big or small, Jesus teaches us to be strong and courageous, knowing that He is with us. We can trust Him and let go of our fears because He will guide and protect us.

Jesus also taught us that when we have worries or fears, we can talk to God about them. In the book of Philippians, 4:6, it says, "Do not be anxious about anything, but in every situation, by prayer and petition, with thanksgiving, present your requests to God." This means we can bring our worries and fears to God in prayer, and He will listen to us and give us peace.

Philippians 4:6 NIV "Do not be anxious about anything, but in every situation, by prayer and petition, with thanksgiving, present your requests to God."

So, remember, Jesus taught us that we don't have to be afraid because God is with us, He loves us, and we can talk to Him about our fears. We can be brave and trust in God's love and care for us!

Fear Is The Opposite Of Faith

Fear and Faith are two very different things, and they can have a big impact on our lives. Let's imagine that you are standing at the edge of a swimming pool, and you want to jump in. Fear will make you feel scared and unsure, making it difficult for you to take that leap into the water. On the other hand, Faith will give you the confidence and trust to jump in, believing that everything will be okay.

In the Bible, there are many verses that talk about fear and faith. One of them is from the book of 2 Timothy 1:7, which says, "For God has not given us a spirit of fear, but of power and of love and of a sound mind." This means that God does not want us to live in fear, but rather in faith, knowing that He has given us power, love, and a clear mind to face any challenges.

Another verse is from the book of Hebrews 11:1, which says, "Now faith is the assurance of things hoped for, the conviction of things not seen." This means that faith is about having confidence in things we cannot see, like believing in God and His promises, even if we can't physically see Him.

2 Timothy 1:7 "For God has not given us a spirit of fear, but of power and of love and of a sound mind."

Hebrews 11:1 "Now faith is the assurance of things hoped for, the conviction of things not seen."

So, Fear and Faith are opposites because fear makes us doubt and be afraid, while faith gives us confidence and trust. It's important to remember that we can choose to have faith instead of fear, knowing that God is always with us and will guide us through any situation.

Jesus taught us about fear is that it is the opposite of faith. Fear and Faith cannot exist in the same space.

Jesus taught us that fear and faith cannot exist together. They are opposites.

In Mark 4:40, Jesus asked why his followers were so scared and lacked faith. He wanted them to be brave. When we talk about faith, we mean what we believe in and how it can make things happen in our lives.

In Luke 17:6, Jesus said that even a little bit of faith, like a tiny mustard seed, can do amazing things. He said that if we truly believe in our hearts, we can make things happen, just like Jesus showed us and Luke tells us in the Bible. But if we let our fears control us more than our faith, then our fears become our reality.

Luke 17:6 "If you have faith as small as a mustard seed, you can say to this mulberry tree, 'Be uprooted and planted in the sea,' and it will obey you."

Mark 4:40 KJV, And he said unto them, Why are ye so fearful? how is it that ye have no faith?

We see this again in Matthew 8:26 where Jesus says, "You of little faith, why are you so afraid?".

In this verse, Jesus is saying "your fear is the opposite of faith, where is your faith". What you believe, what you have faith in, becomes your truth, becomes your life.

In other words, if you focus on what you are afraid of, this fear will come to be; the fear will become your life, your reality.

Instead focus on what you want to happen and what you want to happen, the good, will become your life, your reality.

This is what Jesus is trying to teach us with these lessons on fear and faith.

Matthew 8:26 KJV, "And he saith unto them, Why are ye fearful, O ye of little faith? Then he arose, and rebuked the winds and the sea; and there was a great calm."

A CHILDREN'S GUIDE TO A GODLY WAY OF LIFE

Forgiveness

Forgiveness is when we choose to let go of anger, resentment, revenge and hurt feeling we have towards someone who has done done something wrong or hurtful to us. Forgiving allows us to move forward and have peace in our hearts.

Forgiveness, is a very important concept that we can learn from the Bible. It is when we choose to let go of any anger or hurt feelings we have towards someone who has done something wrong or hurtful to us. Forgiveness is a way to show kindness, love, and compassion towards others.

In the Bible, there are many verses that talk about forgiveness. Here are a few examples:

Ephesians 4:32: "Be kind to one another, tenderhearted, forgiving one another, as God in Christ forgave you." This verse teaches us that just as God forgives us for our mistakes, we should also forgive others.

Ephesians 4:32 "Be kind to one another, tenderhearted, forgiving one another, as God in Christ forgave you."

If You Want God's Forgiveness, You Must Forgive

Matthew 6:14 says, "For if you forgive others their trespasses, your heavenly Father will also forgive you." In the Bible, trespass refers to doing something wrong or sinful against God or others. It's like not following God's commandments or hurting someone intentionally.

Jesus teaches us in Matthew 6:14-15, to forgive everything; if you don't forgive or are unable to forgive, it robs you of the happiness of life. He tells us, if you forgive the sins of others against you, your heavenly Father will also forgive you. Jesus teaches us that if we want God to forgive us, we must also forgive others. It means not holding grudges or seeking revenge, but instead showing love and mercy.

Holding grudges and not forgiving separates us from God's love and this robs us of all joy and love found in life. This in turn robs us of real life at all.

Matthew 6:14–15 NLT, "If you forgive those who sin against you, your heavenly Father will forgive you. But if you refuse to forgive others, your Father will not forgive your sins.

Don't Judge

Luke 6:37: "Judge not, and you will not be judged; condemn not, and you will not be condemned; forgive, and you will be forgiven." This verse encourages us to not hold grudges or judge others but instead choose forgiveness.

Luke 6:37 "Judge not, and you will not be judged; condemn not, and you will not be condemned; forgive, and you will be forgiven."

God Loves Us So Much, He Forgives Us

God's love for us is so great that He forgives us when we make mistakes or do wrong things. He wants us to forgive others in the same way, showing them love and understanding. This verse tells us that we should be patient with others and forgive them, just as God forgives us. God's love for us is so great that He forgives us, so we must also forgive others. It means not holding grudges or seeking revenge, but instead showing love and mercy.

Colossians 3:13 "Bear with each other and forgive one another if any of you has a grievance against someone. Forgive as the Lord forgave you."

Choosing Not To Hold On To The Hurt & Anger

Forgiveness doesn't mean forgetting what happened, but it means choosing not to hold on to the hurt and anger. Instead, we should treat others with kindness and forgive them, just as God forgives us.

Matthew 18:21-22 "Then Peter came to Jesus and asked, 'Lord, how many times shall I forgive my brother or sister who sins against me? Up to seven times?' Jesus answered, 'I tell you, not seven times, but seventy-seven times.'"

To Bring Healing & Peace To OurHearts

Sometimes, it can be hard to forgive others, especially if they hurt us deeply. But God gives us the strength to forgive, and when we do, it brings healing and peace to our hearts.

Ephesians 4:31:32 "Get rid of all bitterness, rage and anger, brawling and slander, along with every form of malice. Be kind and compassionate to one another, forgiving each other, just as in Christ God forgave you."

Remember, forgiveness is not always easy, but it is a way to show kindness and love towards others. When we forgive, we let go of negative feelings and make room for healing and reconciliation. Forgiveness is a beautiful act of love and a way to follow God's teachings. Forgiveness is an important virtue that helps us strengthen our relationships with others and bring us closer to God.

Luke 23:34 gives us one of the most perfect examples Jesus gave us of forgiveness. When Jesus was on the cross in absolute agony, He cried out to God saying "Forgive them, Father! They don't know what they are doing." Can you imagine the pain Jesus must have been in at that moment? But instead of focusing on His pain, He choose to ask our Creator to forgive those that were hurting Him instead. This verse shows us the incredible forgiveness and love that Jesus had, even in the midst of his suffering on the cross.

In Luke 23:34, Jesus says, "Father, forgive them, for they do not know what they are doing." This verse shows us the incredible forgiveness and love that Jesus had, even in the midst of his suffering on the cross.

Just like Jesus, forgiveness means choosing not to hold a grudge or seek revenge when someone hurts us. It means trying to understand that the person who hurt us might not fully understand the impact of their actions, just like Jesus thought about the people who were hurting him on the cross.

Remember, forgiveness doesn't mean that what the person did was okay or that we forget about it completely. It means that we choose to let go of our anger and treat the person with kindness and love, just like Jesus did.

So, Luke 23:34 teaches us about the power of forgiveness and how Jesus showed us this incredible love and forgiveness even when he was being hurt.

Luke 23:34 ESV, And Jesus said, "Father, forgive them, for they know not what they do." And they cast lots to divide his garments.

LADY KIMBERLY MOTES DOTY, AURORA BRAND & CONOR FINNEGAN

Grace

Grace is a gift we can never earn or deserve. Grace is a spontaneous gift from God to people – "a generous, free and totally unexpected and undeserved gift" – that takes the form of divine favor, love, clemency, and a share in the divine life of God. It is an attribute of God that is most manifest in the salvation of sinners.

Grace is defined in the Bible as "a spontaneous gift from God to people – "generous, free and totally unexpected and undeserved" – that takes the form of divine favor, love, clemency, and a share in the divine life of God. It is an attribute of God that is most manifest in the salvation of sinners." It can also be defined as "God's favor toward the unworthy" or "God's benevolence on the undeserving." Or "Grace is a favor from God that is not earned."

Grace is a beautiful concept that we find in the Bible. It is a special gift from God that shows His love and kindness towards us, even though we don't deserve it. Imagine you made a mistake, like accidentally breaking your mom's favorite vase. Normally, you might expect to get in trouble or be punished for it, right? But instead, your mom forgives you and doesn't get angry. She shows you grace by not giving you the punishment you deserve.

In the same way, God shows us grace when we make mistakes or do things that are wrong. He loves us so much that He sent His Son, Jesus, to die for our sins on the cross. Through this sacrifice, God offers us forgiveness and a fresh start. He doesn't hold our mistakes against us but instead gives us another chance. It's like a big warm hug from God saying, "I love you no matter what!"

Grace is a gift that we can never earn or deserve. We simply have to accept it with a grateful heart. It's like receiving an amazing present that we didn't do anything to earn, but we are overjoyed to receive it anyway. When we accept God's grace, it brings us peace, joy, and a deep sense of love and belonging.

It's important to remember that grace doesn't mean we can do whatever we want and not care about our actions. Instead, it teaches us to be grateful and strive to live in a way that pleases God. We can show grace to others too, by being kind, forgiving, and understanding, just like how God shows us grace.

So, grace is a beautiful gift from God that reminds us of His unconditional love and forgiveness. It's like a second chance to start fresh and make things right with God and others.

The Bible verses Titus 3:5, Galatians 2:16, Romans 11:6, and John 6:28-29 are clear that salvation is entirely by grace through faith, and not earned by good deeds.

We begin in Titus 3:5 where it tells us that it is "His own mercy, by washing of regeneration and renewal of the Holy Spirit" and "not because of works done by us" that "He saved us".

Titus 3:5 ESV, "he saved us, not because of works done by us in righteousness, but according to his own mercy, by the washing of regeneration and renewal of the Holy Spirit,

Galatians 2:16 is very similar in verse where it says "a person is not justified by works of the law but through faith in Jesus Christ, so we also have believed in Christ Jesus, in order to be justified by faith in Christ" and not by works of the law, because by works of the law no one will be justified" telling us it is not what we do by by our faith in Jesus that we are saved.

Galatians 2:16 ESV, yet we know that a person is not justified by works of the law but through faith in Jesus Christ, so we also have believed in Christ Jesus, in order to be justified by faith in Christ and not by works of the law, because by works of the law no one will be justified.

Romans 11:6 continues with this thought where it says, "But if it is by grace, it is no longer on the basis of works, otherwise grace would no longer be grace." Grace by definition is "A spontaneous gift from God to the people that is generous, free and totally unexpected and undeserved."

Romans 11:6 ESV, But if it is by grace, it is no longer on the basis of works; otherwise grace would no longer be grace.

Jesus tells the crowds in John 6:28-29 that it is not the material things that He does, such as feeding the multitudes on the day before, the "works" he performs but it is to listen to the things He says "that ye believe on Him who He hath sent" in order to be "work the works of God".

John 6:28-29 KJV, Then said they unto him, What shall we do, that we might work the works of God? Jesus answered and said unto them, This is the work of God, that ye believe on him whom he hath sent. In other words, it is by our "faith" in Jesus that we are saved.

When we put all of these verses together regarding Grace, we see it is not our works but our faith, our believing in Jesus that gives us salvation, we begin to understand that our Salvation is

Entirely by Grace, this undeserved gift from our Creator to us, Through our Faith in Jesus.

Healing

Healing in the Bible means restoring someone's health, both physically and spiritually. When someone is sick, injured, or struggling, healing is the process of making them whole again. It involves not only curing physical ailments but also bringing comfort, peace, and restoration to their hearts and minds.

In the Bible, healing is often attributed to God's power and love. God showed great compassion and performed many miraculous healings through His son Jesus Christ. Jesus healed the blind, the deaf, the paralyzed, and even brought the dead back to life. His healings showed how much God cares for His people and wants them to be well.

Jesus showed us that He has the power to heal all kinds of sickness and diseases throughout the Bible. Jesus cared deeply about people who were hurting and wanted to help them feel better.

Blind Bartimaeus Receives His Sight

One important story is about a blind man named Bartimaeus. In the book of Mark 10:45-52, it says that Bartimaeus was sitting by the roadside, begging for money. When he heard that Jesus was passing by, he called out to Him, saying, "Jesus, Son of David, have mercy on me!"

Jesus heard Bartimaeus and stopped. He asked the people to bring Bartimaeus to Him. Jesus asked Bartimaeus, "What do you want me to do for you?" Bartimaeus said, "I want to see again." And Jesus said, "Go, your faith has healed you." Immediately, Bartimaeus could see again!

This story teaches us that Jesus has the power to heal our physical ailments. When we have faith in Him and ask Him for help, He can make us better.

Mark 10:45-52 NIV For even the Son of Man did not come to be served, but to serve, and to give his life as a ransom for many." Then they came to Jericho. As Jesus and his disciples, together with a large crowd, were leaving the city, a blind man, Bartimaeus (which means "son of Timaeus"), was sitting by the roadside begging. When he heard that it was Jesus of Nazareth, he began to shout, "Jesus, Son of David, have mercy on me!" Many rebuked him and told him to be quiet, but he shouted all the more, "Son of David, have mercy on me!" Jesus stopped and said, "Call him." So they called to the blind man, "Cheer up! On your feet! He's calling you." Throwing his cloak aside, he jumped to his feet and came to Jesus. "What do you want me to do for you?" Jesus asked him. The blind man said, "Rabbi, I want to see." "Go," said Jesus, "your faith has healed you." Immediately he received his sight and followed Jesus along the road.

Jesus Heals A Sick Woman

Another story is about a woman who had been bleeding for twelve years. In the book of Luke 8:43-48, it says that this woman had spent all her money on doctors, but no one could make her better. She thought, "If I can just touch the edge of Jesus' clothes, I will be healed."

So she pushed through the crowd and touched Jesus' cloak. Immediately, her bleeding stopped! Jesus turned around and asked, "Who touched me?" The woman came trembling and fell at His feet. Jesus said to her, "Daughter, your faith has healed you. Go in peace."

This story shows us that Jesus can heal us not just physically, but also emotionally and spiritually. He cares about our well-being and wants us to have peace.

Luke 8:43-48 And a woman was there who had been subject to bleeding for twelve years,[c] but no one could heal her. She came up behind him and touched the edge of his cloak, and immediately her bleeding stopped. "Who touched me?" Jesus asked. When they all denied it, Peter said, "Master, the people are crowding and pressing against you." But Jesus said, "Someone touched me; I know that power has gone out from me." Then the woman, seeing that she could not go unnoticed, came trembling and fell at his feet. In the presence of all the people, she told why she had touched him and how she had been instantly healed. Then he said to her, "Daughter, your faith has healed you. Go in peace."

These are just a few examples of how Jesus taught us about healing in the Bible. There are many more stories that show His compassion and love for us. Remember, whenever we are sick or hurting, we can turn to Jesus for help and healing.

Heaven

Heaven is a wonderful place that the Bible tells us about. It is a place where God lives and where all good and happy things happen. In heaven, there is no sadness, pain or anything bad. It is a perfect and beautiful place where people who believe in God go after they die.

The Bible describes heaven in different ways. Here are some verses that can help us understand it better.

No More Sadness or Pain

Revelation 21:4 says, "He will wipe away every tear from their eyes, and death shall be no more, neither shall there be mourning, nor crying, nor pain anymore, for the former things have passed away."

This verse in Revelation tells us that in heaven, there will be no more sadness or pain.

Revelation 21:4 He will wipe every tear from their eyes. There will be no more death' or mourning or crying or pain, for the old order of things has passed away."

Heaven Has Room For Many

John 14:2-3 says, "In my Father's house are many rooms. If it were not so, would I have told you that I go to prepare a place for you? And if I go and prepare a place for you, I will come again and will take you to myself, that where I am you may be also."

Here, Jesus tells us that He is preparing a special place for us in heaven.

John 14:2-3 My Father's house has many rooms; if that were not so, would I have told you that I am going there to prepare a place for you? 3 And if I go and prepare a place for you, I will come back and take you to be with me that you also may be where I am.

Heaven Is Beyond Our Imagination

1 Corinthians 2:9 says, "But, as it is written, 'What no eye has seen, nor ear heard, nor the heart of man imagined, what God has prepared for those who love him.'"

This verse reminds us that heaven is beyond our imagination, and God has something wonderful prepared for those who love Him.

1 Corinthians 2:9 NIV However, as it is written: "What no eye has seen, what no ear has heard, and what no human mind has conceived"— the things God has prepared for those who love him—

Heaven Brings Us Complete Joy & Eternal Pleasures

Psalm 16:11 says, "You make known to me the path of life; in your presence there is fullness of joy; at your right hand are pleasures forevermore."

This verse explains that being in God's presence in heaven brings us complete joy and eternal pleasures.

Psalm 16:11 11 You make known to me the path of life; you will fill me with joy in your presence, with eternal pleasures at your right hand.

It's important to remember that heaven is a place where we can be with God forever. It's a place of love, joy, and peace. And the most amazing thing is that God wants us all to be there with Him someday.

Matthew 6:33 is also one of the key verses in all of Jesus' teaching "But seek first the Kingdom of God and his righteousness, and all things will be added to you". This verse is one of the key verses because it follows along with the most important commandment, Matthew 22:37-39, which says, "Thou shalt love the Lord thy God with all thy heart, and with all thy soul, and with all thy mind. This is the first and great commandment ".

When I read this verse, "seek first the Kingdom of God" my first thought is the verse Luke 17:20-21 where Jesus tells us the "Kingdom of God is in the midst of you". In this verse, the "Kingdom of God" is meaning Jesus, we'll expand on this further when we cover the "Kingdom of God". In this verse in Matthew 6:33, I believe it is telling us to "Seek Jesus first and His righteousness, and all things will be added to you."

Luke 17:20-21 ESV Being asked by the Pharisees when the kingdom of God would come, he answered them, "The kingdom of God is not coming with signs to be observed, nor will they say, 'Look, here it is!' or 'There!' for behold, the kingdom of God is in the midst of you."

Matthew 6:33 ESV, But seek first the kingdom of God and his righteousness, and all these things will be added to you.

The Kingdom of God is Heaven

The Kingdom of God is Heaven.

We seek the Kingdom of God because we want to be with God and be a part of His special place. We want to be with Him because He loves us very much and wants to be close to us. When we seek the Kingdom of God, it means that we want to be good and kind like Jesus, so we can be a part of God's special place forever.

Here are some Bible verses that talk about the Kingdom of God and seeking it:

If We Put God's Kingdom First, He Will Take Care Of Us

Matthew 6:33 - "But seek first His kingdom and His righteousness, and all these things will be given to you as well."

This verse tells us that if we put God's Kingdom first and try to be like Him, He will take care of us.

Matthew 6:33 NIV But seek first his kingdom and his righteousness, and all these things will be given to you as well.

Have Childlike Faith To Enter God's Kingdom

Mark 10:14-15 - "Let the little children come to me, and do not hinder them, for the kingdom of God belongs to such as these. Truly I tell you, anyone who will not receive the kingdom of God like a little child will never enter it."

This verse reminds us that God loves children and wants them to be a part of His Kingdom. It also teaches us that we need to have childlike faith to be a part of His Kingdom.

Mark 10:14-15 NIV When Jesus saw this, he was indignant. He said to them, "Let the little children come to me, and do not hinder them, for the kingdom of God belongs to such as these. 15 Truly I tell you, anyone who will not receive the kingdom of God like a little child will never enter it."

The Kingdom Of God Can Be In Our Hearts

Luke 17:20-21 - "The kingdom of God does not come with observation; nor will they say, 'See here!' or 'See there!' For indeed, the kingdom of God is within you."

Luke 17:20-21 NIV Once, on being asked by the Pharisees when the kingdom of God would come, Jesus replied, "The coming of the kingdom of God is not something that can be observed, nor will people say, 'Here it is,' or 'There it is,' because the kingdom of God is in your midst."

This verse tells us that the Kingdom of God is not just a physical place, but it is also something that can be in our hearts. When we choose to love and follow Jesus, we allow His Kingdom to be in us.

Remember, even though we can't see the Kingdom of God right now, we can still seek it by being kind, loving, and following Jesus. And one day, when we go to Heaven, we will be a part of His perfect Kingdom forever.

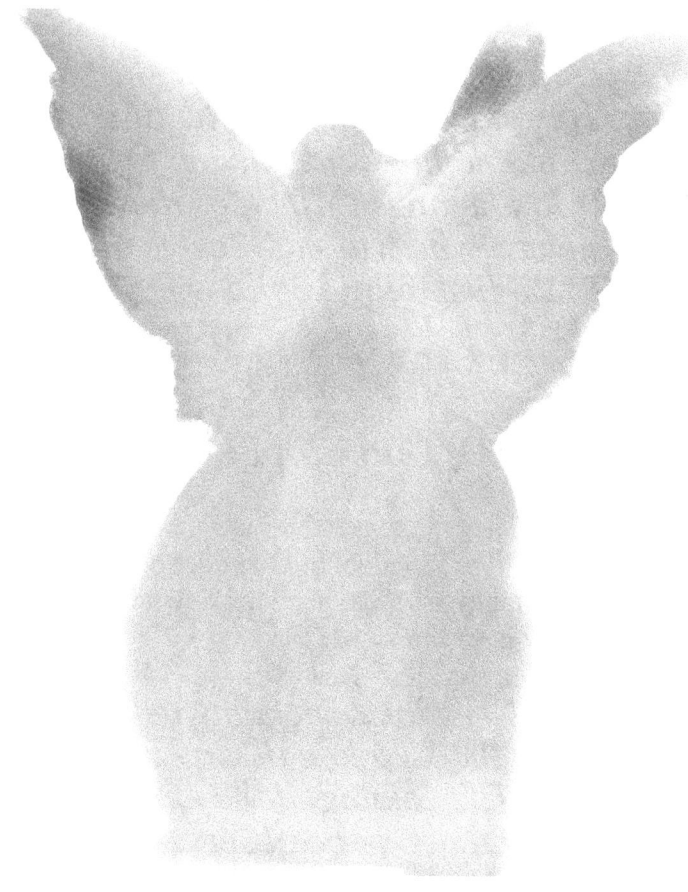

A CHILDREN'S GUIDE TO A GODLY WAY OF LIFE

Holy Spirit

The Holy Spirit is like a special friend that God gives us to help and guide us in our lives. Just like we have friends who support us and encourage us, the Holy Spirit does the same for us, but in a very special way. The Holy Spirit is not something we can see or touch, but we can feel its presence and hear its gentle voice in our hearts. It helps us to make good choices and to be kind and loving to others.

What is the Holy Spirit?

The Bible describes the Holy Spirit as the third person of the Holy Trinity, alongside God the Father and Jesus Christ the Son. The Holy Spirit is often symbolized as a dove and is referred to as a helper, comforter, and guide. So just as we have God and Jesus to help us, we have the Holy Spirit to help us too.

In the Bible, there are several verses that talk about the Holy Spirit:

John 14:26 - "But the Helper, the Holy Spirit, whom the Father will send in my name, he will teach you all things and bring to your remembrance all that I have said to you." This verse tells us that the Holy Spirit helps us learn and remember important things.

John 14:26 NIV But the Advocate, the Holy Spirit, whom the Father will send in my name, will teach you all things and will remind you of everything I have said to you.

Galatians 5:22-23 says, "But the fruit of the Spirit is love, joy, peace, patience, kindness, goodness, faithfulness, gentleness, self-control; against such things there is no law."

This verse shows us that the Holy Spirit helps us grow and develop good qualities, just like a tree bears fruit.

Galatians 5:22-23 NIV But the fruit of the Spirit is love, joy, peace, forbearance, kindness, goodness, faithfulness, gentleness and self-control. Against such things there is no law.

The Holy Spirit, the special friend that God gives us, is always with us, ready to guide and help us. We can talk to the Holy Spirit just like we talk to a friend, and it will always be there to listen and support us.

A CHILDREN'S GUIDE TO A GODLY WAY OF LIFE

Judging

Don't Judge By What You See

John 7:24 says, "Stop judging by mere appearances, but instead judge correctly!"

This means that we shouldn't judge people just by how they look on the outside or by what we think about them. Jesus wants us to look deeper and try to understand them better before making judgments.

Sometimes, we might see someone who looks different or acts differently than us, but we shouldn't make quick judgments about them. Instead, we should try to get to know them and understand them better. Jesus wants us to treat everyone with kindness and not judge them based on how they appear.

So, the commandment from Jesus in John 7:24 is to not judge others by their appearances, but to judge them correctly by getting to know them better.

Don't Judge Others

The commandments of James 2:8-11 talk about not judging others. It means that we should not make fun of or look down on someone just because they are different from us or have made mistakes. We should be understanding and forgiving towards others. We should always speak kindly and avoid saying mean or hurtful things. It's important to use our words to build others up and not tear them down.

James 2:8-11 NIV If you really keep the royal law found in Scripture, "Love your neighbor as yourself," you are doing right. But if you show favoritism, you sin and are convicted by the law as lawbreakers. For whoever keeps the whole law and yet stumbles at just one point is guilty of breaking all of it.

Judging Others

Luke 6:37-42 tells us about some important commandments from God about Judging Others.

Do Not Judge & You Will Not Be Judged

The first commandment says, "Do not judge, and you will not be judged." This means that we should not be quick to make judgments about other people. We should not think we are better than them or be mean to them because everyone makes mistakes sometimes. Instead, we should show kindness and understanding.

Luke 6:37-42 KJV Judge not, and ye shall not be judged: condemn not, and ye shall not be condemned: forgive, and ye shall be forgiven: Give, and it shall be given unto you; good measure, pressed down, and shaken together, and running over, shall men give into your bosom. For with the same measure that ye mete withal it shall be measured to you again. And he spake a parable unto them, Can the blind lead the blind? shall they not both fall into the ditch? The disciple is not above his master: but every one that is perfect shall be as his master. And why beholdest thou the mote that is in thy brother's eye, but perceivest not the beam that is in thine own eye? Either how canst thou say to thy brother, Brother, let me pull out the mote that is in thine eye, when thou thyself beholdest not the beam that is in thine own eye? Thou hypocrite, cast out first the beam out of thine own eye, and then shalt thou see clearly to pull out the mote that is in thy brother's eye.

Do Not Judge Or Criticize Others

In Matthew 7:1-5 Jesus is teaching us more commandments about judgement.

Imagine you and your friends are playing a game, and sometimes you might get upset if your friend does something you don't like. But in this commandment in Matthew, Jesus is telling us that we shouldn't be quick to judge or criticize others. He wants us to be kind and understanding towards everyone.

Jesus says that before we point out the mistakes of others, we need to look at ourselves and see if we have made any mistakes too. It's like looking in a mirror and seeing our own reflection. We need to remember that nobody is perfect, and we all make mistakes sometimes.

Jesus also tells us that instead of judging others, we should try to help them and be kind to them. If we want others to be kind to us, we need to show kindness to them first.

So, the commandment from God in this verse is to treat others with kindness, not to judge or criticize them, and to remember that we also make mistakes. It's important to love and help others just like we would want them to do for us.

Matthew 7:1-5 KJV Judge not, that ye be not judged. For with what judgment ye judge, ye shall be judged: and with what measure ye mete, it shall be measured to you again. And why beholdest thou the mote that is in thy brother's eye, but considerest not the beam that is in thine own eye? Or how wilt thou say to thy brother, Let me pull out the mote out of thine eye; and, behold, a beam is in thine own eye? Thou hypocrite, first cast out the beam out of thine own eye; and then shalt thou see clearly to cast out the mote out of thy brother's eye

Love Peace & Truth

Zachariah 8:16-17 NIV says "These are the things you are to do: Speak the truth to each other, and render true and sound judgment in your courts; do not plot evil against each other, and do not love to swear falsely. I hate all this," declares the Lord."

Now, let's break it down so it's easier to understand these commandments.

Speak the truth to each other

This means that God wants people to always tell the truth and be honest with each other. He also wants them to be fair when they have to make decisions in their courts or when judging others.

Render true and sound judgment in your courts

This means that when people have problems or disagreements, they should go to a court or a judge to make a fair decision. The judge should listen carefully, think about what's right, and make a fair judgment or decision.

Do not plot evil against each other

This means that God doesn't want people to plan or think of doing bad things to each other. He also doesn't want them to say lies or false promises. God really dislikes all these things because they hurt and harm others.

Instead, God wants people to love peace and truth. He says, "So, love truth and peace." This means that God wants people to value and cherish honesty and peace. He wants us to live in harmony with each other, being kind, and treating others the way we would like to be treated.

Do not love to swear falsely

This means we should not make promises or say things that are not true. It's important to keep our word and only say things that we mean and can do.

Zachariah 8:16-17 NIV "These are the things you are to do: Speak the truth to each other, and render true and sound judgment in your courts; do not plot evil against each other, and do not love to swear falsely. I hate all this," declares the Lord."

Miracles

Miracles are amazing things that happen that can't be easily explained by science or logic. They show us that God has special powers and can do things that we can't do on our own.

One important thing Jesus taught us about miracles is that they can happen when we have faith in God. Faith is believing in something even if we can't see it. Jesus often performed miracles when people had strong faith in him and believed that he could help them.

In the Bible, there are many stories of miracles that Jesus performed. Here are a few examples with the corresponding Bible verses:

Jesus Turning Water Into Wine

In the book of John 2:1-11 tells the story of how Jesus attended a wedding and turned water into wine. This was an incredible miracle that showed Jesus' power and ability to provide for people in need.

John 2:1-11 NIV On the third day a wedding took place at Cana in Galilee. Jesus' mother was there, and Jesus and his disciples had also been invited to the wedding. When the wine was gone, Jesus' mother said to him, "They have no more wine." "Woman,[a] why do you involve me?" Jesus replied. "My hour has not yet come." His mother said to the servants, "Do whatever he tells you." Nearby stood six stone water jars, the kind used by the Jews for ceremonial washing, each holding from twenty to thirty gallons.[b]Jesus said to the servants, *"Fill the jars with water"; so they filled them to the brim. Then he told them, "Now draw some out and take it to the master of the banquet." They did so, and the master of the banquet tasted the water that had been turned into wine. He did not realize where it had come from, though the servants who had drawn the water knew. Then he called the bridegroom aside and said, "Everyone brings out the choice wine first and then the cheaper wine after the guests have had too much to drink; but you have saved the best till now." What Jesus did here in Cana of Galilee was the first of the signs through which he revealed his glory; and his disciples believed in him.*

Jesus Feeding 5,000+ With A Few Loaves & 2Fish

In the book of Matthew 4:13-21, it describes how Jesus fed a large crowd of people, over 5,000 with just five loaves of bread and two fish. This miracle demonstrated Jesus' ability to multiply food and take care of people's needs.

Matthew 14:13-21 NIV When Jesus heard what had happened, he withdrew by boat privately to a solitary place. Hearing of this, the crowds followed him on foot from the towns. When Jesus landed and saw a large crowd, he had compassion on them and healed their sick. As evening approached, the disciples came to him and said, "This is a remote place, and it's already getting late. Send the crowds away, so they can go to the villages and buy themselves some food." Jesus replied, "They do not need to go away. You give them something to eat." "We have here only five loaves of bread and two fish," they answered. "Bring them here to me," he said. And he directed the people to sit down on the grass. Taking the five loaves and the two fish and looking up to heaven, he gave thanks and broke the loaves. Then he gave them to the disciples, and the disciples gave them to the people. They all ate and were satisfied, and the disciples picked up twelve basketfuls of broken pieces that were left over. The number of those who ate was about five thousand men, besides women and children.

Jesus Healing The Sick & Raising The Dead

Throughout the Gospels, we read about Jesus healing many people who were sick or disabled. He also raised some people from the dead, like Lazarus in the book of John 11. These miracles showed Jesus' compassion and power to bring healing and life.

John 11:14-17 NIV So then he told them plainly, "Lazarus is dead, and for your sake I am glad I was not there, so that you may believe. But let us go to him." Then Thomas (also known as Didymus) said to the rest of the disciples, "Let us also go, that we may die with him." On his arrival, Jesus found that Lazarus had already been in the tomb for four days. Now Bethany was less than two miles[b] from Jerusalem, and many Jews had come to Martha and Mary to comfort them in the loss of their brother. When Martha heard that Jesus was coming, she went out to meet him, but Mary stayed at home.

John 11:41-44 NIV So they took away the stone. Then Jesus looked up and said, "Father, I thank you that you have heard me. I knew that you always hear me, but I said this for the benefit of the people standing here, that they may believe that you sent me." When he had said this, Jesus called in a loud voice, "Lazarus, come out!" The dead man came out, his hands and feet wrapped with strips of linen, and a cloth around his face. Jesus said to them, "Take off the grave clothes and let him go."

These are just a few examples of the miracles Jesus performed. They teach us that God's power is limitless and that he can do amazing things in our lives too.

We need to have faith in God and believe that he can work miracles in our own situations, just like he did during Jesus' time on Earth.

LADY KIMBERLY MOTES DOTY, AURORA BRAND & CONOR FINNEGAN

Outcast

An outcast is someone who is rejected or discard as defective or useless; throw away, as from home or from society or in some way excluded, looked down upon, or ignored.

Being an outcast means feeling like you don't belong or fit in with others. It can make you feel lonely, sad, or left out. The Bible talks about outcasts and how God cares for them.

Jesus Talks With a Samaritan Woman

In the Bible, there are stories of people who were outcasts, like the story of Jesus and the Samaritan woman. In John 4:7-9, Jesus meets a Samaritan woman at a well. Samaritans were looked down upon by the Jews at that time, so the woman was an outcast. But Jesus treated her with kindness and showed her that God accepts everyone.

John 4:7-9 NIV When a Samaritan woman came to draw water, Jesus said to her, "Will you give me a drink?" (His disciples had gone into the town to buy food.) The Samaritan woman said to him, "You are a Jew and I am a Samaritan woman. How can you ask me for a drink?" (For Jews do not associate with Samaritans.)

The Parable of the Lost Son

Another story is about the prodigal son in Luke 15:11-32. The son wanted his inheritance early and left his family. But when he lost everything and felt like an outcast, he returned home. Instead of being rejected, his father welcomed him with open arms, showing us that God is always ready to accept us back, even when we feel like outcasts.

Luke 15:11-32 NIV Jesus continued: "There was a man who had two sons. The younger one said to his father, 'Father, give me my share of the estate.' So he divided his property between them. "Not long after that, the younger son got together all he had, set off for a distant country and there squandered his wealth in wild living. After he had spent everything, there was a severe famine in that whole country, and he began to be in need. So he went and hired himself out to a citizen of that country, who sent him to his fields to feed pigs. He longed to fill his stomach with the pods that the pigs were eating, but no one gave him anything. "When he came to his senses, he said, 'How many of my father's hired servants have food to spare, and here I am starving to death! I will set out and go back to my father and say to him: Father, I have sinned against heaven and against you. I am no longer worthy to be called your son; make me like one of your hired servants.' So he got up and went to his father. "But while he was still a long way off, his father saw him and was filled with compassion for him; he ran to his son, threw his arms around him and kissed him. "The son said to him, 'Father, I have sinned against heaven and against you. I am no longer worthy to be called your son.' "But the father said to his servants, 'Quick! Bring the best robe and put it on him. Put a ring on his finger and sandals on his feet. Bring the fattened calf and kill it. Let's have a feast and celebrate. For this son of mine was dead and is alive again; he

was lost and is found.' So they began to celebrate. "Meanwhile, the older son was in the field. When he came near the house, he heard music and dancing. So he called one of the servants and asked him what was going on. 'Your brother has come,' he replied, 'and your father has killed the fattened calf because he has him back safe and sound.' "The older brother became angry and refused to go in. So his father went out and pleaded with him. But he answered his father, 'Look! All these years I've been slaving for you and never disobeyed your orders. Yet you never gave me even a young goat so I could celebrate with my friends. But when this son of yours who has squandered your property with prostitutes comes home, you kill the fattened calf for him!'
"'My son,' the father said, 'you are always with me, and everything I have is yours. But we had to celebrate and be glad, because this brother of yours was dead and is alive again; he was lost and is found.'"

The Lord Is Near The Brokenhearted

In Psalm 34:18, it says, "The Lord is near to the brokenhearted and saves the crushed in spirit." This verse reminds us that God is close to those who feel like outcasts. He sees our struggles and is there to comfort us.

So, even if you ever feel like an outcast, remember that God loves you and cares for you. He accepts everyone, and you are never alone.

Jesus was really good at teaching us important things. One thing He taught us is that we can be mad about something or mad at someone, but it doesn't mean we hate them. We can learn this from the way Jesus handled His anger. Being angry at someone is never a reason to make them feel like an outcast or worse to hurt or harm them in anyway.

We see how Jesus taught us to deal with anger. It says in Jeremiah 30:17 that nobody wants to be an outcast. Being called an outcast is very hurtful and makes you feel abandoned and hopeless. It's really lonely to be an outcast, with nobody caring for you and no hope.

An Outcast - Whom No One Cares

Jeremiah 30:17 ESV For I will restore health to you, and your wounds I will heal, declares the LORD, because they have called you an outcast: 'It is Zion, for whom no one cares!'

In Matthew 9:2-8, Jesus saw a man who was an outcast and also had a problem with being paralyzed. He needed forgiveness and healing. Jesus gave him both forgiveness and healing, just like He will do for us when we ask Him.

Jesus Forgives and Heals a Paralyzed Man

Matthew 9:2-8 NIV Some men brought to him a paralyzed man, lying on a mat. When Jesus saw their faith, he said to the man, "Take heart, son; your sins are forgiven." At this, some of the teachers of the law said to themselves, "This fellow is blaspheming!" Knowing their thoughts, Jesus said, "Why do you entertain evil thoughts in your hearts? Which is easier: to say, 'Your sins are forgiven,' or to say, 'Get up and walk'? But I want you to know that the Son of Man has authority on earth to forgive sins." So he said to the paralyzed man, "Get up, take your mat and go home." Then the man got up and went home. When the crowd saw this, they were filled with awe; and they praised God, who had given such authority to man.

Give Yourself The Gift Of Self Love

Embrace the beautiful gift of Self Love, allowing yourself to become a confident, loving individual with strong values and morals. By nurturing this self-love, you will be able to share your whole, radiant self with your loved ones, shining with the light of our Creator. Self love means honoring the needs of your body, mind, and soul, providing the essential care for the journey of life. It is the unwavering belief that you are inherently valuable and deserving. Embracing self love means embracing your inner and outer beauty, graciously acknowledging your own worth without guilt, arrogance, or entitlement. It is an unconditional outpouring of love, gratitude, and self-acceptance.

Remember, self love does not entail elevating oneself above others. Instead, it involves setting healthy boundaries, understanding your values, and steadfastly upholding them throughout your lifetime.s throughout your lifetime.

Self love empowers us, as we embrace the pure love our Creator has for us and cultivate a deep sense of love for ourselves. This enables us to stay true to our values and morals, as we shine brightly for our Creator. Recognizing the significance of self love on our journey of becoming a light for our Creator is crucial. When we truly love ourselves, we prioritize self-care, understanding that we are caring for a precious child of our Creator - ourselves. Each day, as we seek forgiveness for our mistakes and experience the renewal and perfection found in Jesus Christ's boundless love, we reinvigorate our inner light and fortify our unwavering faith, allowing us to steadfastly uphold our values and morals.

Outcast

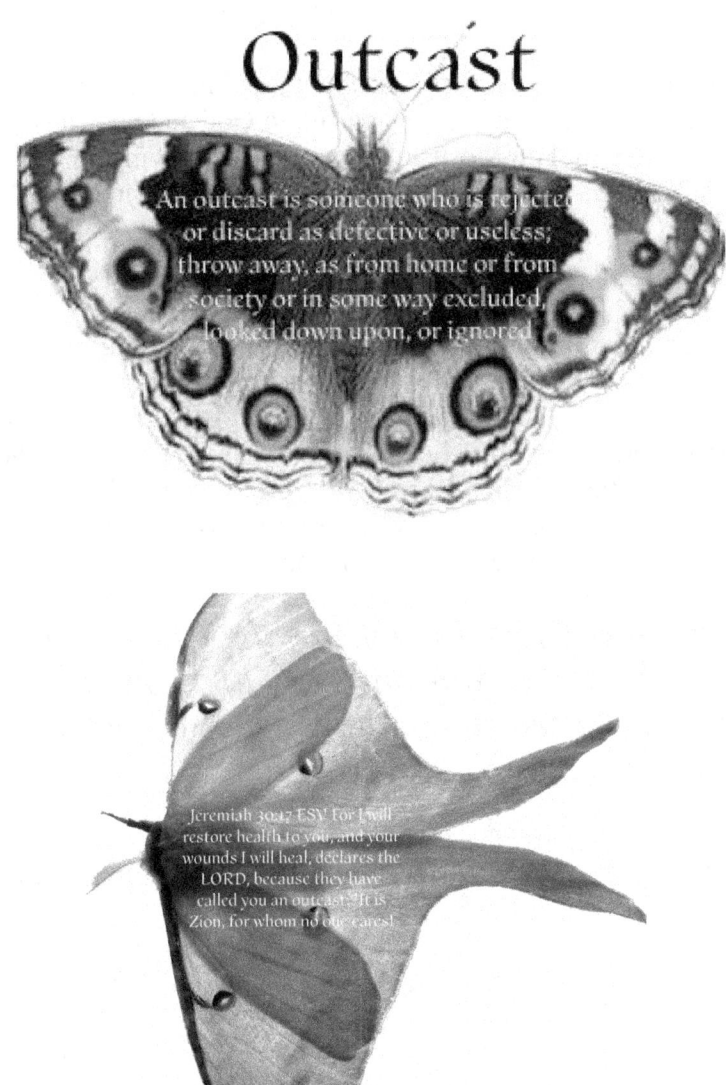

An outcast is someone who is rejected or discard as defective or useless; throw away, as from home or from society or in some way excluded, looked down upon, or ignored.

Jeremiah 30:17 ESV For I will restore health to you, and your wounds I will heal, declares the LORD, because they have called you an outcast: "It is Zion, for whom no one cares!"

Pray

Prayer is a way to talk to God and have a special close connection and friendship with Him.

Jesus taught us many things about praying in the Bible. He showed us that prayer is a way to talk to God and have a special connection with Him. Jesus often spent time praying, and He encouraged His disciples and followers to do the same.

Where To Pray

One important thing Jesus taught us about praying is that we should pray with sincerity and humility. In the book of Matthew 6:6, Jesus says, "But when you pray, go into your room, close the door and pray to your Father, who is unseen. Then your Father, who sees what is done in secret, will reward you." This means that we don't need to pray to show off or impress others, but rather to have a personal conversation with God.

Matthew 6:6 NIV But when you pray, go into your room, close the door and pray to your Father, who is unseen. Then your Father, who sees what is done in secret, will reward you.

Have Faith & Believe That God Answers Our Prayers

Another lesson Jesus taught us about praying is to have faith and believe that God will answer our prayers. In the book of Mark 11:24 Jesus says, "Therefore I tell you, whatever you ask for in prayer, believe that you have received it, and it will be yours." This verse reminds us that God hears our prayers and will answer them according to His will.

Mark 11:24 NIV Therefore I tell you, whatever you ask for in prayer, believe that you have received it, and it will be yours.

The Parable of the Persistent Widow

Jesus also taught us to be persistent in our prayers. In the book of Luke 18:1-8, Jesus tells a parable about a persistent widow who kept asking a judge for justice. Eventually, the judge granted her request because of her persistence. This teaches us that we should never give up on praying, even if it seems like our prayers aren't being answered right away.

Luke 18:1-8 NIV Then Jesus told his disciples a parable to show them that they should always pray and not give up. He said: "In a certain town there was a judge who neither feared God nor cared what people thought. And there was a widow in that town who kept coming to him with the plea, 'Grant me justice against my adversary.' "For some time he refused. But finally he said to himself, 'Even though I don't fear God or care what people think, yet because this widow keeps bothering me, I will see that she gets justice, so that she won't eventually come and attack me!'" And the Lord said, "Listen to what the unjust judge says. And will not God bring about justice for his chosen ones, who cry out to him day and night? Will he keep putting them off? I tell you, he will see that they get justice, and quickly. However, when the Son of Man comes, will he find faith on the earth?"

Overall, Jesus taught us that prayer is a powerful way to connect with God, express our needs and desires, and seek His guidance and help. We can find many more teachings on prayer in the Bible, so it's always a good idea to read and learn from it.

Remember, prayer is a special and personal way to talk to God, and He always listens to our prayers with love and care.

How To Pray To God

The most important thing Jesus taught us was how to talk to God. We talk to God through prayer. When we pray, we are talking to God.

He taught His disciples The Lord's Prayer and by doing so, He taught us how to talk to God in Matthew 6:9-13 and Luke 11:1-4. The Lord's Prayer is the model for how we are to talk to God, our Creator.

Luke 11:1-4 One day Jesus was praying in a certain place. When he finished, one of his disciples said to him, "Lord, teach us to pray, just as John taught his disciples." He said to them, "When you pray, say:

"Father, hallowed be your name, your kingdom come. Give us each day our daily bread. Forgive us our sins, for we also forgive everyone who sins against us. And lead us not into temptation..."

Matthew 6:9-13 KJV, After this manner therefore pray ye:

Our Father which art in heaven, Hallowed be thy name. Thy kingdom come, Thy will be done in earth, as it is in heaven. Give us this day our daily bread. And forgive us our debts, as we forgive our debtors. And lead us not into temptation, but deliver us from evil: For thine is the kingdom, and the power, and the glory, for ever. Amen.

Luke 11:1-4 One day Jesus was praying in a certain place. When he finished, one of his disciples said to him, "Lord, teach us to pray, just as John taught his disciples." He said to them,

"When you pray, say:

"Father, hallowed be your name, your kingdom come. Give us each day our daily bread. Forgive us our sins, for we also forgive everyone who sins against us. And lead us not into temptation...."

Salvation

Salvation is this special gift God offers to us out of His love. We just need to believe in Jesus, accept Him into our hearts, and ask Him to be our Savior. Then, we can have eternal life with God in heaven.

What Is Salvation?

Salvation is like receiving a special gift from God – the gift of eternal life and forgiveness of our sins. Just like when someone gives you a present, you have to accept it to have it. In the same way, we have to accept God's gift of salvation to have it.

Everyone Has Sinned

The Bible tells us that everyone has sinned, which means we have done things that are wrong. But God loves us so much that He sent His Son, Jesus, to save us. Jesus lived a perfect life and died on the cross to take the punishment for our sins. This way, we can be forgiven and have a close relationship with God.

To Accept The Gift Of Salvation

To accept this gift of salvation, we need to believe in Jesus and ask Him to be our Savior. The Bible says in John 3:16, "For God so loved the world that he gave his one and only Son, that whoever believes in him shall not perish but have eternal life."

When we believe in Jesus and accept Him into our hearts, we become God's children. Romans 10:9 says, "If you declare with your mouth, 'Jesus is Lord,' and believe in your heart that God raised him from the dead, you will be saved."

Once we have this amazing gift, we can talk to God through prayer, read the Bible to learn more about Him, and live our lives in a way that pleases Him. We can also share this good news with others so they can have the gift of salvation too!

Remember, salvation is this special gift that God offers to us out of His love. We just need to believe in Jesus, accept Him into our hearts, and ask Him to be our Savior. Then, we can have eternal life with God in heaven.

John 3:16, "For God so loved the world that he gave his one and only Son, that whoever believes in him shall not perish but have eternal life."

Self Love

Self love is giving yourself what your body, brain, and soul needs for the marathon that is life

What Is Self Love

Self love means taking care of yourself in every way, your body, your brain, and your soul. It's like preparing for a long race called life. Self love is believing that you are important and valuable. It means recognizing and appreciating both the inside and outside parts of yourself, and saying nice things to yourself without feeling bad or thinking you're better than others. It's about loving yourself no matter what.

But self love doesn't mean being better than others or thinking you're more important. It's about knowing your own limits, knowing what you believe in, and sticking to those beliefs throughout your life.

When we love ourselves, it makes us feel good about who we are. We know that our Creator loves us too, and that makes us love ourselves even more. This feeling of love and confidence helps us stay true to what we believe in and be a good example for our Creator. That's why it's important to understand self love as we grow up and become a good person for our Creator. When we love ourselves, we also take better care of ourselves because we know that we are taking care of a special person that our Creator made. Every day, when we say sorry for the wrong things we've done and ask for forgiveness, we become strong again in Jesus Christ's love for us. This helps us keep our values and morals strong.

How Do We Know God Wants Us to Have Self Love?

How do we know God wants us to have Self Love? He told us in Romans 12:1-3 to Take Care of Ourselves, this is what Self Love is, it's taking care of ourselves.

Taking Care Of Ourselves

Romans 12:1-3 tells us three important commandments that we should follow about taking care of ourselves and giving ourselves self love. Romans 12:1-3 is the essence of Self Love which we will talk about later in a chapter entitled Self Love.

Take Care Of Your Body

The first commandment says, "Offer your bodies as a living sacrifice." Now, I know that sounds a bit strange, but it means that we should take care of our bodies and use them for doing good things. We don't want to harm ourselves or others but instead use our bodies to help people and make the world a better place.

Make Good Choices

The second commandment tells us, "Do not be conformed to this world." This one is a bit tricky, but it means that we shouldn't just follow what everyone else is doing if it's not right. We should think for ourselves and choose the right path, even if it's not the popular one.

Keep Learning & Growing To Become Better

The third commandment says, "Be transformed by the renewing of your mind." This means that we should always try to learn new things, be open to new ideas, and think in a positive way. We should try to be better and change for the good, just like a caterpillar transforms into a beautiful butterfly.

So, to help remember these three commandments from Romans 12:1-3 about Self Love and taking care of ourselves:

- Take care of your body and use it for good things
- Make good choices, even if others are doing something wrong
- Keep learning and growing to become a better person

Romans 12:1-3 NIV Therefore, I urge you, brothers and sisters, in view of God's mercy, to offer your bodies as a living sacrifice, holy and pleasing to God—this is your true and proper worship. Do not conform to the pattern of this world, but be transformed by the renewing of your mind. Then you will be able to test and approve what God's will is—his good, pleasing and perfect will. For by the grace given me I say to every one of you: Do not think of yourself more highly than you ought, but rather think of yourself with sober judgment, in accordance with the faith God has distributed to each of you.

Walk As Children Of Light

When we talk about being called to "Walk as children of light," in Ephesians 5:8, it means that we are supposed to be like a bright light in the world. We are like a special light that shows everyone how much God loves us. This light comes from inside us and shines out into the world. It is so bright and beautiful that nothing can make it less bright, not even when it's dark outside or really sunny. It's like a lighthouse that guides ships in a stormy sea. This light is God's light shining through us because His Holy Spirit lives inside us. When we love ourselves and let God's Holy Spirit live in us, we feel peaceful and others can see the light shining from us. It's a special change that people can see and feel.

Ephesians 5:8 ESV, For at one time you were darkness, but now you are light in the Lord. Walk as children of light

Sins

According to the Bible, a sin is when we do something that goes against what God wants us to do. God has given us rules to live by, these rules are his commandments, and when we break those rules, it is called sinning.

God has given us His rules or commandments that He expects us to live by and not break his rules or commandments. When we break His rules or commandments, this is called a sin. When we break God's rules it is breaking one of God's "laws". Here are a few examples of what the Bible says about sin:

Breaking God's Laws

1. In 1 John 3:4, it says, "Everyone who sins breaks the law; in fact, sin is lawlessness." This means that when we sin, we are breaking God's law.

1 John 3:4 "Everyone who sins breaks the law, in fact, sin is lawlessness."

No One Is Perfect

2. Romans 3:23 says, "For all have sinned and fall short of the glory of God." This means that every person has sinned at some point because nobody is perfect.

Romans 3:23 "For all have sinned and fall short of the glory of God."

A CHILDREN'S GUIDE TO A GODLY WAY OF LIFE

7 Things God Hates

Proverbs 6:16-19 talks about some things that God really doesn't like. It says, "There are six things the Lord hates, seven that are detestable to him: haughty eyes, a lying tongue, hands that shed innocent blood, a heart that devises wicked schemes, feet that are quick to rush into evil, a false witness who pours out lies and a person who stirs up conflict in the community." So, these are some examples of things that are considered sins.

Now, let's break it down in a simpler way. The passage is telling us about things that make God sad or angry. It lists seven things that are really bad and that God doesn't like.

Haughty Eyes

The first thing is "haughty eyes," which means being proud and looking down on others, thinking you are better than them. God wants us to be humble and treat everyone with kindness and respect.

Liars

The second thing is a "lying tongue." This means telling lies, not telling the truth. God wants us to always be honest and truthful, even if it's sometimes hard.

Murderers

The third thing is "hands that shed innocent blood." This means hurting or harming others who did nothing wrong. God wants us to love and protect others, not hurt them.

Hearts That Devise Wicked Plans

The fourth thing is a "heart that devises wicked plans." This means thinking of bad things to do or planning to do something wrong. God wants us to have good thoughts and make good choices.

Rushing To Do Something Bad

The fifth thing is "feet that make haste to run to evil." This means rushing or going quickly to do something bad. God wants us to stay away from doing things that are wrong or hurtful.

False Witness

The sixth thing is a "false witness who breathes out lies." This means saying things that are not true about others or telling lies about them. God wants us to speak the truth and not say things that can hurt people.

Those Who Cause Fights Or Arguments

And the last thing is "one who sows discord among brothers." This means causing fights or arguments between people who should be friends or getting people to not get along. God wants us to be peacemakers and help others to get along and be happy together.

So, overall, this passage is teaching us about things that we should avoid doing because they make God unhappy. Instead, God wants us to be kind, honest, loving, and helpful to others.

Proverbs 6:16-19 NIV 16 There are six things the Lord hates, seven that are detestable to him: haughty eyes, a lying tongue, hands that shed innocent blood, a heart that devises wicked schemes, feet that are quick to rush into evil, a false witness who pours out lies and a person who stirs up conflict in the community.

Things God Wants Us To Do

But don't worry! The Bible also tells us that God loves us and wants to forgive us when we make mistakes and sin. In 1 John 1:9, it says, "If we confess our sins, he is faithful and just and will forgive us our sins and purify us from all unrighteousness." This means that if we admit our sins to God and ask for forgiveness, He will forgive us and help us do better next time.

1 John 1:9 is a verse from the Bible that says, "If we confess our sins, he is faithful and just to forgive us our sins and to cleanse us from all unrighteousness."

Now, let's break this verse down in a way that is easy to understand.

Confess Our Sins

When it says "If we confess our sins," it means that if we tell God about the wrong things we have done, the mistakes or sins we have made, and the times we have not been kind or honest, He will listen to us.

God Is Fair & True To His Word

The verse also says, "he is faithful and just." This means that God is always fair and true to His word. He always does what He promises, and one of the things He promises is to forgive us when we tell Him about our sins.

God Will Forgive Us Our Sins

So, when it says "to forgive us our sins," it means that God will pardon us and not hold our mistakes against us anymore. He loves us so much that He is willing to forgive us if we ask Him sincerely.

Help Us Become Better People

Lastly, it says "to cleanse us from all unrighteousness." This means that God will not only forgive us, but He will also help us become better people. He will help us to make good choices and do the right things.

So, overall, 1 John 1:9 teaches us that if we admit our mistakes to God and ask for His forgiveness, He will forgive us and help us become better. It's a beautiful reminder of God's love and grace towards us.

Remember, nobody is perfect, and we all make mistakes sometimes. The important thing is to learn from our mistakes, ask for forgiveness, and try to do better.

1 John 1:9 NIV "If we confess our sins, he is faithful and just to forgive us our sins and to cleanse us from all unrighteousness."

Everyone Has Made Mistakes

Romans 3:23 tells us that everyone, including you and me, has made mistakes and done things that are not right according to God's rules. These mistakes are called sins.

So, it's like when you accidentally break something at home or say something mean to your sibling. Those are examples of mistakes or sins we make. And because we all make these mistakes, we fall short of the glory of God, which means we don't meet His perfect standards.

But don't worry! The verse from Romans is not meant to make us feel bad, but to help us realize that we need God's help and forgiveness. Even though we make mistakes, God still loves us very much. He sent His son Jesus to teach us how to live and to save us from our sins.

When we break one of God's rules and make a mistake or sin do you know what that means? God's rules are his commandments and the other guidelines He sets forth for us in the Bible and the example Jesus set for us by the way He lived His life while He was here on earth.

So, when we understand that we have done wrong things, we can ask God to forgive us and help us become better. He is always ready to forgive us and give us a fresh start. And that's why it's important to remember Romans 3:23, to remind ourselves that we all make mistakes, but God's love and forgiveness are always there for us.

Romans 3:23 NIV There is no difference between Jew and Gentile, for all have sinned and fall short of the glory of God

About the Authors

Lady Kimberly (Mamaw) & Aurora

A CHILDREN'S GUIDE TO A GODLY WAY OF LIFE

Lady Kimberly Motes Doty

Lady Kimberly, a force of inspiration and wisdom, wears many hats in her quest to uplift and transform lives. With a warm smile and contagious enthusiasm, she seamlessly transitions from being a Certified Natural Health Professional to an Inspirational Speaker, Ordained Minister, Life Coach, and Spirituality Coach. Yet, her journey doesn't end there.

As a best-selling author, Lady Kimberly has penned over a dozen books that have captivated readers worldwide. However, with her latest masterpiece, she decided to embark on a unique collaboration. Joining forces with her beloved grandchildren, Aurora and Conor, she co-authored "*A Children's Guide to a Godly Way of Life.*" This enchanting book carries the essence of divine wisdom, tailored to young minds eager to embrace spirituality.

Lady Kimberly's literary prowess extends beyond the realm of children's literature. Her top-twenty bestseller, "A Godly Way of Life," resonates with readers seeking to align their thoughts, actions, and reactions with divine principles. Within its pages, profound wisdom and guidance unfold, offering a roadmap to live a purposeful and fulfilling existence.

When not immersed in her writing and coaching endeavors, Lady Kimberly finds solace and inspiration strolling along the pristine shores of the Gulf of Mexico and the Carolina's beaches. These morning walks serve as a sacred ritual, a time for heartfelt prayers and reflections that fuel her creativity and passion.

Lady Kimberly's presence radiates positivity and empowerment. Her holistic approach to life encompasses the mind, body, and spirit, as she seeks to empower others to unlock their limitless potential. With her infectious spirit and unwavering commitment, Lady Kimberly continues to touch hearts and souls, leaving a profound impact on all who have the privilege of crossing paths with her.

Aurora Brand

Aurora Brand, a captivating force of creativity and boundless imagination, is a name that demands attention. As the granddaughter of the illustrious Lady Kimberly, her destiny was etched in the stars from the moment she took her first breath. With a heart filled with wonder and a pen that dances across the pages, Aurora has fearlessly stepped into the realm of writing, leaving a trail of enchantment in her wake.

A driving force behind the mesmerizing masterpiece, "*A Children's Guide to A Godly Way of Life*," Aurora's words effortlessly weave together wisdom and whimsy, captivating readers young and old alike. Together with her indomitable grandmother, she has crafted a literary creation that serves as a guiding light, illuminating the path to a more meaningful existence.

But Aurora's insatiable thirst for storytelling doesn't stop there. With the ink of ambition coursing through her veins, she embarks on a solitary journey to pen her first full-length book. A tantalizing secret whispers in the air, promising a narrative that will transport readers to unexplored realms and ignite their imaginations like never before.

Nestled in the vibrant heart of Tampa, Aurora finds solace in the company of her beloved Mamaw, embarking on enchanting walks along the sun-kissed shores, in search of treasures hidden within the sand. With wide-eyed wonder, she seeks the elusive perfect sand dollar, a symbol of life's endless possibilities.

Aurora Brand is a name that resonates with magic, a storyteller poised to leave an indelible mark on the literary world. With each word she writes, she invites readers to escape the ordinary and embark on a journey of self-discovery and boundless imagination. So, brace yourselves, for in the realm of Aurora's imagination, the extraordinary becomes the norm, and the impossible becomes possible.

Lady Kimberly (Mimi) & Conor

Conor Finnegan

Meet Conor Finnegan, the creative force behind "*A Children's Guide to a Godly Way of Life.*" As a young Catholic student, Conor's inquisitive nature led him to seek answers about God and his Bible studies. But instead of turning to textbooks, Conor called upon his Mimi, his wise and loving grandmother, for guidance. Little did he know that these conversations would spark a remarkable collaboration that would captivate the hearts of children everywhere.

Conor's journey as a writer began with "*If the Alphabet Grew Out of the Sea,*" where he lent his artistic talents as an illustrator alongside his Mimi. The experience ignited a passion for storytelling within him, and he hasn't looked back since. Conor's vivid imagination and ability to communicate complex ideas in a simple, engaging manner make him a natural-born writer.

But there's more to Conor than just his way with words. A true explorer at heart, Conor's love for nature extends beyond the written page. As an avid shell collector, he spends his free time combing sandy shores, seeking out the treasures that lie beneath the waves. It is through these adventures that Conor finds inspiration, connecting him to the beauty and wonder of the world around him.

With his unwavering curiosity, artistic talent, and love for the natural world, Conor Finnegan embodies the essence of a young, creative soul on a quest to inspire and educate. As he continues to share his gift with the world, there's no doubt that Conor's infectious enthusiasm will leave an indelible mark on the hearts and minds of readers of all ages.